SPY GOVERNMENT

SPY GOVERNMENT

The emerging police state in America

OMAR V. GARRISON

LYLE STUART ::: NEW YORK

To Gina dear:
Gratitude in fair proportion . . .

The system of espionage being thus established, the country will swarm with informers, spies, delators, and all the odious reptile tribe that breed in the sunshine of despotic power. The hours of the most unsuspected confidence, the intimacies of friendship or the recesses of domestic retirement, will afford no security. The companion whom you must trust, the friend in whom you must confide, are tempted to betray your imprudence; to misrepresent your words; to convey them, distorted by calumny, to the secret tribunal where suspicion is the only evidence that is heard.

REP. EDWARD LIVINGSTON
Annals, 5th U.S. Congress (1798)

Contents

SPY GOVERNMENT

1
Say privacy, say freedom

Not just an idea, but a condition designed to be coeval
with the birth of America itself—engendered, created, and
simultaneous with the very air and word America. . . .
WILLIAM FAULKNER

One night not long ago, three men, moving with stealth and secrecy, approached a modest office building in the town of Washington, Pennsylania.

One of the men stationed himself as a lookout, while the other
two let themselves into an attorney's office in the building, using a
passkey that had been made earlier from an impression in clay.

Once inside the lawyer's office, the two prowlers quickly and
silently set to work. Operating with the expert skill that comes from
training and experience, they installed a miniature radio transmitter or "bug" behind one of the bookcases that lined the wall of the
law office.

For two weeks thereafter, the transmitter remained in the attorney's private office, where he conducted his most personal affairs—
conversations that included confidential lawyer-client relationships,
intimate family matters and casual remarks to friends and employees.

Who were these faceless intruders? Blackmailers? Members of

the dread Mafia? Disgruntled ex-clients, out to get the attorney?

No, none of these. And, though their names were hardly known outside a certain office in Pittsburgh and one in Washington, D.C., perhaps they ought to be ushered into the full light of day and introduced to Americans countrywide. For they, and an invisible legion like them, play an increasingly sinister part in the lives of every American.

The invaders were, in fact, Special Agents Jack Schwartz, Steve Balen and a man named Richman—all of the U.S. Internal Revenue Service.

Later, put under oath and questioned about the incident, Schwartz admitted that when the agents slipped into the attorney's office to plant the bug—and later to remove it—they had no search warrant, no legal writ or process of any kind.

"Did you not feel just a little embarrassed about being a party to a group illegally entering an office, breaking into an office?" Senator Edward V. Long asked Schwartz when he appeared before a Senate subcommittee investigating government invasions of privacy.

"I never gave it a thought, sir, to be honest with you," Schwartz replied. Then he went on to say, "And I think anything that would have been asked, we would not have thought about the consequences." [1]

During his testimony, Schwartz revealed that the two agents who had installed the secret transmitter in the attorney's office were experts in that type of work, sent from the IRS national office in Washington to do the job.

Special Agent Schwartz told how he had deceived the superintendent of the office building to get possession of a passkey long enough to take an impression of it. An IRS team had previously rented office space in the building, which they had used as a secret surveillance point for operations outside their regular office. The superintendent's suspicions were not aroused, therefore, when Schwartz expressed interest in inspecting the suite of rooms again.

"He gave me the key off his key chain, on his person, and I took this key back and saw the space that I had in mind. I then made a fast impression in clay, and had a key made."

During the course of the intensive investigation conducted by Internal Revenue, the attorney suddenly dropped dead. Whether he would have died at that time anyway, or whether his death was, in part at least, a result of pressures from the IRS probe, is a matter of conjecture.

In any case, death did not end the ordeal for the attorney's family. Schwartz and another special agent named Caruso went to the funeral, where they took down the names of all the mourners.

Nor did this bizarre stratagem conclude the case, so far as IRS was concerned. The deceased attorney's legal representative, former U.S. Attorney Hubert Teitelbaum, related yet another act in the ghoulish drama.

He said that after the lawyer-suspect's death, "while he was stretched out in the funeral parlor, and with his grieving widow present, agents of the Internal Revenue Service came to his office with a criminal search warrant which they had obtained after he died.

"I do not see what crime a dead man could commit. But they got one. And with that search warrant, they went into his office.

"They went in and they seemed to know exactly what they were looking for. They went through personal files . . . files referring to his clients' affairs. These are privileged matters, but the agents went right into them anyway. They scooped up all kinds of stuff and they took it out of the office and they took it to Pittsburgh."

The foregoing story is only one of hundreds and perhaps thousands of dramas that are in progress across the nation today. Not only the Internal Revenue Service, but a host of other federal, state and local agencies are engaged in a massive intrusion into the privacy of the individual citizen.

They can and do intercept and open private, sealed correspondence, sent through the mails.

They can and do illegally tap telephones and spy upon the innocent and guilty alike with such devices as subminiature transmitters, snooperscopes, telephone pen-registers (which record every number dialed) and a frightening array of highly sophisticated gear for electronic prying.

They can and do don various disguises in order to entrap a suspect or even to encourage him to commit a crime.

They can and do break into and enter private homes, offices and automobiles in order to plant listening devices which will record all that man says or woman whispers.

They can and do harass defense attorneys; investigate prospective jurors; and seek to intimidate even federal judges.

They can and do use bugged conference rooms, equipped with secret microphones and one-way mirrors to monitor privileged conversations between citizens and their legal counselors and accountants.

Many of these acts are committed in flagrant violation of federal and state laws, and are just as much crimes as though perpetrated by mobsters and common thieves.

Others—and these include an alarming number of intrusions that employ sneak devices against which there is no defense—are legal under existing laws and according to court decisions.

The real reason, however, that these sinister practices continue is public apathy.

Few Americans seem to be deeply disturbed by the growing array of ugly evidence that our society is undergoing a serious change. The most typical reactions to accounts of bugging and wiretapping are wry amusement or an eager desire to join the game.

During a coast-to-coast radio broadcast, a well-known news commentator recently discussed some of the more advanced space-age gear now used for eavesdropping and spying. The response to his newscast was not a wave of public indignation and misgivings. Instead, he received a flood of letters asking for the address of the manufacturer, so his listeners could buy the equipment to spy on their neighbors.

The most disquieting aspect of the surveillance problem, in fact, is its acceptance by the general public, by the courts and by the news media as a way of life.

A New York joint legislative committee, appointed to study the problem of wiretapping, reported:

"We recognize that there is some human disposition to shrug off, or to minimize the importance of such matters because of the often shabby character of the participants."

And it is true that many Americans still deceive themselves with the notion that only racketeers, gamblers and members of the underworld ever have their privacy invaded by government agencies.

When I cited evidence of the growing use of secret devices to penetrate our private lives, a businessman replid:

"So what? Let them have their fun. I've got nothing to hide."

But how valid is this assumption that "the innocent have nothing to fear"?

The short answer to that question is: They have everything to fear. The instances of clandestine surveillance, intimidation and entrapment recounted in the following pages happen to people like you and me every day of every year. The fact of innocence is no safeguard.

When the full impact of the spy system is eventually felt by an individual citizen, his indifference often gives way to cries of outrage and alarm.

On April 14, 1965, a California newspaperman discovered that a letter sent to him by sealed, first-class mail, had been delivered to and opened by the Internal Revenue Service, before reaching him.

He was shocked and indignant. He was not and never had been, he said bitterly, a tax delinquent. Nor, for that matter, had he ever been arrested. The letter in question contained nothing unlawful or suspicious. It was, in fact, an Easter greeting and a note congratulating him on his fourth wedding anniversary.[2]

There are two points of focus in the newsman's reaction that are significant. First, the expression of surprise coming from the telegraph editor of a daily newspaper at such unwarranted intrusion into his private life strikes one as naive. Just the day prior to the newsman's receipt of the intercepted letter, Representative Durward G. Hall had appeared before a Senate subcommittee to testify that postal officials had admitted to him that on request they had diverted personal, first-class mail to the IRS in cases involving "tax evaders."

Congressman Hall had summed up the situation thus:

"I am personally and very deeply concerned about the fact that 'Big Uncle' is not only watching over us, but on occasion, he is also seizing and reading our mail. And reading our mail before it has been delivered.

"I make no defense for any tax delinquent, certainly. His debt to the government should be paid, and all authorized enforcement methods pursued to insure this collection on the part of the people in government. But a five-cent stamp placed on a sealed envelope entitles him, in my opinion, to the same protection from the invasion of privacy that every other citizen expects." [3]

Hearings before the committee which, under the chairmanship of Senator Edward V. Long of Missouri, was investigating the invasions of privacy by government agencies, had been in session periodically for several months. Had none of the testimony been reported by the wire services whose budget of news was daily placed upon this editor's desk for evaluation and editing?

Probably very little. In fairness to the newspaperman, it should be borne in mind that the shocking revelations brought out by the committee hearings caused little stir in the Fourth Estate. Unless the testimony involved some glamour gadget of the electronic age or had a sex angle, as in the case of the bugged bedroom, it was not considered worthy of in-depth coverage.

The second point worth noting in the editor's statement is his implied belief that *had* he been a tax delinquent or a person with a record of arrest, the IRS would have been justified in opening his private correspondence.

Such an attitude is hardly surprising when even the courts appear to be confused and inconsistent in determining just how much protection the Constitution affords us against invasion of privacy. In defending the action of the postal authorities who turned over first-class mail to the IRS, Harvey H. Hannah, deputy general counsel for the Post Office Department, asserted:

"It has been established that judicial seizures of mail do not violate the Constitutional guarantees of the Fourth Amendment to the Constitution." [4] He cited several court rulings to support his position.

As a result of the frightening disclosures during the Senate hearings already alluded to, a rider was attached to an act to reduce excise taxes, then before Congress. Included as Section 82 of the bill, it amended the Internal Revenue Code to prohibit seizures of first-class mail in transit.[5] However, in view of IRS agents' past record of disregarding both federal and state laws, one cannot avoid the suspicion that they will find some means of continuing the odious practice.

The climate of public opinion in the United States today favors such incursions into our private lives because it has not been widely recognized that such acts indicate a radical change in our deeply entrenched ideas of liberty.

Even carefully documented books and magazine articles on the subject often overlook the more ominous meaning of privacy invasion. Some have deplored it because it is, in the words of Justice Oliver Wendell Holmes, a "dirty business." Others have held that even official snooping is a form of voyeurism and therefore immoral.

The purpose of this book is to examine the more sinister implications of surveillance. The questions to be raised and—it is hoped—answered, include:

Is the annihilation of privacy the antecedent state of an emerging police state in America?

Does tyranny always establish itself by choosing first an unpopular victim, or by pleading that invasion of privacy is necessary to combat organized crime?

How extensive is the network of spies and informers in the United States today? What devices do they use? Are they themselves beyond the reach of the law?

In a free society, where does bureaucratic shepherding end and despotic control begin?

How can we protect ourselves against secret prying and interference with our right to personal freedom?

Contrary to a widespread belief that industrial spies and private eyes do most of the unauthorized snooping, there is mounting evidence that law-enforcement officials and agency functionaries—on federal, state and local levels—are constant practitioners of the "art." Representatives of the largest suppliers of sneak devices have stated under oath that their biggest customers are government agencies.

The records of one manufacturer of spy equipment may provide a good example. They show that from December, 1960, to May, 1964, the Washington, D.C., sales office of this manufacturer alone sold Internal Revenue Service a total of $43,876.42 worth of electronic surveillance equipment. A single order from IRS for a single item (transmitter-receiver kits) amounted to $11,925.[6]

How many other purchases of spying gear IRS made from the more than two-score makers of similar devices is not known. Yet, even with this plethora of clandestine gadgets at their disposal, the IRS office in Kansas City on one occasion had to borrow additional equipment from a private agency—the International Bureau of Investigation.[7]

In sworn testimony before a Senate investigating committee, the manufacturer already mentioned (Fargo Company) under questioning admitted large sales of secret intrusion devices to other nonsecurity agencies of the U.S. government. The agencies named were: Food and Drug Administration; Bureau of Customs; Bureau of Narcotics; Treasury School of Technical Aid (a school in which agents are taught to pick locks, tap wires and use bugging apparatus); U.S. Information Agency; Atomic Energy Commission; and the General Services Administration.[8]

These, of course, were not the only agencies buying such equipment. They were merely the customers of the Washington, D.C. sales office of a single manufacturer.

Time magazine has estimated that total sales of bugging equipment and related gear to all purchasers (government and nongovernment alike) amount to $20,000,000 a year.

Thus, even though government agencies are the big buyers, competitive businessmen and private eyes are not far behind.

Politicians, industrial executives, jealous marriage partners, insurance and credit sleuths, labor unions—all are engaging in undercover activities on an ever expanding scale.

But it is the government itself that sets the pace. As Justice Louis D. Brandeis pointed out, "Our Government is the potent, the omnipresent teacher. For good or for ill, it teaches the whole people by its example. Crime is contagious. If the Government becomes a lawbreaker, it breeds contempt for the law; it invites every man to become a law unto himself."

Ordinary citizens are subject to prosecution if they are caught violating laws already in existence, and will be prosecuted if they violate those that are certain to be passed in the near future.

But government agents and law-enforcement officials, on the other hand, have been and will no doubt continue to be outside of and beyond the reach of the law. It is unlikely that future legislation will affect them any more than laws already on the books have affected them.

It is worth noting, for example, that California has had an anti-wiretap law ever since 1905. Yet, police officers in that state have openly admitted tapping telephones to get evidence. Not one to date has been prosecuted.

Similarly, wiretapping has been illegal in Illinois since 1927. Yet, in cooperation with telephone employees, an intelligence unit of the Chicago police set up a veritable wiretap network. High-ranking members of the department told Samuel Dash, who conducted a survey for the Pennsylvania Bar Association, that at one time the unit had forty men deployed throughout the city, where they maintained secret listening posts. They admitted that in the case of rackets and narcotics investigations, such taps were frequently used by police officers for shakedown purposes.[9]

In New York, wiretapping by law-enforcement officials is legal only by court order, issued like any warrant, upon oath of affirmation that there are reasonable grounds for such an action. However, in New York City alone, plainclothes officers are responsible for an estimated 26,000 wiretaps a year. Certainly, no such number of warrants is issued.[10] In some instances, these undercover men set up wiretap dragnets on a huge scale, covering large concentrations of people in railway stations, bus depots and subways.

Commenting upon the New York system, Supreme Court Justice William O. Douglas declared that "it has been used as a means whereby police have obtained guarded confidences of people and used the information for corrupt purposes."

The U.S. Treasury Department (which includes Internal Revenue Service) has banned the use of wiretapping since 1938. But, as Senator Edward V. Long asked not long ago:

"Which of us would not believe that the regulation was made purely for show, to be winked at but not obeyed, when it was the national office of IRS in Washington that possessed and issued the wiretapping equipment, ran a wiretap school, and also sent out the experts to install and remove the equipment?

"When they graduated from that school, they furnished them a set of burglary tools, perhaps as a graduation present." [11]

It is significant that, in those states where wiretapping has been legalized when a court order is obtained for use by law-enforcement officers, they do not obtain such warrants. They apparently do not wish the nature and extent of their activities made a matter of record. In Las Vegas, Nevada, for instance, a judge authorized to sign the wiretap orders said that no such orders had been issued in Las Vegas. Yet it is well-known that wiretapping and undercover sonic techniques are widely practiced in that city.

Without exception, law officers from the attorney general's office down insist that eavesdropping and electronic spying are indispensable weapons in fighting organized crime. They cite case after case of criminal activity that would have gone unsuspected and unpunished without the aid of advanced intelligence equipment.

Such arguments ignore the obvious fact that an extension of that premise would be: Set surveillance over everybody and there will be no crime. Such, in fact, is the concept of all police states.

Moreover, after stating in one breath that espionage is an invaluable means of curbing crime, the same officials deny in the next breath that they make any but limited use of it.

When asked by investigating committees or survey questionnaires whether their departments have equipment for illegal monitoring, they invariably say, "Very little," or "I have no knowledge of any."

A second argument often advanced for peering into our private lives is that dire consequences are sure to follow if it is not permitted. The two venerable standbys of this pleading are subversive activities and narcotics.

The picture painted of what our country would be like if an unknown number of secret agents were not allowed to spy upon and harass a growing segment of the populace is terrifying. It is so unthinkable, in fact, that almost any measures seem justified!

This wolf! wolf! strategy has proved so successful over the years that not only law-enforcement officers but nonsecurity agencies as well, have enthusiastically adopted it.

Recently, George P. Larrick, then commissioner of the Food and Drug Administration, for example, admitted to Senate investigators that his agency indulges in sonic snooping. But he quickly added:

"Peddling of dangerous stimulant and depressant drugs has grown from individual enterprise to organized business. For reasons I am going to give, we have had to employ electronic transmitting and receiving devices to combat these trends.

"We carefully considered the necessity for and the legal and moral aspects of doing this. In my opinion, we cannot give the public the protection it needs without the kind of use that we have made of electronic equipment." [12]

The commissioner then came up with some frightening statistics. He said his agency had estimated that one half the nine billion doses of barbiturates and amphetamines allegedly sold in the United States each year are sold illegally. He cited a report of the House committee on interstate and foreign commerce which states that in some communities the proportion of abusers of the drugs in the total population is between 1 in 100 and 1 in 500, "and in some communities, even greater."

One inference to be drawn from this statement is that one out of every hundred citizens in America ought to be under surveillance as a suspect in the drug traffic.

Commissioner Larrick went on to say that his inspectors were dealing with hardened criminals and that it was necessary in that type of work to use privacy-invading tools.

But no sooner had he so testified than the Senate probers brought to light some additional details about FDA's fight against organized crime. In their pursuit of "hardened criminals," seven FDA undercover agents, armed with an array of secret snooping gear, and accompanied by a secretary who posed as the wife of one of them, swooped down upon a Kansas City supermarket. There they used their concealed transmitter and tape recorder to monitor two young schoolteachers whose "crime" was demonstrating a milk substitute in the market.[13]

Most Americans would agree that criminals must be apprehended and brought to justice. The problem is how to strike a balance between effective law enforcement and constitutional liberties.

Commenting on this dilemma, Pennsylvania's attorney general, Thomas McBride, observed:

"The only question is whether the use of wire-tapping is so essential in the enforcement of law that it overbalances the greater good, undoubtedly, that comes from the feeling of freedom that people have that they are not being listened to. It must be remembered—and it is not just raising a *bete noir*—that indiscriminate wire-tapping in the totalitarian countries is practically their hallmark . . .

"My personal view is that wire-tapping should be banned—that there isn't sufficient good done by it to overcome the harm that is done by that feeling of loss of freedom by decent people."

No accurate study has ever been made to determine just how effective pry-and-spy law enforcement really is, even when used as a means for combating crime. There are data to suggest, however, that it falls far short of the claims made for it.

Consider, for example, the massive campaign against crime in Kansas City, mounted by the Internal Revenue Service. During 1962 and 1963, in a saturation drive, an estimated one hundred and thirty-five IRS undercover agents were assigned to lay a dragnet for big-time racketeers in that area.

After two years of secret investigation that invaded not only the privacy of criminal suspects, but of countless unquestionably innocent persons as well, they had secured only convictions of minor offenders, not of big-time racketeers.

"Those they got were minnows; they were not big fish," said Senator Long.

Cost to the government for the operation was estimated at two million dollars.

As for organized crime in the city, the chief of detectives of the Kansas City police department later testified:

"Well, we still have the same element here today as we had in 1961, yes."

2
Tax and tyranny

The overzealous activity of the agents of many branches
of the Federal Government are such that the Constitutional rights and guarantees and protections of our citizens are in jeopardy. None of us wants a police state in
this country; none of us wants a Gestapo.

U. S. SENATOR EDWARD V. LONG

While kings, despots and dictators of the past have sought dili-
gently but in vain for some effective way of extending their power
into every corner and retreat of society, it remained for a free Republic to discover one.

The graduated income tax is the most perfect instrument of tyranny ever conceived.

The law, as codified and administered in America, bestows upon
a multitude of federal functionaries an awesome power over every
citizen of the United States, as well as many aliens temporarily
sojourning in our country.

Under the guise of ferreting out tax dodgers and racketeers, secret agents of the Internal Revenue Service can pry into the most
intimate affairs, not only of those guilty of tax evasion and fraud,
but of the innocent as well.

They can, at any time they choose, go back any number of years
and "pull" the tax returns of any taxpayer for investigation and
possible penalties. There is no statute of limitations in civil cases,
such as prevails in all other areas of legal process. So the possibility

of inquisition, if not prosecution, hangs over the head of every American taxpayer to the day of his death—and sometimes afterward.

Even in criminal cases, the statute of limitations for income tax offenses is an incredible six years. In actual practice, it is six years and nine months, since the IRS can file a criminal complaint on the last day of the statutory limit and just leave it hanging for another nine months before getting an indictment.[1]

A recent court decision has also ruled that the limitation period does not start when the taxpayer files his return, but on the date the District Director's office acknowledges receipt of it.[2]

There is now indisputable evidence that some enforcement officers of the revenue service have used this implicit threat ruthlessly to coerce those who differ on questions of tax liability, or who challenge the autocratic and sometimes illegal behavior of the agents.

After his Senate Judiciary subcommittee had spent months carefully investigating the practices of the Internal Revenue Service, U.S. Senator Edward V. Long reported that "there appears to be a festering infection in the IRS."

"We hear much about the 'voluntariness' of our tax system, and there is much to be said for it. But frequently these taxes, which are 'voluntarily' paid, are paid because of the roughest kind of threats and the apparent prospect of the great cost and great retribution facing those who choose to disagree with IRS." [3]

A list of the legal powers (to say nothing of the *illegal* ones) granted to IRS tax detectives reads like a passage out of Himmler's manual for the Gestapo. Some of the more frightening ones, as set forth in the Internal Revenue Code, include the following:

Under Section 7608, agents may, at their discretion, execute and serve warrants of arrest, search warrants, subpoenas and summonses. Often the sworn complaints on the basis of which the warrants are supposed to be issued are stated in the vaguest terms, containing nothing that even remotely shows probable cause as required by the Constitution. Sometimes, extensive searches of citizens' homes are made without a warrant at all, in direct violation of the Fourth Amendment.

Take the case of Grover Cooper, a resident of Englewood, New Jersey, who on October 8, 1963, was entertaining guests in his home at 287 Washington Place.

About 8:30 p.m., four Internal Revenue agents named Stolzenthaler, Doyle, Mulroy and Taylor, descended on his house, armed with an arrest warrant charging Cooper with making a false statement in connection with another taxpayer's case.

In the dramatic tradition of gangbusters, Stolzenthaler and Doyle went to the front door of Cooper's home, while Mulroy and Taylor stationed themselves "near the back door."

When Cooper appeared at the screen door in the rear of his home, Mulroy and Taylor "went up the stairs, addressed the man and learned that he was Cooper. They told him that they were Treasury inspectors, that a warrant for his arrest had been issued, and that the warrant was in the hands of an inspector then at the front door."

They then started through the kitchen toward front of the Cooper home, where their fellow agents had been admitted by the front door.

Mr. Cooper asked the four revenue men to come to his bedroom to discuss the matter, in order not to upset his wife, who was not well.

Doyle remained with Mrs. Cooper in the kitchen (although she was not named in the warrant), and the other three agents went with Cooper to his bedroom. There Stolzenthaler handed Mr. Cooper the warrant and, after the latter had read through the document, told him he was under arrest. The IRS agent further instructed Mr. Cooper to sit on the bed, then directed Taylor and Mulroy to search the bedroom.

None of the agents had a search warrant.

Nevertheless, for the next one and a half hours, they ransacked every nook and cranny of the Cooper bedroom, going through drawers, clothing, boxes of personal keepsakes and private papers. When the householder objected to this unlawful invasion of his home, the federal officers put handcuffs on him.

In the course of their pillage, they seized and took away with them a briefcase, notebooks, at least one address book, a number of papers, including tax returns, W-2 tax forms, other IRS tax forms, business cards, slips of paper with names and telephone numbers on them and so on.

After this intensive prying into every secret of the Cooper bedroom, the agents went to the garage, where they made a thorough search of the family automobile.

It is important to bear in mind that Mr. Cooper was not a suspected tax dodger or racketeer. He was merely accused of making a false statement in connection with the tax returns of someone else.

In the court proceedings which followed, District Judge Wyatt ruled that the revenue men's arrest of Mr Cooper was unlawful because their warrant, issued by the tax commissioner, was invalid, having been issued on an insufficient complaint that did not show any probable cause to believe that an offense had been committed and that the defendant had committed it. Said Judge Wyatt:

"The situation is, that on the strength of an invalid warrant of arrest, Internal Revenue Service inspectors—having no authority to execute even a valid warrant—entered at night the dwelling house of Cooper; arrested him, searched his bedroom and seized numerous papers. This seems clearly an unlawful entry and a violation of the Fourth Amendment."

The court further observed that "the papers seized, as set forth in the inventory, seem to have no connection whatever with the offenses for which Cooper was arrested, and thus are not apparently even evidence of the commission of *that* offense.

"The nature of the search, the place, the character of the articles seized—personal and business papers—required the conclusion that there was a lawless invasion of the premises and a general exploratory search in the hope that evidence of crime might be found." [4]

Thus, these four agents of the federal government stand publicly exposed as miscreants who had unlawfully entered a citizen's home, bullied and abused him, illegally invaded his innermost privacy, and seized his personal papers, supposedly safeguarded by the Fourth Amendment of the U. S. Constitution.

Yet there is no evidence that they were ever even reprimanded by their superiors for their acts. It is more than likely that they were excused with that dangerous and threadbare plea that has come to be the stock in trade of law-enforcement officers who ignore the law: They were just a little "overzealous" in their devotion to duty.

It may be argued that Mr. Cooper eventually received full justice when the court denounced the misconduct of the agents and ordered them to return the personal possessions they had seized unlawfully.

But is this not a strange kind of justice, wherein a victim's only redress for ill treatment, anxiety and costly litigation is merely the return of his stolen property?

Another provision of the IRS Code (Section 7608) empowers the agents to dispense with arrest warrants altogether if internal revenue offenses are committed in their presence, or if they have reasonable grounds to believe a felony under such laws has been, or is being committed. The question of what constitutes an offense against the internal revenue law is so poorly defined and diffused over such a multitude of violations that a special agent could conceivably arrest any taxpayer on suspicion at any time.

That the public is becoming aware of these sweeping powers is evident in the grim humor with which tax-law enforcement is sometimes viewed. A recent cartoon by Robert Day shows two prisoners conversing in the exercise yard of a penitentiary. One says to the other: "Well, among other things, my amount on line 12 was larger than my payments on line 17, and I forgot to enter the balance due on line 18." [5]

Section 7608 also legalizes the seizure of property to satisfy tax indebtedness. Property, as defined within the meaning of this statute, can include just about anything except the gold filling in your teeth.

In practice, the government will not seize your home, for the good reason that even the slow-thinking and slower-acting American public would soon rebel at this final turn of the screw. Instead, tax officials file a lien against the property, which prevents your selling or otherwise disposing of it. Even after you have paid the delinquent tax and accrued interest claimed by the revenue service, IRS officials may not vacate the lien unless you or your legal representative follow through to see that it is done. Apparently, the government prefers to retain this hold over your property in case of future tax default.

A newspaper reporter who worked with me in Los Angeles had an experience of this kind. When he decided to sell his former home in another state, he discovered that Internal Revenue still had a lien against it for taxes he had paid off years before. Getting the title cleared cost him considerable trouble and expense.

Where a taxpaper's business or commercial property is concerned, no restraint is imposed. Everything can be seized, down to the last postage stamp. Countless American citizens have found themselves suddenly stripped bare, penniless and without the means of earning a livelihood.

Until the passage of Public Law 89-44 on June 21, 1965, exempting first-class mail from IRS seizure, federal agents had used nothing more than the arrogance of office to have postal employees deliver to them the sealed, private correspondence of a taxpayer who was being defoliated.

Section 7602 of the Internal Revence Service Code gives agents authority to examine any books, records, papers or data they consider relevant to a tax inquiry.

This means that even though your own tax return is not being questioned, and that you are innocent of any wrongdoing, you may be required to produce private papers and personal records to be used in prosecuting someone else. The person actually under investigation could be a former employee, a doctor or lawyer you once consulted, a stranger with whom you had a single business transaction, a relative or friend; or "anyone the agents may deem proper."

If you refuse to respond to such a summons and to produce the documents as directed; or to answer under oath questions that may pry into your personal and private affairs, you can be fined $1,000 and imprisoned for one year.

No doors, it seems, can be closed against the elite myrmidons of the federal government. Acting under authority of Section 7606, they can enter any building during the day (and at night, if it is unlocked—or if they use their own devices), to examine any articles believed to be subject to federal tax. To refuse them entry will net you a $500 fine and will probably result in harassment by the IRS office in the district where your returns are filed.

Having been granted such vast powers, it would be strange indeed if Internal Revenue agents did not sometimes feel, as one irate attorney put it, "fifteen feet tall." It is doubtful whether any Russian commissar or Nazi SS officer was ever given greater authority.

That this authority is sometimes abused is no longer a matter of opinion. During a recent Senate probe into invasions of privacy by government agencies, a number of courageous citizens recounted, under oath, stories of intimidation and harassment.

Consider, for example, the case of Corporal Paul R. Campbell, a Kansas City traffic policeman. One day not long ago, he observed a car exceeding the speed limit in the area near 44th and Gilham streets in that city.

The officer halted the car and asked the driver for his operator's license. With this in hand, he began writing out a citation. The driver identified himself as a member of the Internal Revenue Service, but Corporal Campbell went right on with the summons. The traffic officer's own account of what followed is this:

"After I had written him a summons for speeding, he said, 'Well, we'll have to check your taxes.' I said, 'I don't care. I have paid them.' Following this, shortly thereafter, I received a phone call to bring some information to the tax bureau. Then there was a second trip . . . and then a third time. I got a letter for me to bring all my information on 1960 and 1961. It was just a matter of a few weeks after that that I received another letter that stated the taxes would stand as they were filed, no change."

Not only ordinary taxpayers and policemen on the beat are sometimes reminded of the sword of Damocles that hangs over their heads. During court proceedings in a tax case, Federal Judge Charles Wyzanski commented recently:

"More than once, judges of a court have been indirectly reminded that they personally are taxpayers. No sophisticated person is unaware that even in this very Commonwealth, the Internal Revenue Service has been in possession of facts with respect to public officials which it has presented in order to serve what can only be called political ends, be they high or low. And a judge who knows the score is aware that every time his decision offends the Internal Revenue Service, he is inviting a close inspection of his own returns. But I suppose that no one familiar with this court believes that intimidation, direct or indirect, is effective." [6]

An important factor that would appear to place the taxpayer at a disadvantage in court is the question of impartiality on the part of jurors, who may fear to offend the powerful Internal Revenue Service by rendering a verdict unfavorable to the government.

Bernard Fensterwald, counsel for the Senate Judiciary subcommittee that investigated IRS, declared: "We have discovered in the Pittsburgh area, we think, instances where prospective jurors were not only subject to tax investigations, which I understand is a normal means of proceeding, but also to field investigations by the

FBI, and I just wondered if you could have a completely impartial jury if the prospective juror is subject to this type of investigation."

Gustave Diamond, U.S. attorney for the western district of Pennsylvania, said that in several cases which the government considered to be important, the IRS was requested to check the records of the persons who made up the jury panel "to indicate whether or not they have anything of pertinence, relative to a prospective juror." On some occasions, he said, "we have also requested—generally through the Department of Justice—the FBI to check their indexes, and perhaps on some occasions also to make a credit check."

The word of such inquiries gets back to the prospective jurors, who are fully aware when they go into court that they are "under the gun."

Mr. Diamond said also it was his understanding that in one district, which he thought might be in Delaware, under existing court procedures there are private investigators who conduct investigations of prospective jurors and compile a report which they then sell to interested attorneys "or to anyone who is interested in purchasing it."

Whether a tax defendant could expect a fair and impartial jury under such circumstances is a question which—for a mind innocent of legal sophistry—is not difficult to answer.

Attorneys who have vigorously defended taxpayers in their unequal fight against the massive power of the government, have also complained that they have been singled out for special attention by tax officials.

In one instance, a New York lawyer named Julius November, who represents former heavyweight champion Floyd Patterson, charged that IRS had intercepted a letter written to him by a client in California. The letter had been opened and read, then resealed and marked, "Received in error—District Director, Manhattan 13, N.Y."

The attorney lodged a strong protest with postal authorities, pointing out that the letter was clearly addressed, even having the correct zip code number. Moreover, his office was not even in the same postal zone as that of the district director of Internal Revenue.

"I cannot help wonder how many letters sent to me by my clients, which may furnish leads against my clients, may have gone to the Internal Revenue, been opened and destroyed.

"As a result, of course, of all this, I have the Internal Revenue special agent on my back. Nobody has indicted me. He has just been in my office now to the point where I sometimes tell him that I really have to practice law; otherwise I cannot make money and pay taxes to the government." [7]

Boston attorney Lawrence O'Donnell, who was "uncooperative" with the IRS, was actually made the subject of a criminal investigation by the intelligence division of the tax office. When the investigating agent, Dante Dieso, appeared before a Senate subcommittee hearing, he was asked on what basis he had been assigned to the case. His reply was, "The case was assigned to me as a result of an audit referral, sir."

Attorney O'Donnell had a different story. Speaking under oath, he said: "Mr. Dieso just gave the impression that my case came from audit. It did not come from audit because I was never audited in my entire lifetime."

The lawyer added that "they have never let up for a minute after I appeared in behalf of the third parties in the McGarry case. They became particularly intensive when I went in front of the Federal court, in front of Judge Charles E. Wyzanski, to establish an illegal search and seizure, for threatening to put Donald Lord in jail when they went into his home on April 18, 1962; and after very careful testimony, Judge Wyzanski found that it was in fact an illegal search and seizure."

Mr. O'Donnell said that Special Agent Dieso came into the case when the attorney started to prepare a contempt petition against IRS, because of the agency's failure to return records as ordered by the court. He said that in going to their offices on over seventeen occasions, he had "listened to their threats and what they were going to do to me."

The McGarry case, referred to by Mr. O'Donnell, was a bitterly contested legal proceeding during the course of which it was disclosed that revenue agents had set up an "observation post" in a deserted barn about fifty yards from the home of a taxpayer, where they had spied upon the intimate life of his family night and day and, according to a former special agent who had participated, made illegal entry into the home, where a basement vault was searched.

The Boston attorney said that after he had started representing third parties on the McGarry case, IRS Special Agent Robert Ferrick had informed him: "I'm going to get you, O'Donnell."

During the ensuing investigation of him, Mr. O'Donnell charged, revenue agents sought to destroy his professional reputation by saying that he was the object of an organized crime probe, and was representing unworthy people.[8]

In prosecution of a taxpayer on criminal charges, the voluntariness of testimony by witnesses brought into the case by the Internal Revenue Service is also sometimes subject to doubt.

Such appears to have been the situation in the proceedings against Lawrence Maloney, a Pittsburgh police official. Referring to several convicted felons who testified against Mr. Maloney, Senator Long asked an IRS official appearing before his committee:

"Don't you know the reason they have not been sent to jail is that they [the prosecution] are holding these sentences—or the impostion of the sentences—over them as a sort of blackmail to get them to testify in this particular case?"

Even honest, law-abiding citizens who are asked to testify for a defendant may be given pause by the realization that their own tax files can be "pulled" for scrutiny by an offended revenue agent.

A tax lawyer told me, "Criminal cases are, of course, tried by U.S. attorneys, representing the Department of Justice; and it has been my experience that they are honorable and ethical men who would not knowingly permit coercion of a witness.

"However, defense witnesses sometimes *fear* retaliation, and this can make it difficult to present the strongest possible case for the defendant."

It is a fact that criminal tax cases are the only prosecutions in American courts in which the government holds the potential power of reprisal against any witness who takes the stand.

William Merle Canady of Kansas City, who was convicted on a tax charge, told the Senate Judiciary subcommittee recently:

"You would be surprised the people that are fearful of our government.

"We have people in this community who are so fearful of their Federal government today that . . . it is very difficult for me to testify here because of the fact that people have come to me as a friend and have begged me not to use their names." [9]

Later in the hearings, another witness, who had also been prosecuted on criminal tax charges, was asked by Senator Long:

"Have you ever talked to anyone, as I have—many citizens who owe little amounts of money—and the agents come in and are so rough and so rude, and *the ordinary citizen is so scared of them,* they will go ahead and pay the tax, even though they feel they don't owe it?"

The witness replied:

"Absolutely. This is common knowledge they do this. *People are afraid."* [Emphasis added.] [10]

It is hardly surprising that the American people should fear a machine of despotism so powerful that it can destroy the reputation as well as harass and bankrupt any citizen who incurs its wrath.

It was a former employee of the Internal Revenue Service itself who, after eleven years as special agent, described IRS as "a Goliath that can take the powers that are given to them and grind the rights of the citizen into the ground." [11]

It cannot be too often repeated that one of the distinguishing features of a police state is the punishment—either legal or extra-legal—of citizens who openly protest oppressive measures imposed by the regime, or who challenge the legal authority of its acts.

The emergence of such a pattern of reprisal can already be discerned in recently uncovered acts by the Internal Revenue Service. The vindictiveness of at least some of its agents is a matter of record.

For example, Allen N. Brunwasser, a Pittsburgh attorney, said he found himself "heading for possible criminal difficulty" after he had subpoenaed the chief of the IRS intelligence division to appear in court in one case, and had filed action against an IRS agent in another.

"The matter came up before Judge Gorley, a very learned and respected member of the bench, a district judge," the lawyer recalled. "While the case was going on, he said to me in a fatherly way—and I assumed he was giving me good advice—he said to me in effect, 'You ought to read *How to Win Friends and Influence People*. You have offended the Federal government, and they will investigate you for the rest of your life.' " [12]

Bernard Fensterwald, chief counsel for the Long committee, told me during an interview in Washington, D.C.;

"Anyone who volunteers to aid this committee is in trouble. And we tell them that before they testify."

One of the most dangerous weapons put into the hands of IRS agents is the authority to make prolonged investigations, without bringing the case into court for adjudication. There are cases on record in which the ruthless probe into a taxpayer's affairs continued over a period of years.

Such a taxpayer may never be indicted and therefore *never* have his day in court, where he can confront his accusers and clear his name. Nevertheless, he may be severely and extra-judiciously punished by having agents question scores of his friends and business associates or clients about his "tax matters."

"The seductive process in interrogation," said Bruce I. Hochman, prominent Los Angeles tax attorney, "all too often leaves a third party with a false impression of a business associate's tactics.

"For instance, an agent comes to you and says, 'How many cash transactions have you had with Smith?'

"You reply, 'I've had none,' and the interview is over. The question was a seductive one. The agent may not know that Smith ever had *any* cash transactions, but when he leaves, you're left with the impression: Maybe this guy Smith is a cash artist and I'd better not do business with him." [13]

Another experienced tax lawyer, Ernest R. Mortenson, says of the practice of protracted investigations, "If they can't do it in a reasonable length of time, maybe they shouldn't do it at all."

Such was the sentiment also expressed by Senator Edward V. Long, after two years of hearings across the country:

"Shouldn't there be some remedy, since we are going out of our way in this country to guarantee a citizen a speedy trial so he can be tried before a jury of his peers—but we take this type of investigation that drags along, the man is completely ruined; he loses his job, he loses his reputation, his standing in the community, and then if you say we are not going to do anything about it, you have already punished the man and you have damaged him beyond repair. Would you not suggest that there be some way that an investigation should be made that would protect that man up until the jury found him guilty?"

Unknown to most Americans, revenue agents have a virtual open-sesame to their most private financial records and papers in any bank.

By law, tax investigators are supposed to serve a summons upon the bank, naming specifically those records and documents they wish to examine.

In practice, however, most bankers (who are themselves taxpayers) allow agents a surprising—and unjustified—latitude in going through just about any kind of file or record in the bank.

Agents have admitted that they often walk into a bank without a summons or legal authority of any kind other than their IRS identification and, at their leisure, copy information from deposit tickets, canceled checks, bank statements and so on.

A former agent said that at one bank where he had a friendly relationship, he was allowed to go on a "fishing expedition"—that is, to make a general search through depositors' records.

On one occasion, two tax detectives removed checks during such a general review of bank records, took them across the street to a YMCA and made copies of them, using the Y's Verifax printer.

When Internal Revenue serves levy form No. 668-A on a bank and freezes a depositor's account, the taxpayer is not informed of the fact.

The banker, of course, *could* inform his client, if he were not afraid to incur the displeasure of the federal government. As a banking publication pointed out to its readers, customers rely upon their banker to protect their interests and to have respect for the confidential nature of their affairs.

But for bankers to cooperate with their clients rather than with the revenue service is apparently frowned upon by the IRS.

As a Los Angeles banker explained to me, "The federal government is our biggest depositor; we can't afford to offend their representatives or they will transfer their accounts."

Gordon W. Warren, president of the Pulaski County Bank in Richmond, Missouri, said that on one occasion two special agents came into his office and demanded information concerning one of the bank's customers.

When Mr. Warren announced his intention of notifying the client of their inquiry, the revenue men told him they did not want the customer informed. The banker said one of the agents—named Horn—told him, "If you do it, you are liable to a $10,000 fine and a 10-year imprisonment."

Mr. Warren called the bank's attorney who, after consultation with a tax lawyer, informed him that the Internal Revenue Code contains no such provision. Agent Horn had lied in an attempt to intimidate the banker.

But Banker Warren is a member of that vanishing breed of Americans to whom justice and fair play are more important than the friendly nod of truculent bureaucrats.

He recalled another instance, on March 31, 1965, when an agent came into his bank and presented a levy for $291.06 against a customer's account. The depositor, a small businessman of the town, had a balance of $170.65 on that date. That balance represented the only funds he had to carry on the business of his modest firm.

Mr. Warren suggested that, since the taxpayer's place of business was only about six hundred feet from the bank, the agent ought to take the matter up with him directly. Mr. Warren was certain the man was not aware he owed the government money.

The agent, however, refused to follow the banker's suggestion. He said the service had communicated with the taxpayer by mail and had not received an answer. Mr. Warren pointed out that it had been his experience that customers of his bank sometimes find it difficult to interpret communications they receive from the income tax office.

The IRS agent insisted on levying against the taxpayer's small account.

After the account was thus frozen, two checks in the amount of $21.74 and of $30.47 came into the bank for payment. The customer had issued them in good faith, thinking that he had funds in the bank to cover them. But, because the account had been officially frozen, the bank was obliged to return the checks. This jeopardized the credit standing and good name of the small businessman, who had written the checks to a supplier in payment for merchandise.

Ironically, it was later proved that the taxpayer did not owe the taxes claimed by the government.

The Missouri banker said he remembered another situation in which a revenue agent came into the bank with a levy for $14.92 against a prominent and prosperous farmer of the area. Knowing the taxpayer to be a patriotic citizen, Mr. Warren suggested that it was not necessary to freeze the man's account, because "he doesn't realize he owes you the money."

The IRS man became irritated with the idea of simply asking the farmer for the money, so Mr. Warren paid the $14.92 out of his own pocket. Admitting that "I am a bit of a flagraiser," the banker said, "These people that we have are wonderful people. They love this country. . . . We have people who are interested in these United States of America, and to a man of the type involved here—I felt it would hurt his pride to know that the government had come in and run a levy against his account for $14.92."

As a matter of fact, the government has run levies for even smaller amounts. In one case on record, they issued a levy against a bank account for a claimed delinquency of $2.35.

Another kind of enforcement, which the Internal Revenue Service shares with Soviet Russia and other Communist dictatorships, is one that might be called the scapegoat prosecution.

IRS officials have admitted that a prominent professional or businessman will be singled out for investigation and possible indictment because the wide publicity accorded his difficulty will act as a deterrent to others of his category. They boast that, after such a public example, other taxpayers in the same trade or profession will file amended returns.

Whether these taxpayers believe they owe additional taxes, or pay as appeasement to prevent harassment and investigation, is a matter of debate.

Employing the sacrificial method in California, Internal Revenue agents went after an eminent Kern County physician and secured a conviction which resulted in the doctor's having to pay $12,000 in back taxes, as well as a substantial fine. Later, in an interview with a newspaper reporter, an official of the IRS intelligence division in

Los Angeles, said the publicity value in the physican's prosecution lay in the fact that the doctor had gained national renown as a hole-in-one golf expert! [14]

A former special agent who worked for the intelligence division reported that "the Internal Revenue Service will take a case that happens to be on the back burner of the stove and just cooking slowly, and then bring it forward to the front burner right around the time that tax returns have to be filed; and they get an extra amount of publicity at the time they feel it will do the most good." [15]

In some areas of the country, if not in all, entire trades or callings will be selected for intensive investigation and surveillance. Said Alvin M. Kelley, then district director of Boston, Massachusetts:

"I would like to say this, that we are interested in the psychological impact of our work on voluntary compliance, and we do pick certain occupations and certain strata of income and so on, each year, that we take a special look at." [16]

Like certain other autocratic federal agencies, in their campaigns to frighten the public into uncritical compliance with official decrees, IRS has found a willing ally in the press. Until regulations were changed recently, in response to a good deal of pressure, agents of Internal Revenue's intelligence division would tip off the newspapers when they were about to conduct a raid or make an important seizure. Reporters and photographers were invited to go along in order to give the fullest and most sensational coverage of the event.

Instructions in the closely guarded *Internal Revenue Manual* state:

"In cases pending with the U.S. attorney, the Service will cooperate with him in an attempt to obtain maximum favorable news coverage. In each case presented for indictment, sufficient information will be furnished to the U.S. attorney to permit his issuance of an appropriate release."

With all the foregoing investigative and prosecutive procedures at their command, it would seem to the ordinary person that in any encounter between citizen and the IRS the cards are sufficiently stacked in the government's favor.

Such, however, is apparently not the view of the revenue enforcers themselves. During the past decade, they have turned more and more to electronic surveillance and privacy intrusion.

This police-state practice of seeking for the guilty among a mass of innocent people has been carried out by means of wiretapping, bugging, hidden microphones and tape recorders, concealed cameras, mail covers, disguises, illegal entries and paid informers.

The IRS not only taught its agents these odious techniques of spy government, but supplied its field offices with highly skilled experts from the national office in Washington, to supervise and aid the operations.

Cresson O. Davis, head of the Service's intelligence division in Pittsburgh, told a Senate subcommittee that there was a tacit understanding among agents that, although wiretapping was a violation of the law, as well as of agency regulations, national revenue officials approved of it.

"They conducted a school here in Washington where our agents were brought and taught to wire-tap, taught to build transmitters, pick locks, and the various things that occurred in the schools."

The snoop academy to which Mr. Davis referred is known by the respectable name of Technical Aids School. Since 1955, it has been operated by the U. S. Treasury Department in the Sloan Building on 12th Street in the nation's capital.

There, personnel from various federal agencies, including the IRS, are given a course in basic electronics and the use of intrusion equipment, including lock picks, sometimes referred to as burglar tools.

Burke Yung, senior coordinator of the IRS Intelligence Division, and widely acknowledged among government undercover agents as the country's leading authority on wiretapping and bugging, admitted having served as one of the instructors at the national school.

According to him, the curriculum includes not only lectures and demonstrations but actual work problems to make sure the agents don't bungle their jobs and get caught. In groups of five, the "students" are assigned such tasks as the planting of microphones and the placing of a wiretap on a telephone.

"We have them actually installed without supervision, and then examine the installation afterward," the intrusion specialist said.

"The one year in which I instructed in the wires—I believe it was 1962—we had a box there of some sort, which had four or five different types of pair boxes to familiarize the agents with the type of pair boxes they would run into in the field." [17]

Pair boxes are terminal points where illegal taps are put on telephone wires.

During some courses at the school, a documentary training film called "The Big Ear," is also shown.

There are reported instances of agents being presented with a kit of lock picks, as well as diplomas, at the time of graduation from the government-run espionage lyceum.

In addition to the Washington school, some of the IRS agents added to their education by attendance at another, operated by U. S. Army Intelligence at Ft. Holabird in Maryland.

Although most high-ranking officials of the Internal Revenue Service profess ignorance of the widespread lawbreaking and privacy invasion by special agents, when confronted with the evidence, certain facts clearly undermine the sincerity of their denials.

In the first place, a complete inventory of wiretapping and bugging equipment is maintained in the IRS national office in Washington. It is to this center of the spy web that supervisors in the field turn when they feel the need for expert assistance and tools for secretly invading a taxpayer's home or office.

Although an extensive inventory of up-to-date eavesdropping

devices is kept in storerooms on the seventh floor (in dead center of the IRS headquarters building), and in the basement of the same location, Internal Revenue Commissioner Sheldon S. Cohen disclaimed any knowledge of the gear until it had been uncovered by Senate investigators.

The ordinary citizen cannot help sharing the view of Senator Long, who told the commissioner:

"With all due respect to you (I realize you have been in your present position a relatively short time), how the officials of that department, with all this type of activity going on around them, did not know of the activities of their agents, is very difficult for me to understand."

As a matter of fact, according to intelligence chief Cresson O. Davis of the Pittsburgh division, high officials of the IRS were knowing participants in at least two wiretaps in his area.

He recalled telephoning Robert A. Manzi, assistant national director of the intelligence division in Washington, when he wished to have taps placed on telephone wires in 1961 and 1964.

In both instances the IRS national office obligingly dispatched electronics specialist Burke Yung with equipment to make the taps.

Davis reluctantly admitted under questioning that agents had rigged one wiretap so that it could be monitored in the first-floor den of his home. His wife was excluded from the room while a special agent for four months recorded confidential conversations from three telephone lines.

Pennsylvania has a statute outlawing all wiretapping by enforcement officers, whether they are federal, state or local, but this did not deter the Internal Revenue men. As in other states having similar laws, they apparently did not feel themselves within the cognizance of courts of law.

"I do not think I have concerned myself about state laws," Burke Yung declared.

Another ranking IRS official, Joseph Harmon, deputy chief of intelligence, admitted that this disregard for law was nationwide.

Even in those states where wiretapping by law officers is legal, provided agents get a court order, he said, "I know of no instance where we ever have."

In one instance, uncovered in the East, Washington provided funds for a district office to purchase a truck equipped for wiretapping, which was painted to resemble a telephone vehicle. Agents then disguised themselves as telephone men so they could tap lines without arousing suspicion.

Investigation has brought to light facts that suggest that the revenue service frequently resorts to impersonations and disguises in its surveillance of taxpayers.

One special agent in southern California posed as a recruiter for an aircraft company in order to spy upon the employees. Another passed himself off as an unscrupulous lawyer.

In Boston, an IRS undercover man named Henry Foderaro donned a Coast Guard uniform and for two months masqueraded as a petty officer, despite the fact that it is a federal crime for anyone to impersonate an officer of the Coast Guard or of the U.S. military services.

Sometimes persons from outside the revenue service are recruited to serve as spies, decoys and informers.

There was, for example, Mrs. Bonnie Holeman (née Johnson), an attractive former waitress, who worked for IRS agents in the San Francisco area from October, 1964, through May, 1965.

During that time, Mrs. Holeman (then Miss Johnson) acted as an informer, and was set up by the revenue service in a bookmaking business for the purpose of ensnaring those who might be engaged in accepting illegal wagers.

Miss Johnson's first assignment was to eavesdrop and spy upon a number of innocent citizens with the hope of discovering someone guilty of crime.

She said Special Agent Larry Miller took her to the vicinity of a bar and told her to go in and mingle with the patrons and see if she could find out anything.

Later, the IRS agents rented an apartment for Miss Johnson at 995 Pine Street in San Francisco, directly across the hall from one occupied by them. They paid her rent ($180 a month), and gave her a salary of $80 a week, which was later raised to $100. Although employees of the federal government are customarily paid by check, Mrs. Holeman said she was paid in cash, sometimes by Agent Miller and on other occasions by Agents Henry Veit and Fred Pinocci.

Mrs. Holeman said her duties were to sit in her apartment and record telephone calls, record wagers and pass them on to another person (apparently a bookmaker, who believed the young woman was his employee).

Asked whether she had entertained guests in the apartment, Mrs. Holeman replied:

"The people I was investigating would stop by the apartment occasionally, and also members of the Intelligence Division (of IRS) would stop by the apartment."

She acknowledged that the agents had placed a concealed microphone in her living quarters, which they could monitor in their own apartment across the hall. She admitted that they had listened to (and presumably recorded) everything said in her apartment.

On some occasions, when Mrs. Holeman's activities apparently took place outside the apartment, IRS agents provided her with a tiny transmitter, which she concealed under her arm.

It is reasonable to suppose that all the magnetic tapes on which unguarded conversations with Miss Johnson were recorded have been carefully preserved in some secret archive and conceivably could be fed, along with other data, into some future electronic dossier.

Such secret transcripts are not confined to field investigations and penetrations into homes and offices. No taxpayer who has visited an IRS office in any of twenty-two cities across the country can be certain that a taped record of his interview there may not be filed away somewhere among IRS confidential memoranda. These recordings may even be of privileged conversations between the taxpayer and his lawyer, accountant, wife or business associate.

An Internal Revenue conference room in Boston was equipped with two-way mirrors for observing and photographing taxpayers; and with microphones hidden behind electric outlet plugs to monitor and record conversations. The room was also equipped with a polygraph or so-called "lie-detector."

In Pittsburgh, a certified public accountant named Robert J. Arnold told how he, a partner, a taxpayer and an attorney accidentally discovered a permanently installed two-way mirror in the conference room, where IRS agents interview taxpayers.

He said that in August, 1963, during a tax investigation of one of his clients, the revenue intelligence unit asked that his client appear at 1 P.M. on August 8 for a formal question-and-answer session pertaining to the client's income tax.

The taxpayer was accompanied to the meeting by Mr. Arnold, by one of the latter's business partners and by George Kiester, an attorney.

"Prior to attending this conference," said Mr. Arnold, "I had a meeting with the taxpayer and the attorney, at which time I advised them of the rumors that I had heard to the effect that the room was bugged, and that there would be a one-way mirror available for picture taking. The attorney became quite indignant at these remarks on my part—wouldn't believe it, wouldn't listen to it, and I was taken to task."

At the meeting, the taxpayer and his representatives sat around a table with Special Agents Driscoll and Eddy.

Agent Driscoll informed them that it was to be a formal question-and-answer conference, so he would ask his secretary to come in, and would place the taxpayer under oath.

At the same time, he requested the attorney, who had seated himself on the side of the table with the revenue agents, to move around and seat himself beside the taxpayer, so that if the taxpayer wished to ask questions of his attorney, it would not disturb the conference.

Attorney Kiester arose and started to pass behind the agents to the other side of the table. On the wall behind him was a picture of the Statue of Liberty, with an American flag draped around it. Accidentally, the attorney's shoulder brushed the picture and it fell to the floor, revealing what had been concealed behind it; a two-way mirror.

According to the accountant who related the incident, "there was a considerable amount of embarrassment" on the part of Special Agent Driscoll. He retrieved the picture and tried to rehang it over the spy-hole mirror, but the nail that had held it had also fallen.

Mr. Arnold said he took the picture and placed it on the table between the taxpayer and the government agents. He quietly suggested that, in the circumstances, there be no formal questions and answers. The taxpayer, he told the IRS men, was there to discuss his problem and to answer questions honestly. The "formal procedure" was not necessary.

"The American flag lay between us on the table while we concluded our question-and-answer session," the accountant said.[18]

Internal Revenue officials have tried to justify the police-state type of surveillance equipment installed in IRS conference rooms by asserting that such devices are necessary when dealing with criminals and racketeers.

It was one of their own agents, however, who declared:

"Racketeers don't talk to us. They don't come in and give sworn statements." [19]

While revenue agents insist upon recording (sometimes secretly) their interrogations of the taxpayer, they will not permit a citizen to bring with him his own stenographer to take down exactly what is said during the proceedings.

He can obtain a copy of the IRS transcript only after he has signed it. If he does not sign it, under oath, he is not allowed to have a copy of his own statement.

In every encounter of the ordinary citizen with federal agents, he is expected to "cooperate like a patriotic American."

What such cooperation can mean was illustrated not long ago when revenue agents in Kansas City wished to bug an apartment in Armour Towers there. After the U.S. attorney had advised them not to enter the private apartment, the agents went to the owner of the building and prevailed upon him to "cooperate" by taking a clandestine transmitter into his tenant's apartment and concealing it under a couch.

The IRS team—Intelligence Supervisor Lawrence B.. Bennett and Special Agent Everett W. Trost—then placed a receiver in a vacant apartment of the building, where they tried to monitor conversations taking place in the bugged suite.

Transmission was not satisfactory, so the agents enlisted further cooperation; this time from the tenants who occupied the apartment adjoining the one they had under surveillance.

Agents Trost and Bennett placed their receiver and recorder in the living room of the requisitioned apartment.

For a whole week thereafter, the family which occupied the apartment turned over the use of their living room, night and day, to the two federal agents for the purpose of eavesdropping on their neighbor.

There is now irrefutable evidence that Internal Revenue agents were wiretapping and using privacy-invading tools as far back as 1942, if not earlier.

Burke Yung, the government's top expert in the installation of devices for electronic espionage, testified that he was first instructed in his "art" by an IRS agent named William Mellon in 1942. Mellon was a former telephone company employee; and his sole duty in the revenue service, according to Agent Yung, consisted of wiretapping and planting microphones.

Invasion of privacy on a massive scale did not get into full swing, however, until 1961. It was in February of that year that the U.S. attorney general made IRS part of the government's so-called organized crime drive.

Prior to that date, the Internal Revenue Service did not have a national hobgoblin with which to frighten the public into accepting unconstitutional practices in law enforcement. The Narcotics Bureau has always had the specter of wholesale drug addiction by the nation's youth; the FBI has had the menace of communism with which to plead justification for trampling on the people's rights. But until OCD (Organized Crime Drive) was born, the revenue service had only tax collection.

And taxes were not enough. As government officials themselves have admitted, the American is a model taxpayer. Estimates of unreported income suggest that the citizens of this country voluntarily report 95 per cent of all their income. Robert K. Lund, IRS intelligence chief in Los Angeles, gave even a higher figure for his own area. He said 97 per cent of federal tax returns in southern California are "reasonably" accurate.

Such compliance with the law, even by those who regard it as confiscatory, certainly provided no basis for what the Service calls "saturation type" investigation.

Organized crime, on the other hand, was a different matter. During the Kefauver and the McClellan hearings, the general public learned that big crime syndicates were operating a billion-dollar-a-year business in gambling, narcotics and prostitution. They had inter-related setups in all the major cities, where they corrupted police and public officials and threatened to take over even legitimate businesses and reputable corporations. Statistics issued by the FBI, dramatic news accounts of narcotics seizures and of the secret gathering of crime overlords such as the Apalachin meeting—all contributed to the growing fear that mobsters and Mafia or Cosa Nostra chieftains would soon control the destiny of the nation itself.

Drastic measures were called for, and most Americans could

only applaud any move by the government that would curb the "growing and fearsome force" of organized crime.

Attorney General Robert F. Kennedy had barely taken over as head of the Department of Justice before he announced a broad plan to smash the power of the bankrollers and kingpins of the underworld.

The basic technique of this anti-crime drive was to select the most important figures in organized crime and to batter them with the combined strength of many government agencies which have investigative powers. These agencies included the FBI, Secret Service, Bureau of Narcotics, Immigration Service and Internal Revenue Service. Eventually, twenty-six agencies reportedly funneled information into Justice's organized crime section.

This OCD section began to compile what is called a master list of persons suspected of being members of the criminal hierarchy.

When a person's name was placed on this list, he was assigned an OCD number, and each of the participating agencies was instructed, in the words of one Justice Department lawyer, "to investigate the guy up to his eyeballs."

With the mass of information resulting from such a finely woven dragnet, the organized crime section would decide what, if any, possibility existed for successful prosecution.

On February 24, 1961, Mortimer M. Caplin, then Commissioner of Internal Revenue, issued a directive to regional commissioners and district directors of the Service across the country.

It stated that, as a part of the government's drive against organized crime, the attorney general had requested IRS to give top priority to the investigation of the tax affairs of *major racketeers*. [Italics supplied.]

"I cannot emphasize too strongly," Commissioner Caplin said, "the importance I attach to the success of the Service's contribution to this overall program."

The directive also contained the following instructions:

"In conducting such investigations, full use will be made of available electronic equipment and other technical aids, as well as such investigative techniques as surveillance, undercover work, etc. If the manpower or other resources of a district are not sufficient to cope with the volume of special racketeer work assigned to it, the district director shall immediately request assistance from the regional commissioner through the regional coordinator."

Most, if not all, agents in the Internal Revenue Service apparently interpreted this portion of the commissioner's directive as approval for the use of any privacy-invading tools available. Wiretapping and eavesdropping, not only of racketeer suspects, but of an unknown number of innocent persons, followed.

In this connection, it is important to trace the evolution of that Justice Department master list of "major racketeers" that were to be singled out for special treatment.

At the outset, the general public was given to understand that these dangerous "kingpins" were limited in number. In an early news account, Attorney General Robert Kennedy was quoted as saying there were "around one hundred."

As in the case of all similar police-state procedures, however, once established (on the basis of unpopular "public enemies"), the list was gradually expanded until it could include anybody.

According to James E. Miggins, former IRS special agent, who resigned from the Service in 1963 after seventeen years' service, "anyone that has a bad reputation was put on this list, and they were given intensive investigation.

"Someone who could be a legal businessman, say in Boston, could be put on that list—even though he was not a racketeer. He would be classified as a breaker of the law. Practically anyone, in fact, could be on this list. *Anyone in public office could be put on it also.*" [Emphasis added.]

Mr. Miggins said he was presently employed by a law firm that represents a corporation, a member of which had had his tax returns questioned by the revenue service.

"I understand these individuals are on the racketeers list. These people have never been arrested, never been in any illegal business. Yet they are classified as racketeers on the list. They have been given intensive investigation where the agents have practically been given carte blanche expenditures and go wherever they want."

Was it advantageous, then, to an IRS agent to have a large list of OCD cases?

The former agent said it would appear so, since agents assigned to an OCD case had overtime pay and could travel all over the country. He said, "I believe the budget for the OCD program comes from another source [outside IRS] and they have unlimited funds."

Mr. Miggins revealed that even one of the Internal Revenue Service's own agents had been put on the list.[20]

At a Senate subcommittee hearing on July 13, 1965, Nicholas deB. Katzenbach, who succeeded Robert F. Kennedy as attorney general acknowledged that when Internal Revenue came across "racketeering figures," in the course of investigations, "it could request that they be added as priority subjects."

Senator Long described this procedure in blunt terms. He said, "it has been the testimony before this Committee that an agent can write to Washington and say, 'Put Mr. Smith on the OCD list,' and that's it. . . . It is just a matter of someone's opinion. No jury says a man is guilty and is OCD." [21]

Attorney General Katzenbach said, nevertheless, that the Department of Justice continued to maintain a priority list and that "we will continue each of these functions because they represent the only way to fight organized crime successfully." [22]

Aware that revenue agents had admitted illegally tapping telephones, breaking and entering and engaging in a nationwide electronic espionage that in its scope would shame the most dedicated member of the Gestapo, the attorney general said:

"I want to put clearly on the record my admiration and respect for the devoted intelligence agents of the Service. I say this in full knowledge of the improper extremes reached in cases which prompt this hearing."

Commissioner Sheldon S. Cohen likewise defended the IRS agents, describing their illegal activities as "emanating from the highest motives."

In fairness to the revenue service as a whole, it should be pointed out that not all IRS agents were happy about instructions from their superiors who, while urging them to engage in practices repugnant to the American people, at the same time told them that if they were caught, "you're on your own."

Some had the courage to dissent, even at the cost of forfeiting chances for promotion and of harassment by their supervisors. Some quit the service in disgust.

One former member of the Internal Revenue rackets squad commented thus on being assigned to telephone taps and to hours of eavesdropping:

"I think the general feeling of the special agents was that they resented being put on this detail, but they had no other choice." [23]

Donald J. Young of Melrose, Massachusetts, another IRS agent who resigned after seven years and nine months in the Service, declared:

"I felt that the circumstances had become such that I could no longer wish to be associated with the Service."

Unfortunately, a study of the psychological impact upon the undercover agent, of being directed to perform duties that are deeply inimical to his moral sense, has never been made. For the agent with a police-state mentality—the so-called overzealous official—such tasks are, of course, welcome. But it is reasonable to suppose that, for a man who believes in the constitutional guarantees of liberty, the emotional conflict resulting from espionage assignments must be severe.

As for positive results of the organized crime drive in terms of criminal kingpins convicted, they appear to be small indeed.

The only area for which we have considerable documented evidence (thanks largely to the Senate Judiciary subcommittee) is Kansas City. It is quite likely typical of the others.

There, in October, 1965—more than four years after the drive was started—the chief of detectives of the Kansas City Police Department testified that only one important local racketeer was in prison. And he was serving a short sentence.

Who, then, were the other seventeen persons convicted, whose combined jail sentences totaled only thirty-one months?

A clue to answering that question may be found in the sworn statement of a former IRS special agent who was assigned to the OCD program in the San Francisco area.

"I noticed that after we arrested what was supposed to be book-making Mr. Big, we would find out he would turn out to be a part-time janitor or a dishwasher or a bartender or some other lesser individual; and I don't mean to speak disparagingly about the occupations I just mentioned. But they happened to be people who would have these large taxes levied against them, sometimes $10,000 and $20,000—and with their salaries or with the amount of money that they made, it would take perhaps the rest of their lives to pay off the levy of the tax against them."

In one case, he recalled, after six days of trial, "I was pertrified because I was afraid that the judge was going to ask me how much money was involved taxwise in that particular case."

The amount was less than $30.[24]

In the Pittsburgh area, and possibly in others, there were indications that the organized crime drive not only had not hurt the Mafiosi and big crime syndicates; ironically, it may even have helped them by removing from the local scene gamblers who had kept them out.

Meanwhile, the decay of moral sense and the corruption of values that inevitably accompany the spy system of government were evident in the reaction of high-ranking Justice Department officials to the disclosures of bugging, trespassing and wiretapping by federal agents.

At the end of four days of Senate hearings on invasion of privacy by Internal Revenue agents, the *New York Times* quoted an important Justice official as saying: "This will kill us."

Commenting on this "strange unconcern for legal procedure by some whose sworn duty it is to foster respect for the law," a *Times* editorial observed:

"Instead of deploring these breaches of law, the prevailing attitude among many top law-enforcers seems to be one of irritation that a Senate investigation caused the nation to learn of their use of outlaw methods to ferret out outlaws."

At a White House briefing for newsmen in July, 1965, presidential press secretary Bill Moyers informed the correspondents that President Lyndon B. Johnson had banned all wiretap and electronic eavesdropping by federal employees except in cases involving national security.

But if officials of the Internal Revenue Service received the directive, their subsequent statements gave no indication of it. The president's directive was issued June 30, 1965. Two weeks later, when asked whether IRS would now dispose of its huge inventory of electronic spy gear, Commissioner Sheldon S. Cohen hedged. He spoke of the devices as having many "legitimate uses."

One of the Service's regional commissioners spelled out the IRS position in plainer terms.

On January 21, 1966, Alvin M. Kelley, former IRS district director of Boston (who was *promoted* to the Chicago post after some of the worst cases of lawless conduct by IRS agents were uncovered in his area) told the *Chicago Daily News* that Internal Revenue would use electronic eavesdropping devices when necessary.

"I would not like to give comfort to those who think we will not continue our use of intensive surveillance techniques," he declared.

What inferences are to be drawn from these statements? It seems to me there are only two possible explanations. Either the Internal Revenue officials regard the president's directive as political window-dressing and therefore not to be taken seriously; or they believe they can flout an executive order with the same immunity with which they have flouted the Fourth Amendment of the U. S. Constitution.

Some Capitol hill observers believe that the president is as sincerely opposed to eavesdropping as he is opposed to sin. But sometimes politics has to accommodate to sinful situations.

If President Johnson had directed the attorney general to prosecute the next federal employee caught wiretapping or bugging (including members of his own organization), the practice would have ceased overnight. One prosecution is a better deterrent than the Constitution of the United States itself. So far, there have been none.

Further insight into Internal Revenue's future policies was revealed when Commissioner Cohen also voiced his opposition to Senate Bill 973, which would prohibit mail covers for any purpose. He asserted that mail cover information had been of great assistance to IRS agents and that, in his view, enactment of S973 would seriously hamper the Service.

Historically, there have been two opposite ways of combating crime, whether organized or not. One is the accusatory criminal procedure we inherited from Anglo-Saxon common law, the essence of which is embodied in the Constitution. Under this system of government, the law merely defines what is actionable; it does not initiate a massive intrusion into the homes and lives of its citizens in the hope of discovering the guilty.

The other method is imposition of an inquisitional or police-state procedure in which a body of secret agents and spies—enjoying in their official capacity rights denied the private citizen—harass and intimidate the innocent and guilty alike.

"We could not wait for crimes to be reported to us," said Attorney General Katzenbach, "in the way that in a more conventional prosecutive setting, bank robberies or murders are discovered.

"It was our belief, in short, that what was required was a program of action law enforcement, rather than the more usual reaction law enforcement." [25]

In his much-neglected work, *Philosophy of Civilization,* R. H. Towner directs our attention to the fact that in every recorded instance of history, when the Asiatic spy system was imposed upon a people, an increase in crime followed with mathematical certainty.

A watched society soon becomes a criminal society.

That a crisis in law enforcement exists, no one will deny. An effective drive against organized crime in America is one deserving of nationwide support, *provided it is undertaken without overstepping constitutional guarantees of liberty.*

But when a national system of surveillance is established, and when just anybody a secret agent does not like can be labeled a member of organized crime, the whole effort becomes a front for police-state oppression.

There are Americans, it is true, who sincerely believe that in order to combat crime, the use of furtive, illegal practices such as wiretapping, bugging, trespassing and compiling secret dossiers on individual citizens is both necessary and justified.

There are others who view such methods as an intolerable encroachment upon American freedom.

The moral distance between the two can be measured in light years.

3

The right to know ... everything

Today our Government is engaged in a more insidious form of search than going into someone's home or through personal papers. We are now searching their minds, trying to pry out the most hidden and intimate thoughts.

U. S. REPRESENTATIVE CORNELIUS E. GALLAGHER

In the totally controlled society of George Orwell's nightmarish novel, *1984*, the individual had one retreat that Big Brother could not penetrate:

"Nothing was your own except a few cubic centimeters inside your skull."

But in America today, even those "few centimeters" of cranial refuge are under siege. If the present trend of mind-searching, personality vivisection and mental wire-tapping is allowed to continue, the day may not be far off when the average citizen finds his innermost self stripped naked in the pitiless glare of forced exposure.

With the support and participation of the federal government, a multitude of subliminal snoopers calling themselves behavioral scientists are assaulting the national psyche. Their instruments include:

1. Psychological tests that probe the secret places of the unconscious mind in an attempt to determine attitudes towards sex, religion, family relationships, health and so on.

2. Polygraphs, the so-called "lie-detectors," once reserved for grilling criminal suspects to detect falsehoods and to uncover guilty knowledge.

3. Brain manipulation procedures that seek to control human behavior by such means as drugs, chemicals and tiny electrodes implanted in the brain. Some of these secret research projects are being carried out by the U.S. military services.

The over-all program, still in its infancy, is already so widespread and so alarming in its possibilities that it has inspired growing public debate, and has touched off a full-scale investigation by Congress.

The legion of psycho-spies who are prying wholesale into people's minds now holds dominant positions in schools, hospitals, armed services, police courts, the U.S. Civil Service Commission, the Peace Corps, the U.S. Office of Education, about one-half of the nation's major corporations and a constellation of federal agencies, most of which have nothing to do with security.

The American people have never been consulted about the claims of the behavior pundits that they are entitled to subject everyone to a mental third degree in the name of science. Yet the lives of many citizens in this country—job, schooling, marriage, reputation—are already being charted by their secret reports.

The basic theory of psychological testing appears to be the same as that of the organized crime drive: Find the guilty (or the incompetent or the mentally defective) by a privacy-invading dragnet that covers the whole population.

Starke R. Hathaway, University of Minnesota medical school professor, who invented the most widely used "personality inventory" probe, compared the tests to chest x-rays and immunization shots. He said, "We are now beginning to advocate general surveys with such psychological instruments as the MMPI [Minnesota Multiphasic Personality Inventory—a controversial test to be discussed later in this chapter]."

To realize such sweeping ambitions, the mind invaders maintain a close but hush-hush liaison with official Washington. A statement addressed to members of the American Psychological Association last year declared:

"Officially, APA has a Central Office in Washington, and one of the reasons for this location is that it is easy for psychologists and others of our staff to get in touch with psychologists and others of various Government agency staffs."

Even more significant was the added information: "We cannot report here the details of the unofficial help given by APA to State [Department] officials in the winter of 1964 and spring of 1965. The APA's operation here may seem mysterious, but it was not—it was merely quiet. Periodically, when it appears that psychologists or psychology may be 'in trouble,' in a Government agency, the Central Office of APA will see to it that Government officials are offered help from recognized psychologists. There are no public statements and no petitions from APA officials. There is no 'official action,' not even a letter. . . . The major APA objective ordinarily is to achieve a desired end—not necessarily to get 'on the record.' " [1]

This sly, cozy relationship between psychologists in and out of government has been very effective in the past in moving the nation towards the brain watchers' ultimate goal to make the soul-baring quiz as common as influenza shots.

During an exhaustive inquiry into psychological testing by the government, a House Operations Subcommittee learned that federal jobholders and applicants have been asked to respond with a Yes or No to such questions as: "I feel that my sexual instinct is as strong as my ambition," and "I have to urinate more often than others."

In 1964, the U.S. Labor Department administered such tests to twenty-one thousand applicants for counseling jobs in youth opportunity projects.

The Department of Defense has a Human Reliability Program in which it has psychologically tested an estimated quarter million men in the Air Force alone.

Employees of the federal Bonneville Power Administration, who were being considered for promotions, were required to answer such queries as: "Which would you rather do: (a) Kiss a person of the opposite sex, or (b) experiment with new things. Choose one."

Similar searching questions about sex, along with religion and biological functions, seem to characterize all of the tests.

The personality probe which came under the most withering fire of both the congressional investigators and the general public was the one called the Minnesota Multiphasic Personality Inventory (MMPI for short)—a 566-question True-False quiz developed in 1942 for use in the treatment of psychopaths.

Dr. Starke R. Hathaway, who developed the test, said that it grew out of a need to evaluate the diagnoses of mental patients who were to be given insulin shock therapy, which was dangerous to the patients and extremely expensive in terms of hospitalization and nursing care.

What was needed at that time, Dr. Hathaway explained, was a personality test that would identify a mental illness and provide an estimate of its severity.

That was what the MMPI was designed to accomplish. The idea of using it to screen job applicants or as a general survey for the whole population of the United States came later.

Nevertheless, the test is basically an instrument for plumbing the depths of the human personality to bring to the surface hidden symptoms of psychopathology.

"The symptoms of mental illness and unhappiness," said Dr. Hathaway, "are represented in verbal complaints or statements that relate to personal feelings or personal experiences or reactions to job and home."

In an effort to lay bare these "personal feelings," the MMPI examiner asks the most intimate questions covering the fields of medicine, psychiatry and religion. Examples (which must be answered True or False):

Medicine
— I have never noticed any blood in my urine.
— I am not bothered by a great deal of belching of gas from my stomach.
— The top of my head sometimes feels tender.
— I have never had any black, tarry-looking bowel movements.

Psychiatry
— I like tall women.
— Once in a while I laugh at a dirty joke.
— Many of my dreams are about sex matters.
— A large number of people are guilty of bad sexual conduct.
— The man who had most to do with me when I was a child (such as my father, stepfather, etc.) was very strict with me.

Religion
— I pray several times a week.
— The only miracles I know of are simply tricks that people play on one another.
— I believe my sins are unpardonable.
— I believe in a life hereafter.
— I believe there is only one true religion.

To deal with cheaters who think they can outwit the test by being untruthful in their answers to some of the prying questions, the quiz contains a "lie scale." This scale consists of questions which any normal person would not hesitate to answer truthfully. For example, "I would rather win than lose in a game."

To some critics of the tests, the notion that a person who might boggle at telling the truth about his sex life would likewise hesitate over a simple-minded question about winning or losing a game seems a little naive.

Others regard the psychologists as modern-day Cagliostros. They say the doodles, inkblots, cartoons, word-teasers, warmed-over jokes and draw-a-man tests are merely updated counterparts of such pseudo-sciences as phrenology, palmistry and Tarot cards.

There is, in fact, a respectable body of opinion among psychologists themselves which holds the view that personality testing may not have firm scientific value when used to screen job applicants or to determine which employee is most deserving of promotion.

Evaluation of test results by independent research teams, retests, experimental sampling of university students have usually resulted in the verdict, "Claims go beyond the data."

Martin L. Gross, in his carefully researched and thorough survey of the subject, *The Brain Watchers,* cites studies made at Northwestern University and at the University of Minnesota, in which a group of randomly selected students scored very high norms on the aberration scales.

Noting that even the faculty man who conducted the tests at Northwestern felt compelled to state that there was no supporting evidence of such abnormalities among the students, Mr. Gross observes:

"These new statistics indicate that possibly thousands of employees have been falsely and irretrievably identified as mentally disturbed in corporations all over the nation."

He might have added that similar files exist by the hundreds of thousands in government agencies.

Despite this skepticism of many professional psychologists, and the searching scrutiny of recent congressional hearings, Michael Amrine, public relations consultant to the American Psychological Association, reported that "use of tests increases steadily."

The reason is probably twofold: High-pressure salesmanship by test purveyors; and the belief of executives and bureaucrats that they can impose quality control upon human beings with the same precision they apply to assembly-line products.

The elaborate mystique of pseudo-scientific gibberish that surrounds many of the tests also exerts a fascination over naive laymen.

The overriding objections to the tests, however, are not concerned with their reliability or scientific value.

Among the more important considerations is the fact that, accurate or inaccurate, they *do* comprise a permanent record that will follow an individual the rest of his life. Eventually, they may very well wind up in a government master file, ready for instant retrieval for purposes other than those for which they were originally made.

For example, the Allport Ascendance-Submission Reaction Study claims to reveal whether the person measured has a tendency to dominate others or is by nature inclined to submit to domination. The results of such a test would conceivably be of great interest to any future dictator or totalitarian regime.

Voicing this same concern, Monroe H. Freedman, a Washington attorney, warned a meeting of the American Psychological Association that the same test answers used today to assess a man's adaptability to new surroundings or reaction to stress might well be used tomorrow to assess other characteristics. Some official or agency might want to know about submissiveness, resistance to suggestion, loyalty, dependence on authority and even reliability from a particular political point of view.

"If one ideal distinguishes the open society from the totalitarian," Mr. Freedman told the psychologists, "it is a recognition that things of the mind and the emotions are inviolably personal." [2]

Another serious objection cited by critics of testing is that personality probes, designed to unmask neuroses and hidden aberrations, may precipitate emotional crises in persons rejected for jobs after taking them. If they had not been obliged to run the psychological obstacle course, such persons might have passed their entire lives without experiencing a breakdown.

To argue that no one is compelled to take the tests and that no tests are made without the subject's consent is very much like saying that no one is compelled to complete a job application blank. No one, that is, who can afford to get along without working.

Likewise, persons who are already employed are not obliged to submit themselves to mind-raking personality "audits." But those who refuse do not have to consult an astrologer to know what the future holds for them with respect to career.

One junior advertising executive told me, "We were informed quite frankly that, while the tests were being offered on a strictly voluntary basis, reports made by the consulting firm which gave them would be considered in selecting future management positions."

But the brutality of requiring someone out of work and seeking a job, or an employee hoping for a promotion, to answer hundreds of impertinent and often humiliating questions about his private life is apparently of little concern to the testers.

In addition to being offensive, some of the questions included in the tests are inappropriate for many persons asked them. Why, for example, should a Jewish job applicant be required to answer True or False to the query: "I believe in the Second Coming of Christ."?

Or what inference, even in a clinical context, could possibly be drawn from the statement: "I think Lincoln was greater than Washington."?

The numerous questions in many of the tests that center about sex and religion seem to indicate a strong Freudian orientation on the part of the psychologists giving them. This despite the fact that today there are many psychiatrists of recognized standing who challenge some of Freud's basic theories.

As for those questions on religion included in the MMPI, Dr. Hathaway explained that "there is a well-recognized pattern of psychological distortion to which we apply the term religiosity."

There is little doubt that, if evaluated by an MMPI test, the saints and illuminati of all the great world religions would be classified as emotionally disturbed, if not outright psychotic. Certainly they would not be "suitable" for a job with, say, the U.S. State Department.

Psychological espionage is not, of course, confined to federal agencies and government departments. It holds a growing fascination for educators as well, who seem to confuse mind-improvement with mind-manipulation.

Thousands of unwary school children have been subjected to the same unsettling intrusion into their emotional lives, under research projects financed by the U.S. Office of Education.

And, although the massive testing program was paid for with tax money, parental consent was neither sought nor given. Washington seemed to share the concept of totalitarian governments that the child belongs first to the state.

The *New York Times* reported that, by 1960, psychological testing programs had grown to a point where an estimated one hundred and thirty million tests had been given in schools during that year alone—nearly three tests for every student from first grade to graduate school.

Oddly enough, parents and parent-teacher groups put up only token resistance to this unrestrained prying into their children's family life, behavior codes, conformity, attitudes towards sex and so on.

Perhaps, like most Americans, they were willing to accept the "personality inventories" because they were presented in the guise of scientific research.

This is the way Dr. Karl U. Smith, professor of industrial psychology at the University of Wisconsin, analyzes the situation:

"The American people have been fooled into believing that a few simple-minded True-False, or multiple choice questions can be used to forecast the careers of their children in school and in the university; and to predict their own careers in work because of two influences . . . mental-medical mumbo jumbo of the psychiatrist and clinical psychologist, and the misleading propaganda of organized psychology in claiming that guesswork and statistical shotgun procedures have medical and scientific significance."

When parents have expressed doubts as to the wisdom of giving naked-mind examinations to pre-teen and teen-age students, they have been ridiculed by school authorities as being behind the times; or have been urged to leave the delicate matter in more competent hands than their own (meaning the testers).

In the Bronx, New York, for instance, early in 1966 parents of all ninth-grade students were informed that their children would be given a psychological test designed to detect neurotics or maladjusted pupils who might later become dropouts.

A mother of one of the students, who was a registered nurse and familiar with the intrusive nature of the test, wondered how the Board of Education could sanction the use of the test without parental consent, especially since each child would be required to sign his name to the in-depth quiz.

In reply to a letter which she wrote to the school principal, expressing her doubts and misgivings, the mother was told that she "would simply have to trust the judgment of the educators." That was one thing, the nurse declared, "which at this point I can't honestly say I want to do."

"I wonder," she mused, "what safeguards are being taken to insure that school children, via the public school system (and I understand, some private schools also) will not become a vast emotional laboratory, serving the quasi-scientific curiosity of anyone who happens to come along with an interesting research project to try out on them."

As a result of this mother's concern, her son was exempted from the probe. Later, complaining because he was not permitted to take the test, the boy said, "I hear it was great. They ask all about your sex life!" [3]

In many instances, teachers and guidance counselors who administer the tests have little or no formal training as psychologists. Publishers of the tests, in effect, simply provide a classroom do-it-yourself psychology kit. Yet many educators view the test results with almost religious awe.

Moreover, test scores and interpretations usually become a part of the student's permanent school record, despite assurances of school authorities to the contrary. The results are first filed on IBM punch cards, then transferred to magnetic tape as part of a continuing electronic dossier, subject to instant retrieval.

As we shall see in the next chapter, these data, along with countless other bits of information being compiled about each individual, may turn up to plague him in later years. As an adult, his character and reliability—even his political posture—may be partly assessed on the basis of a junior high school pupil's answers to such questions as "My parents don't trust me," or "I hear strange things when I am alone."

If a staff psychologist or even a school guidance counselor decides a student is emotionally handicapped or socially a misfit, that stigma, whether imaginary or real, will follow the individual for the remainder of his life.

For government commissars and decision-makers in private management who may feel that results of psychological testing are somewhat less than trustworthy, the mind-ravishers have another tool that often commands more respect—the so-called "lie detector."

A surprising number of government officials and company executives who have no faith in the quiz games, believe that some of the same questions asked while a subject's breathing, blood pressure and sweating are monitored, will provide the basis for predicting future performance as a public servant or employee.

There are several types of instrument employed for this purpose. The most widely used, and the one that has caught the fancy of official Washington, is the Keeler polygraph.

It is an apparatus first developed back in the roaring 20's by the late Leonarde Keeler to extract information and confessions from criminal suspects.

During his studies as a psychology major at Stanford University, Keeler learned of a theory announced in 1895 by Italian criminologist Cesare Lombroso, which held that during police interrogation, changes in a suspect's blood pressure could be used to determine whether he was lying. The celebrated Swiss psychiatrist, C. G. Jung, agreed with Lombroso, and added his own speculation that deception could be detected by a *psycho-galvanometer*—a device for measuring the skin's response to low-energy electric current.

After leaving the university, Keeler joined the Berkeley, California, police department. There he evolved a device that was basically the same as that which bears his name today. He called it a polygraph, a Greek-derived term meaning "many writings" or lines. But in popular parlance it soon came to be called a lie detector.

Law-enforcement officers adopted it with enthusiasm as a refined successor to the rubber hose and blackjack, which had often proved ineffectual against hardened criminals.

The polygraph in use today is a coordinated recording of three sensing instruments attached to the subject's body. One, the pneumograph, is a rubber tube fitted around the chest or stomach to record the breathing rate. Another is a baglike rubber cuff with the jaw-breaking name of sphygmomanometer. It is wrapped around the upper arm to record involuntary changes in blood pressure, as well as the strength and rate of the pulse. Finally, a pair of electrodes or metal contacts are attached to the hands to measure galvanic skin response (GSR), or flow of perspiration.

As questions are put to a subject during interrogation, three pens, activated by impulses from the instruments, graphically register responses on a continuous roll of paper. Some polygraphs are provided with a fourth pen, which is used to mark the point at which a given question was asked. The record paper, imprinted with time markings, moves at a constant speed of six inches per minute.

With the subject thus trussed up and wired to a mysterious apparatus, the examiner repeats a number of questions, which ordinarily he has run through with the subject before harnessing him to the chair.

Some of the questions are irrelevant to the inquiry. They are of such a noncontroversial nature that anyone would answer them truthfully. The examiner may ask, for example, "Have you ever attended a movie?" "Do you own an automobile?" "Are you an only child?"

The peaks and valleys registered on the graph by responses to these queries establish a pattern of nonguilty reaction.

During the interview, which normally takes from five to ten minutes, questions will also be asked that are designed to trigger an emotional reaction in anyone attempting deception.

In addition to the "lie-detector," polygraph rooms are often provided with one-way mirrors for secret observation and even for photographing with a movie camera of the subject. Auxiliary equipment may also include a concealed microphone and tape recorder to take down his remarks before, during and after interrogation.

In hearings before a congressional committee, federal agents admitted that they did not make it a rule "to inform criminal suspects of this additional gear." They assumed, they said, that all Americans knew their constitutional rights (even when they have no way of knowing that such rights are being grossly abused!).

The crucial and controlling fact about lie detectors is that the apparatus does *not* detect lies or hidden guilt; the examiner does. Evaluating responses on the graph is a highly skilled and complex undertaking. It has been compared to interpreting a medical electrocardiogram (EKG), which is used for diagnosing heart troubles; or the electroencephalogram (EEG) for measuring brain waves. Yet, as Dr. H. B. Dearman, a psychiatrist, pointed out to House investigators, an internist requires eight years of training, while the polygraph examiner is taught the fundamentals of his delicate task in courses of study ranging from six weeks to six months.

Researchers at Fordham University, who made a careful survey of the subject, reported that a computer could not replace the human examiner in polygraph tests because there were no objective criteria for judging what particular pattern of response on the graph really indicated guilt or deception.

Are the three thousand polygraphers in the United States competent, then, to make such qualitative readings? The chief supporters of lie-detector infallibility who say yes base their opinions largely on anecdotal evidence. The examiners themselves think they are great.

Professor Fred E. Inbau of Northwestern University law school, himself an advocate of the polygraph and coauthor of a text on its use, thinks otherwise. He estimated that 80 per cent of the examiners currently in practice are unqualified. While staunchly defending the polygraph as an investigative tool when used for the proper purpose by a proficient examiner, Professor Inbau warned that in unskilled or unscrupulous hands, it could be a dangerous instrument.

The difficulty is that experts widely disagree on what, exactly, constitutes a qualified examiner. Professor Inbau himself, when asked by a House subcommittee to define examiner capability, replied in only the broadest and most nonspecific terms.

An examiner, he said, should have integrity, a good background, maturity, a college education and a sense of values, with respect for the feelings and rights of individuals.

Whereupon, Porter Hardy, Jr., U.S. Representative from Virginia, threw up his hands. "How do you measure the moral fiber of the individual who administers the test?" he asked. "Isn't that the key question?"

Many persons who have never laid eyes on a polygraph certainly have all the qualifications cited by Professor Inbau.

The House committee's inquiry showed that, while polygraph testing has been spreading through federal agencies, there was no government-wide policy governing its use. There were no established standards for examiners. There were no over-all specifications for the equipment itself. Nor were there any criteria to be met by testing firms which the government might contract for polygraph services.

Use of the lie detector by Washington goes back as far as 1948, yet in all that time no study was undertaken to determine objectively the accuracy of the instrument.

A technical report issued July 31, 1962, by Dr. Jesse Orlansky of the Defense Department's Institute for Defense Analysis revealed that in the previous ten years the Department of Defense had given two hundred thousand lie-detector examinations, but that objective data to determine just how effective an instrument the polygraph was had not been compiled by the agencies using it.

"Up to this time," the report declared, "it has proved impossible to uncover satisfactory performance data to support the view held by polygraph examiners that lie detection is an effective procedure."

Dr. Harold Brown, director of Defense's own Defense Research and Engineering section, voiced a similar opinion. In a memorandum dated April 13, 1965, he observed that "despite the weight which has been placed on polygraph data in arriving at decisions of considerable importance, little if anything, is known about what they contribute to the accuracy of an investigation."

Even the most doctrinaire polygraph theorists concede that there are countermeasures possible; that is, ways "to beat the machine."

Those who try to justify the government's massive intrusion into the minds of its citizens on the grounds that such a procedure is necessary to smoke out Communists and homosexuals might well heed the admonition of Dr. Stefan T. Possony, director of international studies at the Hoover Institution on War, Revolution and Peace.

Dr. Possony warned that, ironically, by using the lie detector to screen prospective employees, the Central Intelligence Agency had opened the field of espionage to homosexuals who feel no guilt about being deviates, and to Soviet secret agents, who are trained in many ways to outwit the instrument.

One polygraph expert explained that the best way to hoodwink the lie detector is to show emotion about questions that are not really exciting. "Think of something that is exciting to you, in a manner that will make it hard for the examiner to guess what number (that is, what question) you have in mind."

In experiments with twenty subjects who used this technique, the researcher reported that accuracy of the polygraph was reduced to between 15 per cent and 25 per cent.

Similarly, tests carried out in 1962 showed that by tensing the muscles of the feet or by use of self-exciting images, polygraph subjects reduced examination accuracy from 75 or 80 per cent to a low 20 per cent. In 55 to 70 per cent of the cases, the subjects were able to direct the attention of the examiner to a decoy question rather than to the relevant one.

Two other methods of circumventing the lie detector have been widely discussed by examiners, but little is actually known about their effectiveness. They are hypnosis and a kind of self-induced trance that Hindus call *samadhi*.

Some of the feats of mind and body control I have personally witnessed in India leave no doubt in my own mind that anyone fully accomplished in yogic techniques could govern his autonomic responses during interrogation. The number of such yogis in America, however, is small indeed.

As for preconditioning the subject by hypnosis, Dr. William S. Kroger, psychiatrist and leading authority on medical hypnosis, told me:

"There is a valid basis for believing that a person could, through hypnotic and posthypnotic suggestion, be trained to produce both false positives and false negatives on the polygraph. Given a good hypnotic subject and a hypnotist thoroughly familiar with polygraph methodology, you might in time come up with the perfect liar, so to speak."

Some lie-detector examiners say that when evasive tactics are used, they can detect unusual characteristics in the record. An abnormal pattern alerts them to the deception. This claim has never been proved under rigid field conditions, however.

Even if a subject does not try deliberately to play a double game with the lie detector, experts say that other factors may result in the examiner misreading the graph. Some of the things which produce confused or unreliable readings are: excessive fatigue, fear of revealing guilty knowledge, extreme nervous tension, prolonged interrogation, physical abuse, tranquilizers and drugs.

Similarly, serious physical or psychological disorders preclude a trustworthy examination. Most, but apparently not all, polygraph authorities agree that ailments such as high or low blood pressure, heart disease, respiratory disorders, hyperthyroidism and mental illness may seriously undermine accuracy of a test.

Difference of opinion on this point is usually kept within the professional fraternity. But sometimes the importance of a proposed test will bring it to the attention of the press.

There was, for example, the recent case of the late Jack Ruby, slayer of Lee Harvey Oswald, President John F. Kennedy's assassin.

Dying of cancer in a Dallas hospital, Ruby reportedly asked for a final lie-detector examination to prove that in killing Oswald he had acted on his own and not as part of a conspiracy. FBI agents had given him two previous tests, but evaluation of his answers has never been made public.

When Ruby's request was announced, Andrew L. Smith, head of Truth Verification, Inc., a Dallas-based firm which administers over one hundred thousand polygraph tests a year, said it would be useless to give Ruby such a test. For results to be reliable, he claimed, a subject must be in good health.

"You can't even run a valid test when you have someone with a fever," Smith said, "let alone someone who is in the last stages of cancer."

Two other lie detector experts sharply disagreed with this opinion. Cleve Backster of New York and Chris Gugas of Los Angeles sent a telegram to Texas Attorney General Waggoner Carr, urging that Ruby be given the final test "in the interest of history."

If such a final examination was ever given, the public has never been told of it.

Turning to private enterprise for an assessment of lie-detector and mental wiretap techniques, researchers have found no compelling evidence that such methods improve the over-all quality of personnel. Psychologically tested engineers still sometimes go over the fence with patents, which they sell to competing firms. Key jobholders still leave the company for better pay and greener pastures. A certain number of workers still have sticky fingers.

Dr. Alan F. Westin, professor of law at Columbia University, together with a group of colleagues studying the impact of modern technology on privacy, recently took a long and searching look at the problem. After a comprehensive survey, they reported that "there has not been the slightest proof that employees selected by organizations that do not use personality testing are less effective, successful or adjusted, than those from companies that have bought the fad of personality testing."

Reporting on a study of two hundred and eight industrial firms made in 1965, Dr. Westin said that 53.6 per cent of those covered in his inquiry were not using personality tests. This, he pointed out, indicated a trend away from the practice in some important areas of private business.

Among the big firms that felt they could operate efficiently without forcing entry into the personal lives and beliefs of their employees were American Motors, Bristol-Myers, Du Pont, Florida Power and Light, A & P, Gulf Oil Company, Litton Industries, Metropolitan Life Insurance, Northern Pacific Railroad, Pabst Brewing Co. and RCA.

Dr. Westin observed that none of these giant companies—and thousands of others like them—seem to be centers for emotionally disturbed employees or executives.

Unhappily, official Washington does not seem to share this enlightened view of employees as individuals with deep human feelings, who should be protected against forced confessions to federal quidnuncs.

Response to a questionnaire sent to 58 U.S. government departments and agencies revealed that during the fiscal year of 1963 alone, 19 agencies owned 512 "lie detectors," acquired at a cost of $425,000. A House subcommittee found that during the same year, 24 federal agencies employed 656 examiners to administer 23,122 tests. These figures did not include security agencies such as the CIA and NSA, which reportedly also make extensive use of the polygraph.

The latest information available at the time of this writing shows that the government has been spending more than $5,000,000 a year to operate the instruments that some critics have called refined models of medieval torture devices.

Senator Sam Ervin, Jr., of North Carolina, for one, likened the tests to ordeals for discovering witches: "Does the flesh of the applicant burn when a hot iron is applied to it? Heaven help us if we are reduced to alchemy as a technique of screening applicants for highly sensitive positions in the Federal bureaucracy."

Not only "sensitive" positions, however, require the applicant to be grilled while strapped into a chair and wired for emotional response. Representative Cornelius E. Gallagher cited the case of a seventeen-year-old girl, just out of high school, who was subjected to the lie-box treatment when she applied for a job with the government as a clerk-typist. During the interview, the polygraph examiner asked her highly personal questions concerning her family life and attitudes towards sex. The congressman said the young girl had suffered a humiliating experience from which, several years later, "she seems not to have recovered."

Another prospective federal employee to whom the emotional stomach pump was applied, said afterward he was beginning to think the middle letter of the agency designation (NSA) must stand for "sex." While a multiple-pen subsystem recorded his reactions on a roll of graph paper, he was asked, among other things:

"When was the first time you had sexual relations with a woman?"

"How many times have you had sexual intercourse?"

"Have you ever engaged in sexual activities with an animal?"

"When was the first time you had intercourse with your wife?"

"Did you have intercourse with her before you were married? How many times?"

It is precisely this unwarranted invasion of privacy that makes the question of the technique's accuracy irrelevant.

Furthermore, one cannot escape the chilling suspicion that "confidential" information and arbitrary judgments resulting from the tests will creep into a future electronic dossier farther down the line.

Because of mounting public concern, six states—Alaska, California, Massachusetts, Oregon, Rhode Island and Washington—now have laws prohibiting the use of the lie detector as a condition of employment. These laws, however, presumably are not applicable to operations of the federal government.

To protect federal employees, a bill was recently introduced in the Senate which, among other things, would outlaw all interrogations, psychological tests and lie detector interviews designed to elicit personal information from employees and job applicants.

Meanwhile some of the brain watchers have turned their attention to an even more frightening area of research—mind control by drugs, chemicals and electrochemical stimulation.

The research is still in its infancy. But results already achieved are so awesome that one behavioral scientist has compared discoveries in "this grand new enterprise, this brave new science of mind" with development of the atomic bomb.

Addressing a symposium on brain research, Dr. David Krech of the University of California at Berkeley reminded his colleagues: "I don't believe that I am being melodramatic in suggesting that what our research may discover may carry with it even more serious implications than the awful (in both senses of the word) achievements of atomic scientists. Let us not find ourselves in their position of being caught foolishly surprised, naively perplexed, and touchingly full of publicly displayed guilt at what they have wrought."

Only a part of what brain researchers have wrought so far has ever been made public. Much of their work in developing ways of conditioning and controlling social behavior is locked behind the iron turrets of classified government projects.

But scientific reports from research centers such as those at Yale, Harvard, M.I.T., University of Michigan, Tulane, UCLA and Emory, all point up the alarming fact that mind control is no longer a daydream of the future. It is here now.

A noted research psychologist, Dr. James McConnell at the University of Michigan, says categorically that "the time has come when, if you give me any normal human being and a couple of weeks—maybe a couple of months, but I don't think so—I can change his behavior from what it is now to whatever you want it to be, if it's physically possible. I can't make him fly by flapping his wings, but I can turn him from a Christian into a Communist and vice versa."

Dr. McConnell admits that the implications of imposing behavior patterns in this way "scares hell out of people when they first hear about it." But he hopefully believes that the benefits to be derived from it in reducing the rising crime rate and treating mental illness make such research worthwhile.

Other bright rewards being held out to us by the scientists to justify widespread modification of human behavior are vastly improved thinking, memory, learning and problem-solving; as well as better treatment of anxiety, depression and a host of other mental illnesses.

But looming ominously over all these benefits to mankind is the sobering fact that, by the same procedures, the behavior of whole populations could eventually be controlled without their knowledge or consent.

Geneticists say that the personality and social attitudes of even the yet unborn can conceivably be predetermined by genetic manipulation. They predict that some day, by modifying the chemical compound that makes up genes and carries the inheritance code, they will "pre-program" individuals, eliminating hereditary defects and producing special talents.

But the question has been asked: Suppose some future dictator or evil political genius wished to pre-program whole sections of the population—some individuals to be submissive, some aggressive, others to perform tasks ordinarily repugnant to civilized men? Could preselection and mind-control techniques result in such a slave society?

Many knowledgeable scientists answer with a cautious, "Perhaps, but not likely."

In another area of behavior management, control by electro-chemical triggering of mechanisms in the brain has already shown startling results.

Not long ago, an emotionally disturbed man mingled with normal people of his city, performing his routine tasks and taking part in the community's social life like everyone else.

Yet, unknown to the people around him, beneath a cap he wore to conceal them, tiny electrodes had been implanted in his brain. Each time he sensed the onset of morbid feelings that had formerly taken possession of him, he pressed a button on a small black control box, concealed beneath his jacket. Suddenly the black mood would disappear. He felt good. He smiled again, and the world smiled back.

Others, similarly implanted with hair-thin wires leading into deep brain centers, had their emotions manipulated by researchers at Tulane University, using remote-control radio signals.

At last report, more than fifty persons—most of them suffering behavioral disorders—had had aggressiveness, melancholy, rage and pleasure switched on and off at the will of a psychiatrist operating electronic controls.

Engaged in the same kind of research at Yale, Dr. Jose M. R. Delgado controls implanted patients by sending radio signals to a miniaturized wireless receiver worn by the subjects.

Several years ago, Dr. Delgado attracted worldwide attention when he demonstrated his brain-control technique in a bull ring. After implanting electrodes in the skull of a brave bull, bred for fighting in the ring, Dr. Delgado entered the arena armed only with a matador's cape and a small, hand-held radio transmitter. He incited the bull with the cape, just as professional bullfighters do. The bull lowered its head and went charging toward the professor. Just before the animal reached him, Dr. Delgado triggered an electrical stimulus by radar to the rage control center of the bull's brain. The animal halted its charge within a few feet of him, reared backward, then peacefully trotted away.

Dr. Delgado reported another experiment in which two male cats that enjoyed a feline friendship were gradually turned into snarling enemies. The smaller cat was accustomed to lie close to the larger one and purr affectionately. When a certain brain center in the smaller animal was stimulated, however, it would start growling and would attack the larger one. The latter responded defensively, retaliating with punishing blows of unsheathed claws. The fight would continue as long as the stimulation was applied. The smaller cat would always start a fight, even though it always came off second best.

Dr. Delgado observed that "after several stimulations, a state of mistrust was created between the two animals, and they watched each other with hostility."

Dr. Delgado minimizes the possibility that techniques developed in such research would ever be used to control the behavior of whole populations. He points out that the procedures require specialized knowledge, refined skills and a complex exploration of each individual because people vary from person to person in their psychological makeup.

He said, however, that because brain stimulation is clinically useful, its use as a research and therapeutic tool will continue at an accelerated pace.

While most of us would agree with Dr. Delgado that "scientific discoveries and technology cannot be shelved because of real or imaginary dangers," there remains the urgent question of how legally and ethically to control this awesome power.

Restraint of its applications does not mean a hysterical attack on the researchers themselves, like the outraged villagers of fiction who march on the mad scientist's house and destroy his laboratory.

At the same time, an impressive number of laymen and responsible scientists alike are asking: Once fully developed, how are these mind-control techniques to be kept out of the hands of incompetent federal agents and reckless military leaders?

The sobering fact is that many research programs using both drugs and electrochemical stimulation are being pursued in laboratories sealed by security classification.

Furthermore, military research is rarely aimed at what could be called humanistic goals.

The actual nature and scope of these secret projects are unknown outside a limited official circle. Occasionally, however, data seeping into unclassified literature, or inadvertently revealed at scientific symposia, give some idea of what is going on.

Recently, for example, I learned from a reliable source that the government had queried an electronics research firm in Santa Monica, California, as to the feasibility of developing a remote-control device to be used during interrogations. Unknown to the subject, an invisible beam directed at his head would confuse his thoughts and presumably lead to self-revelation.

My informant said that similar experiments have been carried out, using an inaudible tone, directed at the person's ear. Another subliminal technique involves a visual pattern imprinted upon a table used for interrogation. The design on the suspect's side is one specially worked out by psychologists who claim it will heighten emotional involvement during questioning.

Other experiments being conducted in laboratories, prisons and military hospitals involve the study of pain and sensory isolation as well as drugs when used as stressors to stimulate autonomic responses to tests.

Specialists have also used the Macworth camera and corneal reflections to tell what a person is looking at and how important it is to him.

Hidden motion picture cameras have been employed to make a photographic record of subjects undergoing lie-detector tests for later visual study.

Several scientific teams are using an electronic model of the human nervous system in an effort to find out how our nerve cells work to govern our movements, impulses and thoughts.

A growing number of local police departments (and, no doubt, other law-enforcement agencies) are turning to hypnosis as an investigative tool. Suspects are rarely told that they are to be hypnotized, since they would usually resist. Instead, a trancelike state is induced indirectly by a device called a brainwave synchronizer; or the suspect is informed after prolonged questioning that the "Doc" will relieve his nervous tension by "progressive relaxation."

The man referred to as "Doc" (implying that he is a physician) may be a professional hypnotist, a psychologist or a real doctor; or simply another detective who has had a course in hypnotism.

A work just published on the use of hypnosis in criminal investigation relates a typical case.

A youth of seventeen, suspected of muggings and murder, was grilled for hours by detectives in an effort to extract a confession. But the boy remained indifferent to their questions. Finally, one of the detectives, with signs of resignation, said the suspect might as well be taken back to his cell. A fellow officer agreed, but observed that it was too bad the youth's mother would have to see him the way he was. She would be the one to suffer.

As the guard appeared to take the boy back to his cell, one of the detectives, pretending to be struck with an idea, suggested that they get "Doc" Arons to come down and help the kid relax long enough to see him through his mother's visit. "After all, the kid does not really want his mother to suffer needlessly. Do you, kid?"

"Doc" Arons (a professional hypnotist, not an M.D.) then entered and suggested that he and the suspect be left alone. By prior arrangement the detectives monitored the interview that followed, on a hidden tape recorder.

The hypnotist told the youth he was there to help him put on a good front for his mother, so she would not be distressed at seeing him in his present state. This could be accomplished, he said, by a psychological procedure called progressive relaxation.

He then began "the procedure which is familiar to most hypnotists."

Under hypnotic manipulation, the suspect suddenly began to sob, blurting out: "I can't stand it any more! I'll talk—I'll tell them everything. . . ." [4]

What of the subject's constitutional right to protection against self-incrimination? Referring to the antagonistic attitude of the legal profession towards hypnosis, the writer waves it aside as "prejudice born of ignorance and misinformation."

Since 1936, however, the high courts have tended to reject involuntary confessions of this kind. In one case the court found inadmissible a confession made to a police psychiatrist, even though outright hypnosis had not been used.

An even more odious indignity to the individual is the use of narco-interrogation—that is, the administering of drugs to a suspect to elicit information.

It has been reported that secret police in Communist countries have used such pharmaceuticals as sodium amytal, scopolamine and pentothal for brainwashing prisoners and for forcing confessions.

In the United States, too, there is creditable evidence that researchers are quietly experimenting with mind-modifying drugs. Because of the public's hostile attitude towards experiments of this kind, they are kept in the background as much as possible.

Not only in the field of so-called "mind drugs," but in other areas of medical research, recent disclosures of serious abuses have raised the specter of Hitler's concentration camps.

Early in January, 1967, New York State Senator Seymour R. Thaler charged on the floor of the Senate that doctors in certain New York City hospitals were performing experiments on indigent patients and mentally retarded children, without their consent.

During his angry, hour-long speech, Senator Thaler charged that "the medical establishment has presumed to act as God over the health and lives of the medically indigent. . . . How often are people used as guinea pigs without their knowledge and consent? The data suggest that the practice is widespread."

The legislator said he had "searched my soul and conscience," before making public his shocking disclosures. He told his colleagues that he had in his possession documentary proof of the following incidents:

—At Willowbrook State Hospital on Staten Island, five hundred mentally retarded children, aged three to nine years, had been injected with live hepatitis virus as part of a hepatitis research program being carried out under a federal grant.

—Five out of a thousand alcoholics and derelicts taken to New York's Bellevue Hospital died after hospital personnel took liver biopsies from them for its research program.

—A twenty-three-year-old pregnant woman at Harlem Hospital

had a hysterectomy (removal of the womb) performed on her to demonstrate the operative procedure to interns and residents.

In answer to Senator Thaler's charges, the responsible doctors claimed that no experiments were conducted without the patient's consent.

While acknowledging that parents of some of the mentally retarded children had given their consent for the experiments, Senator Thaler added, "I doubt whether the parents of 500 children gave their consent." [5]

He might well have raised also the broader question of what kind of persuasion, if any, was brought to bear upon those parents who did give their consent.

Less than a year prior to Senator Thaler's indignant charges, the New York State Department's board of regents had placed two other doctors on probation for a year, after they were found guilty of "fraud and deceit in the practice of medicine."

In more specific terms, the deceit referred to giving experimental drugs to patients without their knowledge and consent. The charge against one of the doctors was that he had supervised the injection of live cancer cells into the bodies of twenty-two old and helpless patients in a Brooklyn hospital.

In his testimony, the physician conceded that he had not mentioned the word "cancer" to the patients, and had instructed his associates not to do so.

Far from being a disreputable practitioner on the fringes of his profession, the doctor belonged to an elite group of medical researchers who have determined the direction and policies of cancer research in America for more than a decade. His *curriculum vitae* included, among other important posts, that of special consultant to the U. S. Public Health Service and to the National Cancer Institute (both federal agencies), research advisory panelist for the World Health Organization, a full member of the Sloan-Kettering Institute medical staff, associate professor of medicine at Cornell University and so on. He had written a chapter of the report issued by President Lyndon B. Johnson's 1965 Commission on Heart Diseases and Strokes.

In an article that discussed the inadequacy of rules governing medical experiments on humans, *Saturday Review* said that such rules must include the Nuremberg Code. Observing that four Nazi doctors had been hanged for violating the code, the magazine noted that an American was chief prosecutor at the trial.

Nuremberg Rule No. 1 requires the consent of human subjects who take part in medical experiments. Before acceptance of such consent by the experimental subject, "there should be made known to him the nature, duration and purpose of the experiment; the method and means by which it is to be conducted; all inconveniences and hazards to be expected; and the effect upon his health or person which may possibly come from his participation in the experiments." [6]

The extent to which experimental drugs are being administered to patients without their informed consent is not known. When cases of the kind come to public attention, they almost always involve tax-supported institutions or federally financed research programs.

Mental patients in at least one U.S. government hospital were subjected to narcoanalysis. A French writer, Jean Rolin, who had access to a report of the study, said it was undertaken to explore the possibility of using narcosis as an instrument of interrogation.

In his work *Police Drugs,* Rolin reports that the research was carried out at Tilton General Hospital in Ft. Dix, New Jersey. In all, seventeen service men, most of them prisoners or under scrutiny by military police, were the guinea pigs.

The patients were not told that narcoanalysis would be performed on them until a few minutes before the procedure was begun. Even then, it is doubtful whether the men were fully informed as to the nature and extent of the research. It was explained to them merely that they would be given a drug which would make them drowsy and encourage them to discuss personal matters that would enable the doctor to help them.

The Ft. Dix report, apparently written by the doctors who supervised the experiment, states that "the doctor was positive, forthright, but considerate. He indicated by his manner that the patient had no choice but to submit to the procedure. . . ."

Despite the doctor's thus "pulling rank" on the men, not all of them were ready to comply.

Only six obeyed without question. Three were suspicious, but offered no verbal protest. Three others made it clear that they regarded the "treatment" as unnecessary, and asked to be excused. Four were openly hostile, objected to the violation of their rights and demanded to see the Inspector General. One serviceman flatly refused to be given the drug, but sullenly submitted under a direct military order to comply.

In each case, the patient was given one gram of sodium amytal in 10 cc. of distilled water, injected into the antecubital vein.

During the ensuing state of semiconsciousness, each man was interrogated about crimes with which he was charged or of which he was suspected.

The researchers were careful in their report to emphasize that none of the material developed during the drugged interviews was used in subsequent prosecution of the subjects who faced criminal charges. Such use, they declared, would be a breach of medical ethics as well as a violation of the patient's civil rights as guaranteed by both the Constitution and the Twenty-fourth Article of War.

True, but how confidential will those long, detailed files of drug-elicited confessions remain? It has become virtually axiomatic that any government file, no matter how inviolate it is at the start, sooner or later is made available to other government agencies for purposes not intended in its original use.

Even worse, the material resulting from confessions made under narcosis is known to be untrustworthy. The psychiatrists themselves warned that modification of consciousness by a narcotic is characterized by bewilderment, disturbed memory, loss of time sense and inability to discriminate between what is real and what is illusory.

Rolin stated the case in more Dantesque terms. He wrote: "Everybody will agree that with this kind of truth, we are traveling towards a world which is both strange and disturbing. When consciousness is dismembered and out of control of itself, its intimacies lying open to the eyes of everybody, everything must be at once both false and true. Nothing is concealed, but nothing is in its proper place. The light which abolishes all shadow also abolishes all outline. Everything is known, none of it makes sense: it has the transparency of a phantom.

"The icy clarity which removes all mystery thereby destroys all reality. Forced consciousness is falsified consciousness. The kind of reality that rules in hell must be of this order."

4
Filed . . . for eternity

||||||||||||||||||||||||||||||||||||||||||||||||||||||||||||||||||||||||||||||||||||||||||||||||||||||||||||||||||||||||||||

Secret dossiers are paraphernalia of the police state.
ALAN BARTH

One of the "weaknesses" of Operation Close-Watch, as presently carried out by the government, is the wide dispersion of its files.

Each federal, state and local agency keeps its own set of records, in which vital information—factual and fanciful—about all Americans is stored.

As a safeguard of the citizen's privacy and freedom, this fragmentation is a good thing. The many items of intelligence about us are, in the words of Representative Frank Horton of New York, "scattered in little bits and pieces across the geography and years of our life."

For any single agency or official to bring together everything that is known or has been reported about us would require a great deal of time and considerable work. Individual files now number in the billions.

Even the mammoth dossiers of the Federal Bureau of Investigation and the Internal Revenue Service lack many items that have been gathered by census takers, license bureaus, banks, schools, hospitals, courts, credit services, insurance firms and personnel offices.

The ideal setup—at least from Big Brother's point of view— would be a giant, computerized data bank where all this information could be pooled for instant retrieval.

Thanks to electronic technology, at the push of a button, your whole life story (as told by the snoopers) would be instantly available for official scrutiny.

The first step towards creation of just such a centralized storage system has already been taken by the government. Under study by a top-level task force appointed by President Johnson are plans for a National Data Center. The proposal calls for a vast computer complex in which would be preserved on magnetic tape statistics about every living American.

For openers, data already compiled by some twenty federal agencies would be integrated in the bank. Collectively, these agencies have one hundred million coded file cards and thirty thousand magnetic tapes on which they have recorded various kinds of information about individuals and businesses.

Included among the twenty charter members of the bank are such government departments as Treasury (which embraces Internal Revenue, Customs, Narcotics Bureau and Secret Service, all of them having police powers); Health, Education and Welfare (with wide access to psychological tests, medical histories, school records etc.); Labor Department; Bureau of Old Age and Survivors Insurance; and so on.

These twenty organizations actually represent access to far bigger information stockpiles than merely those they hold in their own files.

Mutual exchange of information among government agencies on all levels has long been an established fact.

The federal file builders have solemnly assured everyone within earshot that the purpose of the Center is merely to improve storage and access to information they need for statistical uses. It would not be used, they say, to build up dossiers on individuals.

Opponents of the system think otherwise. They feel certain that, once in operation, the centralized files will be expanded to include an ever-growing reservior of intelligence, constantly fed by our data-stream society.

During House hearings on the proposed super computer, Representative Cornelius Gallagher warned that "secret reports on marital affairs, I.Q. tests, school grades, illnesses, forgotten comments by teachers and former employers; records covering credit, travel and adolescent indiscretions could easily be added, once the Center is set up."

Assurance by government spokesmen that the "raw," unevaluated data about us, filed forever in the great complex, would be held in strictest confidence, cannot be taken seriously. Bureaucrats are as agile as alley cats in getting around departmental regulations and constitutional safeguards.

It doesn't require a very long memory to recall that their brethren made similar pledges about our Social Security number and about the sacredness of our federal income tax returns.

We were told when the Social Security program was initiated that the number assigned to us would never be used for any purpose other than to identify our account. Today, our Social Security number has become almost as available as our automobile license plates. It is required on credit and job applications, tax returns, health insurance claims and for many other purposes. It will be used as a matter of course to identify us in the files of the new Data Center.

In the matter of our federal tax returns, it was the same story. Official promises that the returns would remain forever inviolate were soon repudiated in practice.

In fact, the history of federal tax "confidentiality" can provide a sound idea of what happens to personal information we are obliged to confide in *any* official agency or government department.

Executive agencies can get permission to examine them almost at will. This means not only security agencies, but other arms of the government as well, among them: U. S. Civil Service Commission; Social Security Administration; Health, Education and Welfare; Small Business Administration; Interstate Commerce Commission; Labor Department; Securities and Exchange Commission; and the Housing and Home Finance Agency.

Various congressional committees have also asked for and received permission to inspect the federal tax returns of citizens in whom they had an interest—legitimate or otherwise. One House committee was authorized to scrutinize anyone's returns over the past sixteen years (1947 to 1963).[1]

Unknown to most Americans, bureaucrats of the various states have had access to their Internal Revenue returns since the very beginning of federal taxation.

At first, to give the impression that the information was indeed closely guarded and hard to get, state government personnel were required to go personally to Washington. There, acting under terms of an *informal* agreement between federal and state functionaries, they were allowed to examine the returns on file in the nation's capital.

This procedure was later given legal sanction by enactment of the Revenue Act of 1926. Even then, scrutiny of federal returns by state officials was authorized only at the request of state governors. In practice, state employees were allowed to make transcripts of federal audit reports *or to purchase photostatic copies.*

After the Internal Revenue Service decentralized in 1953, setting up field offices throughout the United States, federal records became even more accessible to state tax officials.

Eager to foster a mutual exchange of information about taxpayers, the government in 1950 initiated a formal federal-state cooperative program. At first, agreements were negotiated with only two states—North Carolina and Wisconsin. Then, during the ensu-

ing two years, three more—Colorado, Kentucky and Montana—
were added.

In this original, foot-in-the-door program, the agreements covered only an exchange of income-tax data. But when Minnesota
joined the pool in 1957, terms of the accord were expanded to
include other kinds of information—a broad provision that permits
the trading of any kind of intelligence about the taxpayer.

By the end of 1965, the Internal Revenue Service had signed
information-sharing agreements with forty states and the District of
Columbia.[2] Ten of the states do not have broad-based personal
income tax. But the opportunity for trading confidential information about the citizen apparently seemed too good to pass up.

Referring to the federal-state information swap, an October,
1965, report of the Advisory Commission on Intergovernmental
Relations comments: "To date the progress has been chiefly in the
direction of strengthening the enforcement arm of the State."

In simpler terms, this means that when the IRS uses intimidation
to collect more taxes than a citizen really thinks he owes, the information is passed on to authorities of his state, so they can do likewise. In this way, the initial wrong to the taxpayer is compounded.

So close is the federal-state liaison in some cases that a number
of states (California is one) are now using Internal Revenue tapes
of taxpayers filing from their areas to prepare their own mailing
lists.

Washington officials have said quite plainly that electronic record-keeping by the huge new IRS computer in Martinsburg, West
Virginia, will significantly broaden the scope of information ex-
changed among federal and state agencies.

The vast Martinsburg configuration is one of the world's largest
computer systems now fully operative. One of its two main com-
plexes, the IBM 7074, can enter or retrieve 30,000 ten-digit words
of information in 0.0000004 of a second. The other, the IBM 1401,
will read and write through the medium of magnetic tape at rates up
to 62,500 characters per second.

According to an IRS official, it is planned to operate the colossal facility around the clock, using three labor shifts a day throughout the year. In this way, all data and documents will be added to the tapes as fast as they come in. The master file will be updated every seven days to include the new information received.

Linked up with this centralized "brain," are satellite, feeder computers in the nine Internal Revenue regional offices.

Despite the growing importance of this kind of electronic data processing in both government and industry, computer technology is scarcely twenty years old. And the most rapid development has occurred in the past decade.

David Sarnoff, board chairman of RCA, was quoted not long ago as saying that in just ten years the typical data processor has become ten times smaller, one hundred times faster, and one thousand times less expensive to operate.

Looking ahead, experts in the computer field predicted that, in the decade between 1963 and 1972, cost of data processing would decrease 85 per cent; cost of storage in computer memories would decline by 97 per cent.

In 1951, there were fewer than one hundred computers operative in the United States. By 1956, about one thousand of them had been installed in government accounting offices, schools, factories and laboratories. Today, it has been estimated that there are at least a quarter million or more in use—four times the number in all the rest of the world combined. Their total value amounts to approximately eleven billion dollars.

The biggest single user of this most subtle and powerful tool ever devised by man is, and has been, the federal government. A Bureau of the Budget report to the president in 1965 noted that "in the short span of a decade, the electronic computer has had an unprecedented effect upon conduct of Government activities. Use of the equipment has enabled the Government to carry out programs never before possible."

The same report disclosed that Washington spends a billion dollars annually to buy, use and maintain 1,767 of the machines. This number represents about 10 per cent of all the computers in the nation. Not included in the inventory is about an equal number of systems employed by the military establishment, including top secret computers in the Pentagon. Still another group of equal size is operated by private contractors, who perform work for the government on a cost-reimbursement basis.

Attorney General Ramsey Clark recently announced the establishment of a coast-to-coast communications network that will tie the vast FBI files to police departments across the country.

Clark said that a $406,197 federal grant to fifteen local and state law-enforcement agencies will enable them to join the network by means of which they can feed into and retrieve information from the National Crime Information Center in Washington. The center is operated by the FBI.

Clark said that by the end of 1967 other agencies are expected to have joined the network. Ultimately, the planners intend for the system to reach every state.

Aside from the FBI system, the giant web of government-operated electronic data processing units now occupies 209 separate areas of 48 states and 16 locations outside the United States.

Currently involved in the operation of the non-security data processing computers are approximately 45,000 federal employees. Of these, about 2,300 reportedly know how "to converse with the machine"—that is, to record and retrieve data.

Meanwhile, the Civil Service Commission is operating a computer educational center, where hundreds of computermen will be prepared for future jobs.

Manufacturers of computer equipment confidently predict that state and even local governments will soon follow Washington's lead in setting up electronic files.

There are already indications that their forecasts are correct. In California (which leads the nation in spy government on state and local levels) the county of Santa Clara has established a centralized computer system. Dubbed LOGIC (for Local Government Information Control), it possesses almost unlimited capacity for electronic record keeping.

County spokesmen have said that in the machine's magnetic memory will be stored the following information for each resident: name, alias, birth record, driver's license data, vehicle license number, position (if a county employee), voter and jury status, property holdings; and "other data" if the person has ever been involved with the county welfare or health departments, the district attorney, sheriff, adult or juvenile probation, court "and so on."

Some of the county's nearly one million residents were understandably alarmed to think of so much personal information about them being instantly available to "authorized inquirers."

Assurances by county officials that they would strictly enforce confidentiality of the tapes did not allay the fears of those familiar with the ways of bureaucrats.

One resident, a graduate student at Stanford, in a letter to the *Palo Alto Times,* expressed grave concern over possible abuse of the system.

"Unlimited capacity for information storage, combined with instant retrieval," he wrote, "would seem almost irresistible temptation to record more than is warranted and to retrieve for unethical and/or illegal purposes. The toy could easily become a monster." [3]

He added that he was apprehensive that "many people out there are saying, 'We're going to have to build a case against somebody in the future. Let's start building his history now!'"

An executive of the county's data processing division, who is known as "father of the Santa Clara system," lightly dismissed such misgivings as coming from "the higher educated people—you might call them dreamers."

Why, nobody had any reason to fear anything, he asserted, "if you have no arrests, no outstanding warrants against you, or if you're not on welfare, or if you've stayed out of the clutches of adult probation." [3]

On the level of municipal government, the Los Angeles police department (already bugged from basement to rafters) has announced plans to set up an "electronic rogue's gallery."

Just over the horizon, computer experts foresee the time when all these burgeoning data banks will be linked up in an integrated system, operated through a government-controlled switching center.

If some federal department heads have their way, direct tape-to-tape feeding of information from one computer to another will become common.

Information can also be mutually put in or retrieved from even remote-location computers by simply dialing the telephone. Many computers are already connected across state, national and even international boundaries by communication lines. In the fraction of a second a teletypewriter in Washington can feed information into a computer in Houston, where it is processed with lightning speed and then transmitted to Los Angeles.

A Bell Telephone advertisement in a recent issue of the *New York Times* pictures a man seated at a desk in front of a large computer. He is answering his telephone, and is saying, "Just a minute. I'll put the computer on the phone."

The ad copy goes on to say, "That's just about the way it's done today. Moving information in split seconds is the exciting art of data communications. . . . You name the kind of data you want to transmit. Name *how* you want to transmit it—between computers and people or between computers and other computers." [4]

The prospect of lightning-fast, magnetically whispered gossip about us, moving over a universal network of communication lines has proved too much for even the most level-headed observers.

Vance Packard who, in his book *The Naked Society,* used such low-key terms as "disquieting," "disconcerting" and "questions we must ponder," in discussing privacy invasion by bug and wiretap, came into sharp focus when he viewed a computerized future.

Testifying before a House committee looking into the dilemma, he said: "I think we should all be scared stiff about the possibility that these giant machines would be fed data about individual Americans and that this information would be retrievable by a number of different organizations or groups. I think this would clearly create the preconditions for a totalitarian system."

Packard told the lawmakers that, as more and more people have access to the information, security becomes more difficult. "If you have a lot of people who can get into the computer and take out information," he said, "it will always be harder for any investigating body later to try to trace down how the leak occurred." [5]

That is the specter that haunts some of the computer experts themselves.

Paul Baran, researcher at the Rand Corporation, expressed serious concern about the readout of records stored in widely separated, but interacting, data banks. He warned that this could mean "loss of the individual's right to privacy as we know privacy today." He also voiced the fear that computer-based information systems would permit unscrupulous individuals to use the information for unlawful purposes. He predicted an increase in the already widespread practice of unearthing defamatory bits of information about candidates for political office.

A colleague of Baran's who has also made an extensive study of computer development, reported an even gloomier outlook for individual privacy and justice in the computer age.

"Consider," said M. R. Maron, "what could happen as machines are used to make decisions about people. For example, consider a situation where a computer is programed to decide who should get an education loan, or whether someone's driver's license should be suspended, or who should get a passport, etc."

He pointed out that, as information becomes easily accessible from a number of banks, linked cross-country by telephone, "there will be a natural tendency to use machines for automatic selection or rejection of people, not on the basis of human understanding and sympathy, but according to some pre-programed set of criteria." [6]

In such a mechanized dispensing of justice, how could an individual explain his special case, or plead extenuating circumstances? How could he convince a machine that its preprogramed criteria don't apply in his particular situation?

"Will there be a tendency in the future," asked Dr. Maron, "to create an environment where we treat each other as machines: that is, where there is no opportunity to 'change the system's mind'?" [7]

Looking ahead to the not very distant day when they will be plagued by a host of new legal problems spawned by the computer, a group of New York lawyers held a seminar not long ago to consider some of them.

They wanted to know, for example:

—How can you cross-examine a computer? The machine can and will perform acts and make judgments for which human beings are held accountable under the law. Yet the computer cannot be brought into court to confront the accused or to be held as defendant in a lawsuit.

—What can an attorney do when he subpoenas records vital to the preparation of his case, and the adversary appears in court with an armload of magnetic tapes or coded punch cards? Most, if not all, computers memorize their information in symbols that only an expert knows how to decipher.

In such circumstances, the lawyers decided, they would face the necessity of employing—at a high fee—a specialist to translate the computerized data into words and figures. Such a procedure would add substantially to the client's legal fees.

In an ordinary citizen's fight against the massive power of the federal government, it would make justice even more expensive and difficult of access than it is now.

Noting that a subtle and perhaps unnoticed act of the programer can affect a computer's testimony, a speaker told the lawyers that both attorneys in a case would need an expert programer—one to ask the computer questions and the other to analyze what he asked, so as to detect loaded questions.

—Whom could the law hold legally responsible for an illegal act ordered by the computer? Could a programer "pass the buck" and attribute to the machine his own error—willful or otherwise?

Roy N. Freed, a lawyer and computer expert, cautioned his colleagues that before they became too respectful of the machine's veracity, they ought to bear in mind an axiom designated by the acronym GIGO, meaning "Garbage in, garbage out."

Although amusingly phrased, the attorney's admonition points up one of the most serious threats of the computer when used by the government—the doubtful validity of its primary information.

If the secret files of the FBI and other federal security agencies have taught us nothing else, they should have taught us to be wary of untrustworthy "raw" data.

Much of such information is based upon reports by informers, or as police and law-enforcement agencies call them, "confidential informants." Referring to them in the case of *Peters v. U.S.,* Supreme Court Justice William O. Douglas noted that "they may be venal people, psychopaths . . . who revel in being informers. They may bear old grudges. Under cross-examination, their stories may disappear like bubbles. Their whispered confidences might turn out to be yarns conceived by twisted minds or by people who, though sincere, have poor faculties of observation or memory."

The policeman's point of view (which prevails in confidential file keeping), on the other hand, was expressed by FBI Chief J. Edgar Hoover. In an address before the International Association of Police Chiefs on October 3, 1955, he declared.

"The confidential informant has become an institution of establishing truth. The use of confidential informers is as old as man; in fact, the first recorded use of the confidential informant is found in the Old Testament."

The same can be said of prostitution and murder.

As Bishop Mandell Creighton once remarked, "Gossip is none the less gossip because it comes from venerable antiquity."

Today, amid the growing atmosphere of suspicion and mutual distrust among people in America, there is a marked trend towards informing on one's neighbor, employee or tenant.

An undercover investigator, widely experienced in the practice of gathering information about people, said recently that Americans of a generation ago wouldn't talk about friends or neighbors. "Now they enjoy it. They tell everything they know or have heard."

He said that banks, too, were among his best informants. "I can't recall a bank that has ever refused to give us information."

Insurance companies appear to be moved by the same spirit of cooperation when asked by federal agents for confidential information about their clients. According to Senator Edward V. Long, whose subcommittee investigated the matter, "Quite a number of major insurance companies, without subpoena and solely upon request of local revenue agents, will turn over copies of your statements of finances and income."

Other chatty magpies, eager to provide material for secret files, include ex-spouses, fellow employees, former teachers, political opponents and credit bureaus.

Only priests, attorneys and doctors have held out against the privacy invaders. And of that intrepid trio, some lawyers and physicians have been something less than scrupulous in certain instances.

In the matter of private medical records, which most people (hypochondriacs excepted) would not like to see widely circulated, the future holds little cause for optimism.

Plans now shaping up call for every man, woman and child of the nation to have his entire medical history preserved in a giant computer in Washington.

The advantages of such a system to doctor and patient alike are obvious. If such records were kept up to date, lives might often be saved by having a patient's total medical chronicle instantly available. This becomes especially important to a mobile population like ours, in which few patients are treated by the same personal physician all their lives.

Too, such a file would be invaluable in cases of emergency. If, for example, a man from New York were suddenly stricken with a heart attack in Los Angeles, the California doctor who had to treat him could telephone the Washington data bank and in a matter of minutes have before him a full recital of the medical events—including laboratory findings, allergic reaction to drugs and so on—in his new patient's life.

That is the bright side of the picture. Against it must be weighed the possibility that, once digested by a government-controlled computer, the information would be "leaked" to persons other than licensed doctors, and be used for purposes not originally intended. The history of federally supervised record-keeping in other areas, as we have seen, leaves little room for optimism or trust.

Some of the medical events in a patient's lifetime could be very damaging to his reputation if brought into public view. Part of the record could even be used for blackmail. It was a member of the medical profession who commented: "Let's assume an individual had a nervous breakdown years ago, with subsequent complete recovery. Or even that the person contracted a social disease in his youth. Is this medical record to pop up out of a computer at the touch of a button, say, by that person's employer? What might such medical information mean to an unscrupulous politician out to 'get' an opponent? Rigid safeguards would be needed to protect information in any medical bank." [8]

There is the disturbing thought, too, that doctors are not infallible. A diagnosis of the patient's illness might be, and often is, incorrect. A recent survey revealed that an estimated 25% of all laboratory tests and clinical diagnoses are incorrect. Such errors, if recorded and used as fact by another physician, could lead to fatal consequences.

The same weakness afflicts the closed files of federal security agencies. There is nothing, for example, in the FBI dossiers to indicate that a given arrest record may have been made illegally by the local police reporting it. False or incorrect charges made against an individual and later reduced or dropped don't reveal themselves in the information preserved. It is a record of arrest—period.

Yet in Los Angeles alone, in 1963, of 31,304 adult felony arrests made by the police, 11,283 of those arrested were released without ever having been charged. Nevertheless, on a job application, to the inevitable question, "Were you ever arrested?" they would have to answer, "Yes."

Other arrestees during the same year in Los Angeles, who were booked on charges of burglary and robbery (seemingly favorite categories with the police), later had the charges reduced to disturbing the peace or public drunkenness. It is well established that such misdemeanor charges, unrelated to the original felony charge, is the preferred method of covering up a false arrest.[9]

Such fast-and-loose treatment of citizens' civil rights is not, as commonly supposed, reserved for vagrants and disadvantaged minorities whose activities have traditionally aroused the suspicions of police. It can be, and is, applied to innocent persons "from the right side of the tracks."

For example, a Los Angeles newspaperman was stopped by a traffic policeman in Hollywood for allegedly driving through a pedestrian crosswalk while it was occupied by a pedestrian.

After a routine warrant-or-want radio check with police headquarters, the officer informed the newsman that there was a warrant outstanding for his arrest. The reporter was dumbfounded. He assumed it was a case of mistaken identity. The officer was sympathetic, but asked the reporter to accompany him to the precinct station. Although the matter was handled in an amicable way, the newsman understood that he was, in fact, being taken into custody.

At the police station, a teletype check with centralized records revealed that an arrest warrant had indeed been issued in his name. He was charged with not responding to an overtime parking citation.

The fact was that, in accordance with a policy of his newspaper under which newsmen who received parking tickets during working hours turned them over to the city desk, the reporter had given the two-dollar ticket to his city editor.

What happened to the citation was never disclosed. Nonetheless, the reporter was never informed that it had not been paid. He never received a notice of intention to issue a warrant. He was never served with a summons.

It may or may not have been relevant to the case that the reporter was an outspoken critic of police practices in Los Angeles. He had received the parking ticket, in fact, while his car was parked outside the police building where he was engaged in a long discussion with then police chief William H. Parker. Chief Parker had requested him to pass by his office for a friendly talk, following a lecture the newsman had given at the University of Southern California, in which he had suggested improvement in police methods.

Whatever the background of the case may have been, the indisputable fact is that the newsman was taken into custody, booked and fingerprinted on the basis of nothing more than a piece of paper left under the windshield of his car by a traffic policeman. He now has an arrest record on file with the FBI in Washington.

So much for due process in California.

Another potential source of unevaluated information about individuals that may one day be fed into a National Data Center on a computer-to-computer basis is the public school system.

Manufacturers of computers already in use as technical aids in many schools across the country predict that the next step will be installation of computers for guidance counseling.

Used in this way, the machines would either supplant or supplement the school psychologist and counselor. As now envisioned by the technologists, the procedure would be as follows:

All available personal data about a student—grades, personality inventories (including family affairs, mental aptitude, social beliefs, attitudes towards sex and religion etc.) and general behavior patterns will be fed into the computer.

When a student's profile does not conform to preprogramed criteria, the machine will flash a warning light.

An executive of Systems Development Corporation was quoted as suggesting that the electronic mastermind might, for example, send out the following messages:

"This student should be watched closely. He will probably need remedial courses."

"Student's grades have gone down quite a bit. Ask about this in interview. Possibly there are personal problems." [10]

An examination of all the information being gathered and filed about people will disclose that the greater part of it is derogatory or, at its best, neutrally statistical. There are no bulging file folders, punch cards and magnetic tapes extolling the virtues or accomplishments of the individual. Computers do not egest stories of heroic sacrifice; the tenderness between man and wife; the love, the laughter, the sorrow that make up "the strange and bitter miracle of life."

Theirs is the sordid tale of a robot idiot, full of credit delinquencies, legal skirmishes, academic struggles, marital strife, suspicions, doubts, failures—all signifying nothing.

A computer-based form of government may thus come to be negative, rather than constructive in its relationship with its citizens. There is already a mounting resentment among people at being treated as numbers or statistics.

And there is fear.

A Yale law professor who discussed the proposed national computer system with people of his own city said that, after listening to him describe the Center, a clerk in a dry cleaning establishment exclaimed: "Why, that sounds just like Russia. We are going to have a number instead of a name over here pretty soon and it is not going to be very American."

When the professor asked if he could quote the clerk's remarks in testimony before a congressional hearing on the subject, the clerk replied, "No, I don't want to get into trouble. Don't say a word."

Said the professor: "I thought, there it is. They don't even have the Center yet and this man who just works in a drycleaning establishment in New Haven is afraid. He doesn't want his name mentioned to those anonymous people in Washington, who might write it down and might make some trouble for him some place, somewhere."

Relating this incident to a House committee, Professor Charles A. Reich warned that, if the Washington super-computer is indeed set up, we will increase the number of people who fear their government and will begin to lose what is best in the American character—"people who are willing to speak up, people who are willing to do things and not look around over their shoulders to see who is looking on." [11]

Another major concern about a government-run dossier bank is that it would result in an enormous waste of human talent and resources. Those who once made a mistake in their lives would often be barred from later opportunities to develop their potentialities, or even to serve their country.

Not long ago, for instance, a young man who was graduating from college decided to become an officer candidate in the U.S. Marine Corps. As an honor student, physically robust (standing over six feet), he was well qualified for such a career.

But just prior to his being sworn in, records of a central traffic data bank revealed that there were four parking violations against him, incurred when he was seventeen years of age. This fact, said the Corps, showed a certain instability of character, and he was disqualified even though as his congressman remarked later, "He is not twenty-three years old and appears to have the right to drive to defend his country and get shot at."

Later, the youth applied for officer training with the Navy, but when it was learned that he had been rejected by the Marine Corps, the Navy likewise refused to accept him for service.[12]

The computer itself, of course, is incapable of allowing for teen-age indiscretions. It is not programed to permit such variables as rehabilitation, forgiveness, a second chance.

This despite the fact that today social workers, educators, psychiatrists and even penologists agree with the Judeo-Christian concept of human regeneration. They say that it is possible for anyone, at any age and in any coterie of society, to experience a fundamental change in disposition and character. They point out that, if our society is not to stagnate, everyone must have the right to make a new start, free from the stigma of past mistakes.

It is also an unfortunate but true fact that people today—reared as they are in almost religious awe of scientific achievement—are inclined to regard machines as more reliable than humans. They have been "sold" the idea that computers are superhuman, electronic brains, capable of judgments superior to those of their makers.

They are, of course, no such thing. One computer technologist said that, compared to an ordinary schoolboy, computers are mindless morons. They can, to be sure, perform feats of calculation with blinding speed and accuracy. Their capacity to sort, store and retrieve information bits exceeds that of any man or vast collection of men.

But this provides no logical basis for the assumption that their answers to all questions are any more free of error or even calumny than those of homo sapiens. A man may be defamed by a machine just as easily as by false reports of other men.

In addition to inaccurate or deceptive information programed into the computer, the system is capable of making new errors *within the machine itself.*

J. B. Bessinger of Middleton, Rhode Island, who uses the computer for research in literature, recently wrote that "my colleagues and I have observed (it is a humbling experience) how relentless computers can be in the fixing and multiplication of human errors.

"Lately we have observed also, with growing alarm, that computers and their superb ancillary equipment are capable very occasionally of radical new errors conceived in the machine and blandly printed on the record."

If the machine could assign a false reading to the manuscript of the ancient poem, *Beowulf,* he reasoned, a computerized national data center would likewise be prone to commit radical errors and attach them to the permanent records of innocent people.[13]

Professor Martin Shubik, who teaches the economics of organization at Yale, may have been thinking of the same threat recently when he reminded a conference of computermen that their machine can multiply man's ability to make mammoth mistakes.

Citizens so maligned could not vindicate themselves because they would be unaware that the error had been made. The whole process would be secret; and it is this secrecy that poses one of the greatest menaces to liberty. We shall have no more idea of what has been charged against our name-number account in a computerized record than we have today of what reposes in the secret government files of such organizations as the FBI, Internal Revenue Service, Military Intelligence and so on.

Such dossiers are clearly a violation of our constitutional right to confront our accusers, to cross-examine them and to rebut their testimony.

To say that such a right should be exercised only in court is the rankest kind of police-state sophistry. The person who is denied an opportunity to hold a good job, to enjoy a good reputation in his community and to remain free of surveillance and harassment is often more severely punished than a criminal actually tried and convicted in the courtroom. Yet he is given no trial, no legal counsel, no chance to know what charges have been lodged against him and by whom.

It would seem urgent, then, that before Congress permits or authorizes construction of a centralized super-file to expand the most dangerous feature of spy government, adequate and immutable safeguards must be established to control its use.

The key question is: What steps can be taken to prevent the formation of a bureaucratic elite who can, in Congressman Gallagher's words, "narrow and dominate the corridors of power"?

The minimum acceptable bulwark against abuse would certainly include the following provisions:

1. Confidential information given by an individual to one agency of the government for one particular purpose would not be passed on to another agency or individual, in or out of government.

For example, the Federal Housing Administration may have a legitimate reason to know about the personal finances and background of a person seeking an FHA-guaranteed loan. But that same confidential data should not be handed over to some other arm of the government, possibly to be used against the individual in some other bureaucratic or political frame of reference.

2. Such files ought to have a prescribed useful life and be destroyed at the end of that period. They should not be as they now are, added to a cumulative dossier on each citizen.

3. When information from any government file is necessary for lawful research or statistical purposes, individual identification should be removed before the data are passed along to the researchers.

Such a procedure is apparently not as easy as it sounds. A congressman whose committee had been looking into the matter said he had been told that, in order to build a system that would have any value, the computer had to go back to the basic building block of information—the individual. Even if it does not identify him by name, it will identify him by Social Security number or some other designation.

The computermen say this is necessary to avoid duplication of material.

Programers say that codes can be devised that will change the original number in the system, so that information about a person will never come out tagged with his name or number. The original identity would remain with the agency that first compiled the information.

To build in such safeguards, however, would increase tremendously the cost of the computer system. An informed estimate for programing this kind of privacy into a computer was three to ten times the cost of the system itself.

It is for that reason that many fear what Congressman Gallagher called "a quick and dirty computer," that is, one not built to protect the individual. As for the federal file builders' assurances that they would be able to program out derogatory and confidential information, the congressman remarked:

"What we fear is the ability to program it *in.*"

4. Before the centralized federal system becomes operative, Congress should enact explicit legislation providing that any individual shall have the right to know the entire contents of his own file, even if the information is coded only to his Social Security number.

Too many secret dossiers exist on individual Americans already. Too often in the past they have been used to intimidate and to discredit the innocent.

Merely to propose guidelines of the kind just cited, however, is not enough. As we have seen, both guidelines and administrative regulations are constantly ignored and violated by the *apparachiki* when it suits their own purpose. When they are caught, they go unpunished; when they are interrogated under oath, they quibble and they lie.

Only by putting a strong, unequivocal penal interdiction on disclosure of confidential information (to other bureaucrats as well), *and by prosecuting violations of it,* can privacy be assured.

Even with the most carefully considered safeguards that Congress can provide, the question will remain: Is the super electronic brain really necessary?

Representative Benjamin J. Rosenthal of New York, after a long, hard look at the problem, voiced the feeling of many when he said, "I have yet to be convinced of the necessity for a central bank of highly personal data on all American citizens. I have yet to learn why each agency cannot maintain its own files. And I find it hard to believe that the improved efficiency afforded by the Center would outweigh the clear risks."

Then Congressman Rosenthal posed several questions that all his countrymen might well ponder:

Are we sacrificing too many aspects of our personal lives for limited objectives?

Does the additional knowledge we might gain, yield benefits to society greater than the losses to the individual?

Can adequate safeguards be formulated so that we can benefit from the growth of technology in the area of personal data control?

No thinking person has ever contended that the government should not use computers, which would raise standards of efficiency, cut operational costs and perhaps help to keep our national economy on a more even keel.

Automation is a central fact of our lives today. It has been said that, deprived of computer technology, both government and business operations would fall to bits of their own weight.

From the checking out and setting orbit patterns of spacecraft to helping dentists make false teeth, the computers are accelerating changes in our environment as no other single invention in history has done.

They are being used to obtain insights into human cognitive psychology; to relieve congestion in air and automobile traffic; to answer vexing questions in high-energy physics; for abstraction of documents, processing of business data; and for providing solutions to many complex problems hitherto beyond reach of the un-aided human mind.

By 1990, according to many well-informed observers, a computer terminal will be as much a commonplace in the American home as telephones and television sets today. Their designers say they will provide an electronic aid for housework, shopping, educational homework and entertainment.

The trouble is that some computer enthusiasts are too eager to apply their electronic marvel to every field of human activity. They become impatient with any suggestion that, like almost any radical advance in science, the new technology could also lend itself to serious abuses.

The most serious would be to remove the last vestige of privacy, a fundamental freedom of the American citizen. Furthermore, privacy is perhaps the only protection we have against the government's growing interest in our personal affairs.

An educator, whose field is history, put the problem this way: "Must the miracle of the person succumb to the order of the computer?" [14]

Unless some corrective action is taken, and established in law, it could very well happen.

In a day not far distant, we may find that in the computerized mind of our government, our name is a number, our life a magnetized plastic ribbon, scanned with the speed of light in a computer.

5
How private is our mail?

It is shocking to the conscience to think that the Government, after an indictment is filed, may put a mail watch on the attorney for the defendant. . . .

JUDGE ARCHIE O. DAWSON

On February 5, 1964, as Marie Bolan was about to leave her home in Cambria Heights, New York, the mailman arrived. He was not the regular letter carrier, Charlie, but a stranger substituting for him.

As he handed Mrs. Bolan the day's mail, he asked her if she had been living very long at that address. She replied that she had. He then handed her a slip of paper saying, "I don't know what this is, but perhaps you should have it."

Mrs. Bolan, the wife of an attorney, did not know what to make of the notice handed her by the substitute mailman either. It appeared to be an official memorandum of some kind, and it was plainly marked *Confidential*. On the paper were both her name and that of her husband, together with their address, and the following statement:

"Submit all first-class mail to supervisor. Do not reveal this to addressee or other unauthorized persons."

It also said, across the top, *Indefinite until cancelled.*

Mrs. Bolan took the paper back into the house with the rest of the mail. She was certain her husband would know what it meant when he returned that evening.

It is not surprising that the Cambria Heights housewife could not identify the mysterious communication. She had in her possession a document rarely, if ever, seen outside a narrow official circle—an order to postal employees to monitor a citizen's private mail. Although thousands of such interceptions are carried out year after year, it is only by rare accident that Americans ever learn of it.

Even the power of Congress was not sufficient to pry loose information about the practice from the Post Office Department. A Senate subcommittee looking into snooping techniques of federal agencies asked then Postmaster General John A. Gronouski for a list of persons—twenty-four thousand of them by official estimate —whose mail had been scrutinized during the past two years. Gronouski refused.

Among reasons given by the postmaster for his refusal were: (a) such disclosure would violate the civil liberties of many innocent persons; (b) it would jeopardize national security; (c) it would cripple any criminal investigations.

In reply, the committee wryly observed:

"There is no indication that you feel that the civil liberties of the same persons might have been violated by the placement of mail covers without their permission or knowledge, and without any statutory authority. You also emphasized that a large percentage of the list would consist of the names of persons 'innocent of any crimes.' "

As to the question of security, said the committee spokesman, every committee staff member had been given a full FBI investigation. Furthermore, the committee chairman intended to keep the list locked in his personal office safe when it was not being used by him or a member of the staff.

The letter also pointed out that, when a mail cover is placed on an individual on behalf of a sensitive agency, several members of the postal establishment know of the cover. These employees are not cleared for security information.

Noting that the postmaster had invited the senators to submit reports they had received of alleged abuses, the committee said, "It must have occurred to you that reports of such abuses are rare indeed. How can anyone know of an abuse when mail covers are supersecret, when no central files are kept, when most records are destroyed instantly, and when *all* records are destroyed within two years? Abuses come to light only when a postal employee makes a serious mistake." [1]

When Mrs. Bolan gave her husband, Thomas A. Bolan, an experienced New York attorney, the notice that had been left by the substitute mailman, he instantly recognized it as an order placing a watch on the Bolans' private correspondence. The temporary letter carrier had blundered in turning it over to Mrs. Bolan.

When he explained its import, his wife was gravely concerned. After all, they were not criminals, tax evaders or fugitives from justice. Why should a mail cover be put on them?

Bolan thought he knew why. He was defense counsel for Roy Cohn, the late Senator Joe McCarthy's former investigator, then under indictment for perjury and conspiracy to obstruct justice.

Lawyer Bolan told his wife that getting possession of the mail-watch order might mean a tremendous break for him in his defense of Cohn. He said he had heard about such mail interceptions, but had never before been in possession of documentary proof.

The evidence provided by an erring postal employee would enable him to go into court and bring the whole procedure out into the light of day.

The attorney immediately filed an affidavit with Federal Judge Archie Dawson, requesting a hearing. To the affidavit, he attached the order for the mail cover, together with a statement that he had information and believed that all mail coming into his law office was being intercepted by the government.

The U.S. attorney submitted an affidavit opposing the hearing and asserting that the federal prosecutor's office had nothing to do with placing a watch on Bolan's mail.

Later, in response to a direct query from Judge Dawson, the U.S. attorney admitted that, yes, it was he who had requested a mail watch. He then swore under oath that, when he got the information from the mail cover, he put it away in a locked file cabinet, and did not make any use of it.

After the hearing was concluded, according to Attorney Bolan, the government lawyer sent a letter to Judge Dawson, saying that he had forgotten something. "What he had forgotten," said Bolan, "was that when he got from the Post Office the names of certain banks which Mr. Gottesman (Cohn's co-defendant) had been communicating with, he immediately sent the FBI out to those banks to interview them with respect to Mr. Gottesman. So his testimony there was erroneous also." [2]

Bolan said it was disclosed later that the U.S. attorney had not even given the postal authorities a written request for the mail cover. He had orally asked a postal inspector whom he encountered in the corridor of the U.S. courthouse to do it. It was that easy.

There was the added advantage that, if no written records existed, it would be extremely difficult for the person being spied upon to prove his case.

Chief Postal Inspector Henry B. Montague defined mail covers as the recording from a piece of mail the name and address of the sender, the place and date of postmarking, and the class of mail. The notation is made by a postal employee, but the information is then passed on to the agency or official requesting it.

Inspector Montague insisted that a mail cover is authorized only when there is good reason to believe that it may be instrumental in the solution of a crime.

The truth is, as Postmaster General Gronouski stated in his letter to the Senate committee, thousands and thousands of innocent persons are among those each year whose personal correspondence is scrutinized. In one case in Kansas City, the Internal Revenue Service even ordered a watch on the mail of a ten-year-old boy.

Information brought to light during Senate hearings indicated that mail covers could also be placed on an individual's doctor, priest, minister or attorney.

On February 26, 1965, the *Washington Post* noted that the post office department seemed to have embraced snooping as a universal policy. "Instead of hurrying domestic mail to its destination, it apparently goes sniffing about for smut and feeling envelopes for fraud, peering at postmarks and generally conducting itself like a collection of professional Peeping Toms."

There are indications that not all postal employees are enthusiastic about that kind of work. Jerome Keating, president of the National Association of Letter Carriers, said that members of his organization, when required to cooperate in conducting a mail cover, "feel sullied and besmirched by what they have to do."

Keating added that while the postal inspection service avers that letters subject to a mail check are never opened—not even "steamed open by mistake"—it would be hard to convince the average American that the professional curiosity of the postal inspector is fully appeased by merely noting the information on the outside of the envelope.

The union official said his organization regarded use of the mail cover for any purpose other than national security cases or to insure safety of the mail itself as "both reprehensible and unjustifiable." [3]

A retired postmaster of Poplar Bluff, Missouri, recalled that during his tenure, a federal agent disguised himself in a letter carrier's uniform and went to a home, claiming he had a registered letter that required the addressee's signature. His plan was frustrated because the individual under surveillance was not at home.

Testimony of post office officials at Senate hearings in 1965 disclosed that all federal agencies, as well as any law-enforcement officer from J. Edgar Hoover to a village constable, can order a mail cover.[4]

Various requisition forms, both printed and improvised, are used by different agencies to order a mail watch. The most commonly used, apparently, is POD Form 2008. It carries the official designation: Request For Information Concerning Mail Matter. A space is provided for the date, and one to identify the official or agency requesting the cover. The text of the requisition is worded as follows:

"For a period of ———— days, please furnish me daily on Form 2009, copies enclosed, information concerning ———— class mail received for delivery to the person(s) or addressee(s) listed below. If no mail is received, please so advise at end of period specified.

"Under no circumstances should the addressee or any unauthorized person be permitted to become aware of this action. Do not delay delivery of mail to obtain this information. Destroy this form at end of period specified. Do not retain any copies of Form 2009."

Records of the U.S. government printing office show that in the four-year period between March, 1961, and January, 1964, a total of 835,000 copies of this form were printed for the Post Office Department.

The extensive need for Form 2008, reflected in these figures, makes the official post office estimate of one thousand mail covers a month nationwide seem overly modest, even granting that several forms might be used for a single cover.

Postal authorities have said that normally mail covers are limited to no more than thirty days, and that agencies are encouraged to keep the watch to a maximum of fifteen days. They conceded, however, that it is possible to put a cover on an individual's mail for an indefinite period, as was done in the case of the Bolan cover cited earlier.

Until March, 1964, all postal inspectors (there are 1,028 of them) were permitted to authorize mail covers. But after that date, and no doubt because a Senate investigation of the practice was under way, the regulations were changed.

Today, except for requests involving fugitives from justice, that authority is limited to the chief postal inspector and inspectors in charge of the department's fifteen geographical divisions.

Although the practice of monitoring mail sent or received by citizens has been going on since 1893, postal authorities admit they have no statutory authority for doing it. It is purely an administrative procedure.

They defend the practice by citing custom and usage. Chief Postal Inspector Montague also pointed to paragraphs (1) and (5), Section 501, Title 39 of the U.S. Code as conferring upon the postmaster general authority to issue regulations permitting mail covers.

Actually, the portion of the Code recited does not refer to mail covers, even by implication. It merely empowers the postmaster general to prescribe rules and regulations he deems necessary to accomplish the objectives of Title 39, namely, "to issue regulations to implement the acts of Congress." No act of Congress ever authorized a mail watch.

The U. S. Supreme Court has never ruled upon the legality of mail covers, which many constitutional lawyers hold to be a clear violation of the Fourth Amendment.

Certainly the practice imposes a restraint on the freedom of communication, so necessary to an open society. The citizen who fears that the letter he writes to another may be examined, and the names of both sender and recipient noted down in a secret record, will be hampered in his freedom of expression. He may be afraid to write the letter at all, lest it put him under surveillance as well, or bring to his door some federal agent or law officer to question him about the addressee.

Whatever value such a practice may have as an aid to law enforcement is far outweighed by the general loss of freedom and public confidence.

No group of men in government has ever been more keenly aware of this truth than our country's first lawmakers. In 1789, members of the first Congress passed a law declaring the privacy of personal letters to be inviolate. Still smarting from the injustices that had resulted when the king of England had instructed postmasters in the American colonies to intercept and read correspondence, the founders of the new nation wanted to put an end to the reprehensible practice once for all.

Then as now, however, bureaucratic snoopers apparently regarded themselves beyond the reach of the law; or thought that their flouting the law in secret would never be discovered. Ten years after the Continental Congress had prohibited the scrutinizing of private letters, Thomas Jefferson evidently had reason to believe that his own correspondence was being opened and read. In a private letter to a friend, he wrote: "I pray you always to examine the seals of mine to you, and the strength of the impression. The suspicions against the Government on this subject are strong."

Jefferson had been accused by some of his political enemies of being a "French agent," and the mail cover was probably placed on his correspondence in the hope of uncovering information that would lead to his ruin politically.

That controversial public men, including U.S. senators, may still be subject to mail watch was revealed in the case of the late (and by many, unlamented) Senator Joe McCarthy.

In December, 1954, the Senate appointed a committee, headed by Senators Homer Ferguson of Michigan and Walter George of Georgia, to investigate the use of mail covers on Senator Joseph R. McCarthy "or any other senator."

In their subsequent report to their colleagues of the upper house, the committee disclosed that the private correspondence of McCarthy and certain of his associates had indeed been intercepted and examined.

The mail cover had been imposed, not by the executive branch of the government, but by a subcommittee of the Senate itself: the subcommittee on Privileges and Elections. This was the body which was investigating charges against Senator McCarthy that were to lead to a later vote of censure by his fellow senators.

In the course of their inquiry, the Ferguson-George investigators learned that a mail watch had been placed on all first-class mail incoming to Senator McCarthy at his home address for the period from October 24, 1952, to November 16, 1952. The post office in Washington, D.C., was asked during that period to furnish the names of addressees, the postmarks and the names and addresses of the senders, and to forward that information daily to the Hennings subcommittee, marked for the attention of Paul J. Cotter, chief counsel.

A similar cover was placed on mail addressed to 3032—24th Street N.E., residence of Miss Jean Kerr, a close friend of Senator McCarthy.

Covers were likewise imposed upon mail addressed to Donald A. Surine at 9606 Garland Avenue, Takoma Park, Maryland.

Senators Ferguson and George, obviously embarrassed at finding their own confreres engaged in such scandalous undertaking, stoutly insisted in their report that Senator Thomas C. Hennings, Jr., who chaired the group investigating McCarthy, was never aware that the mail check was put into effect.

It was initiated, they said, by Chief Counsel Cotter and carried out by staff investigators Francis X. Plant and Robert Shortley without the knowledge or consent of Senator Hennings or any other member of his committee.

Letters requesting postmasters in Washington and in Kinsington, Maryland, to place the covers had been written on Senate stationery, it was true; but both original and file copies carried a facsimile signature of Senator Hennings, made by a rubber stamp.

"Your committee is convinced," says the report, "that the representation of Senator Hennings' signature was affixed to the letters without his knowledge or consent."

As to whether mail covers had ever been maintained against

other members of the Senate, the committee found it impossible to make an exhaustive or conclusive finding.

The report noted that evidential determination of such a broad question could be made only after examining the records of every post office in the nation.

The committee left little doubt, however, about their own attitude towards using mail covers to aid congressional probes: "Your committee desires in strong language to condemn the use of mail covers by a Senate committee or its staff."

The senators fully understood the implications of permitting mail interception for any purpose. They realized that if surveillance could be exercised over the correspondence of even an unpopular figure like McCarthy, it could likewise be imposed upon their own.

If they have not expressed their concern in terms of legislation that would outlaw mail checks altogether, except in cases of national security and fugitives from justice, perhaps it is because they have not been pressed to do so by their constituents.

On the other hand, as in the case of so many other government intrusions into our private affairs, the general public has remained, for the most part, unaware of the scope and nature of postal snooping. At the present time, it is doubtful that more than a small fraction of the nation's citizens have any idea what a mail cover is.

This is hardly surprising, considering the strict secrecy under which the surveillance has been carried out. Post office employees have been close-lipped (to save their jobs); and records have been destroyed. As late as April 27, 1964, a memorandum from a federal agency's division of regulatory management, addressed to its district directors, quoted the chief postal inspector as saying:

"The source of information obtained from mail covers should never be disclosed under any circumstances. I am sure that you can appreciate that a careless word, or misuse of information obtained from a mail cover could prove most embarrassing." [5]

The memorandum went on to point out that a few years previously, legislation had been introduced in Congress providing severe penalties for the supplying of information concerning mail covers to any person, including law-enforcement agents. That legislation, warned the inspector, was deferred only "with some difficulty."

About this time, the mail interceptors were also beginning to feel the heat of the Long committee's inquiry into their procedures. When brought into the arena of public hearings on the issue, postal authorities not only stoutly defended the practice, but were considerably less than candid in answering the senators' questions about the extent to which postal espionage had been pushed.

Appearing before the Long subcommittee on February 23, 1965, Chief Postal Inspector H. B. Montague piously intoned:

"The seal on a first-class piece of mail is sacred. When a person puts first-class postage on a piece of mail and seals it, he can be sure that the contents of that piece of mail are secure against illegal search and seizure. *The only time first-class mail may be opened in the postal service is when it can neither be delivered as addressed nor returned to the sender.* [Italics mine.] Then, it is treated by trusted employees in the dead letter office to determine whether it contains any information to establish ownership. A court may issue a search and seizure warrant for a particular letter or letters, but such instances are rare because of the time element involved. Mail cannot be deliberately delayed in the postal service."

Less than two months later, senate investigators had turned up irrefutable evidence, later acknowledged by the Post Office Department itself, that since as far back as 1942, post offices across the country had been turning over to the Internal Revenue Service first-class mail addressed to businesses seized for tax delinquency.

In late 1962, this practice was extended to private, nonbusiness mail.

Revenue officials opened and read the correspondence and, said Senator Long, in one instance even answered one of the intercepted letters.

In making these seizures, IRS agents were empowered by nothing more than an administrative form and the arrogance of office.

The piece of paper which IRS said it regarded as a warrant—"or equal to a warrant"—was simply a form the agency itself had dreamed up. It was not issued upon probable cause supported by oath or affirmation. It was not signed by a judge. It did not specifically describe the things to be seized; rather, it was used to lay hold of *all* mail matter meant for the addressee.

An assistant to the Post Office Department's General Counsel reported that, in a number of cases, the IRS merely wrote "a letter saying, would you please deliver, because this guy owes us some money." [6]

That such seizures were flagrant violations of the Fourth Amendment, there can be no doubt.

As long ago as 1877, the U.S. Supreme Court made it clear (in *Ex Parte Jackson*) that mail enjoys the same constitutional protection as papers in our own homes. To search and seize first-class mail, law enforcement agents must go before a court of competent jurisdiction and obtain a warrant. Said the court:

"Letters and sealed packages of this kind in the mail are as fully guarded in examination and inspection, except as to their outward form and weight, as if they were retained by the parties forwarding them, in their own domiciles. The constitutional guarantee of the right of people to be secure in their papers against unreasonable searches and seizures extends to their papers, thus closed against inspection wherever they may be. Whilst in the mail, they can only be examined under like warrant, issued upon similar oath affirmation particularly describing the thing to be seized, as is required when papers are subjected to search in one's own household.

"No law of Congress can place in the hands of officials connected with the Postal Service any authority to invade the secrecy of letters in such sealed packages in the mail. And all regulations adopted as to mail matter of this kind must be in subordination to the great principle embodied in the fourth amendment to the Constitution."

When publicly confronted with the question of having violated the Fourth Amendment by unlawful seizure of citizens' private papers, the Post Office Department passed the buck. Their argument was that there was no opening of the mail by postal employees themselves. They had done nothing more than deliver unopened mail to the Internal Revenue Service in compliance with their levy. It was the IRS agents who had really opened the mail and confiscated its contents.

As mentioned earlier, the 89th Congress put an end to this travesty of due process by enactment of Public Law 89-44, which went into effect June 21, 1965. Section 812 of that act specifically prohibits seizure and opening of first-class mail by agents of the Internal Revenue Service, or anybody else.

The question of mail covers, however, remains unresolved. When Senator Edward V. Long announced that he might seek passage of his bill (S.973) outlawing mail covers, Internal Revenue Commissioner Sheldon S. Cohen opposed the move. Revenue agents had found the mail watch a valuable investigative technique, he said, in solving tax crimes and determining integrity.

Enactment of the bill, he asserted, would seriously hamper the Service in investigating and enforcing the criminal provisions of the federal tax laws.

Passage of the legislation would also hamper the IRS (and other agencies of the government that engage in the same practice) in their postal surveillance of thousands of innocent persons, in the hope of apprehending a few of the guilty.

6

Authority to bind and to loose

|||||||||||||||||||||||||||||||||||||||||||||||||||||||||||||||||||||||||||||||||||||||||||||||||||||||||||||||||||||||

It [the government] has taken on a vast mass of new duties and responsibilities; it has spread out its powers until
they penetrate to every act of the citizen, however secret;
it has begun to throw around its operations the high dignity and impeccability of a state religion; its agents become a separate and superior caste, with authority to bind
and loose, and their thumbs in every pot.

H. L. MENCKEN

One of the chief purposes of surveillance under the spy system of
government is to make sure that everyone is conforming to officially proclaimed doctrines.

Detailed standards are established for just about everything.
These are then expanded until they embrace every vital aspect of
our lives. Under the guise of promoting general welfare, they have
come to include criteria for determining what we eat, how we conduct our business, the kind of personality our children will have—
even what the architectural style of our homes must be, if a legally
empowered bureau so decrees.

The original concept of police power to enforce only limited
governmental objectives has been gradually and subtly changed
during the past three or four decades. It has come to mean no
longer a power delegated to the government by the people and sub-

ject to their consent; but a sovereign right of the government to establish whatever regulations of living officials deem appropriate, with or without the approval of the electorate.

The Supreme Court did not judicially endorse such a view until 1952. Then came the Day-Brite case in which the court held that police power "is not confined to a narrow category, but extends to all great public needs."

Implied, if not stated in this ruling, is the idea that these great public needs are to be determined by bureaucrats, not by the people themselves.

In 1954, the court went even further and, in the view of many, made a mockery of the Constitution it had sworn to defend. It ruled that the state may set up standards that are "spiritual as well as physical, aesthetic as well as monetary."

Such a broad and arbitrary exercise of power is, of course, in direct conflict with our right to lead our own lives, creatively and in our own way, so long as we do not injure our neighbor.

To insure compliance with the vast flood of rules that has poured forth from regulatory agencies ever since (the federal pandect alone now fills one hundred and ten fat volumes), greater and greater vigilance has been required.

Ellis Arnall, former governor of Georgia, pictured inspectors of the Federal Food and Drug Administration, for example, using "un-American police-state tactics." Comparing FDA agents to James Bond, the celebrated spy of Ian Fleming's novels, Governor Arnall said, "The secret activities of Secret Agent 007 were actually over-shadowed by FDA Agent 41."

He was referring to a case in which an agent had used a wireless device to make a secret recording of interviews while seeking evidence against a company that made a milk substitute.

Governor Arnall told a Senate hearing that his corporate clients had been entrapped, deceived and pilloried by the government agency, which had acted "improperly, unconscionably and illegally.

He said that three members of the FDA Kansas City staff, all seated in the hearing room as he spoke, had committed perjury and were so obviously infamous that the jury from the outset had recognized that both the FDA officials and inspectors were "not only incompetent, but were unworthy of belief under oath."

Arnall's clients were acquitted.

Food and Drug officials who had appeared before the Senate committee earlier admitted that agents used secret electronic equipment in their investigations.

The snooping gear most frequently employed appeared to consist of a radio transmitter about the size of a cigarette lighter, and a tape-recorder unit built into an attaché case.

Committee aides disclosed that the agency owned about twenty such radio-recording combinations, costing about $1,200 to $1,400 apiece.[1]

Governor Arnall said operation of these devices constituted illegal radio broadcasting. He charged that the FDA was a participant in a secret government radio network called IRAC.

In response to questions by newsmen, government spokesmen later revealed that IRAC (Interdepartmental Radio Advisory Committee) was the clearing house for assignment of radio frequencies and call letters to various federal agencies, primarily the military.

The organization is administered by the U. S. Office of Emergency Planning.[2]

Governor Arnall urged strong legislation outlawing the use of intrusion devices by government. He recommended that FDA and other federal agencies, except those guarding national security, be forced to destroy their secret arsenals of electronic snooping gear. He called upon Congress to place restrictions on appropriated funds to prevent the agencies from purchasing such nefarious equipment.

Senate hearings produced evidence that even churches are no longer outside the azimuth scan of Big Uncle's all-seeing eye. Not big churches, of course, because they have political muscle and the money to march the invaders into court, and to keep them there all the way to No. 1 First Street N.E., Washington, D. C.

But for a starter, take a small unorthodox congregation, whose beliefs and practices are somewhere out in theological left field. Plant a spy (probably equipped with a secret transmitter or microphone) among members and ministerial staff. Give him a month's time to "get something" on the church's clergy and teachers.

That's the way it was done with the Founding Church of Scientology at 19th and R. Streets, Washington.

On January 3, 1963, a band of U.S. marshals, acting on orders of the Federal Food and Drug Administration, descended on the church, tramped through the buildings beating on doors, grabbing books out of the arms and hands of religious students and interrupting confessional procedures that were in progress at the time.

They also invaded rooms occupied as residences by the ministers and, without a search warrant, went through closets, bureau drawers and even lifted bed covers to see what might be underneath.

Chief objective of the seizure was a small, electronic device known as an E-meter, resembling the polygraph (the machine so widely used by the Department of Health, Education and Welfare, parent agency of the raiders).

Church officials later said that these small instruments were used during "auditing," a confessional-type procedure, to measure the emotional intensity of the communicant. "When a person is very confused," explained the church's minister, "he really doesn't know what the problem is. With this meter, we can locate the highest point of emotional upset with him, and normally that would be the problem that he is having the biggest trouble with."

Church officials vehemently denied ever having claimed that the E-meter could cure disease, as charged by FDA. Scientologists said that, in fact, each member is asked to sign a written acknowledgment that the device does not diagnose or treat disease.

The sect's attorney said the church had never been asked by the FDA to discontinue the use of the E-meters and, prior to the raid, had not alleged that they were being used unlawfully.

He pointed out that the church, like any other in the Washington area, was incorporated as a nonprofit, religious body under the laws of the District of Columbia, and had been propagating and practicing its beliefs at the same address for ten years.

The attorney suggested that the FDA had staged the raid for its publicity value. The agency had, as usual, tipped off the press, which had responded in force with both reporters and photographers.

Although the raid had occurred two years prior to the Senate hearings in which details were aired, the scientologists' lawyer said the government still retained the church property seized by the U.S. marshals. The government had done this by simply not listing the case for trial.

Meanwhile, he added, the FDA has continued its publicity campaign against the church, an attack based on false statements. As in other instances of the kind, when newspapers have received press releases with the government imprimatur on them, they have not bothered to check out the facts.

The church attorney also charged a continuing effort by federal agents to harass both officers and members of the church through their interrogation regarding the practices of their beliefs.

He said church staff members suspect—"and we have some reason for the suspicion"—that the FDA tapped the telephone lines of the church.

The scientologists further accused the agency of a possible attempt to spy on the mail coming to the church, its personnel and its members.

Observed the attorney: "The rapist, murderer and drug seller is protected. Certainly the private citizen or a church is entitled to a sworn warrant before their premises are invaded, but the courts have held—and I think they have erroneously held—that where it is a civil action, the government can go in under this Food and Drug Act and just invade the premises and take whatever they want and keep it as long as they want it."

Both press and public were apparently satisfied to accept without question FDA's claim that the church's use of E-meters brought it within the purview of the federal agency. But it requires little thought to realize that only a few miles down that same road are the Adventists with their sectarian ideas about nutrition; the Christian Science practitioners; the Evangelical faith healers; and finally—when Big Brother has grown to full size—the Catholic priest with his consecrated olive oil, used in extreme unction for the desperately ill.

In its broadly interpreted mission to protect the public against not only dangerous drugs and adulterated or misbranded foods, but also against their own stupidity and wastefulness, FDA snoopers often resort to curious snares.

Item: Paul C. Bragg, who believes in the efficacy of various dietary supplements, was conducting a series of lectures in Boston. At eighty-four years of age, he was a robust specimen of manhood, known as "the world's strongest great-grandfather." His audience, which probably felt that he was a living testimonial to his own ideas about health and longevity, listened carefully to what he had to say.

So did an undercover agent of the FDA, via an electronic bug planted (with a peculiar sense of propriety) in the flag stand holding the Stars and Stripes.

Bragg had long been regarded by the G-men as a "food faddist," which in the FDA lexicon means anyone whose views on diet disagree with those contained in the pronouncements issued from time to time by the agency.

When the lecturer discovered (quite by accident) that he was "tuned in," he was understandably annoyed. He demanded that the eavesdropper come out of hiding and make his identity known.

But the antisocial agent preferred solitude. It was later learned that the snooping had continued.

Eventually, FDA instituted a seizure of various of Bragg's writings and some food supplement products that were on display.

One of the publications seized was an instruction manual setting forth a special system of breathing exercises developed by the lecturer. Displaying this booklet before the Senate committee, Bragg's attorney said he challenged anyone to find one word in it that would make it subject to FDA control, or which could relate the publication to any product under FDA regulation.

Even so, Bragg had little hope of getting back these and other publications confiscated from him, without expensive and time-consuming court proceedings.

This "harassment by legal proceedings," as it was called by a citizens advisory committee appointed in 1962 to study FDA, can sometimes tie up and hold inventories running into the hundreds of thousands of dollars.

Business firms, as well as individuals, who feel strong enough, outraged enough or wealthy enough to take on the government in court, often find it difficult to enlist expert testimony.

Witnesses who could offer such testimony—doctors, scientists, medical researchers—often fear the consequences of becoming an adversary of a federal agency with the vast powers wielded by the FDA. They are afraid they might lose their hospital associations, incur the displeasure of the AMA or forfeit a fat government research contract.

A New York attorney announced that he had a documented statement concerning just such a case of intimidation. It was litigation in which the FDA was the plaintiff. A prominent and reputable doctor agreed to testify on behalf of the defendant. After the physician's testimony, which presented opinions completely contrary to those of witnesses the government had put on the stand, an FDA official had told the defense attorney that he would see to it that repercussions would follow and retaliatory measures would be taken against the doctor who opposed the agency.[3]

Another enforcement technique of the FDA appears to be entrapment.

Take the case of a small pharmaceutical company which distributed a drug actually made by another corporation. Pondering a decision recently announced by FDA, the firm thought the edict might apply to the product they had on the market.

Following a procedure more or less routine in such cases, the corporation asked the court for a declaratory judgment as to whether the drug could be legally sold. While awaiting judicial decision, the firm voluntarily removed the drug from the market.

Meanwhile, the FDA instructed one of its secret agents in St. Albans, New York, to write a letter to the drug house, posing as a customer urgently in need of the drug.

The company responded to the unusual request. Having thus tricked the firm into a technical violation of the legal restraint, the FDA brought a charge of criminal contempt against the pharmacal corporation and two of its officers. They were convicted, but an appeal court reversed the judgment.[4]

In seeking to defend this kind of trickery, the agency offered the lame explanation that FDA wished to ascertain whether the corporation that orginally brought the action for declaratory judgment was acting in concert with another firm.

One of the striking features of our national life today is the attempt of federal functionaries—from top-ranking officials on down —to bridge the credibility gap with nimble, but implausible vindications.

One of the reasons advanced by FDA for making tape recordings is that (even though they are made secretly) they are for the purpose of "protecting" the individual being bugged by providing a reliable record of what was said. An agent, it has been explained, might have a lapse of memory, or might misunderstand what was actually said to him.

However, when a citizen wishes to have his own stenographer at the hearings to take down what is said for the same purpose—self-protection—the reaction of agency officials is seemingly the same as that of IRS authorities in similar circumstances.

At a hearing before the FDA district director in Denver, the defendant's attorney took along a court reporter because, he said, he suspected that the government office was bugged and that the proceedings would be secretly recorded.

At the hearing, when the district director became aware that a stenographer was transcribing the interrogation, he asked: "Who is this man here?" Upon learning that he was a court reporter, the agency official ordered the U.S. marshal to throw him out.

As the marshal towered above him, the reporter continued taking down a verbatim report of the incident. The defense attorney warned the marshal that if he laid a hand on the reporter, he would not be able to defend all the lawsuits which would follow.

The hearing ended in an impasse. At a later date, perhaps under pressure from his superiors, the FDA district director allowed the court reporter to take down what was said at the hearing.

After a series of shocking disclosures by witnesses appearing under oath during three full days of Senate hearings, the committee chairman publicly castigated the FDA in the strongest language possible.

He said the inquiry had revealed police-state tactics ranging from perjured testimony to gain a conviction, to abusive law-enforcement practices that included intimidation and gross disregard for constitutional rights guaranteed to all Americans.

He took the occasion to note also that prior to the Senate hearings, the FDA had seen fit to be uncooperative, misleading and evasive with the committee.

The ramifications of such wholsesale misconduct, he added, are overwhelming. Instead of FDA shouldering its responsibility to protect the nation's health, the senators had found an agency which was police-oriented, chiefly concerned with prosecutions and convictions, totally indifferent to the rights of individuals and "bent on using snooping gear to pry and to invade the citizen's right of privacy."

After a sweeping rebuke like that, the presumption would be that FDA officials would institute reforms within the agency, and retire their overworked eavesdropping equipment.

Not at all. After the Senate hearings, agency spokesmen clearly indicated their contempt for the proceedings, telling newsmen that those who offered testimony were "well-known quacks and crackpots" (the two epithets most often used by the FDA *apparatchiks* to describe anyone who challenges their exclusive possession of scientific truth).

When an organization change in FDA was made more than a year later, it was to expand that agency's already awe-inspiring police powers, not to restrict them.

With the solid backing of Congress, which has traditionally been susceptible to the big-scare technique, the FDA established a new corps of undercover agents, known as the Bureau of Drug Abuse Control. This is a police arm similar in function to the U. S. Bureau of Narcotics.

The Bureau's duty, according to FDA spokesmen, will be to ferret out and trap those who sell non-narcotic, but dangerous, drugs. Amphetamines and barbiturates were the drugs most often mentioned in appearances before legislators, but in the end the law was broad enough to cover almost any drug the agency chooses to regard as dangerous.

Senator Thomas Dodd, a former FBI agent, who pushed the bill through the Senate after a single day of abbreviated hearings, told his fellow lawmakers that the illegal use of such drugs is increasing at a fantastic rate among juveniles and young adults.

He was quoted as saying, "The use of these drugs is replacing, in many cases, the use of hard narcotics such as opium, heroin, and cocaine." [5]

If true, the latter fact seemed to some observers to represent an improvement in the drug-traffic picture. It would be hard to find a well-informed parent who would not vastly prefer that his youngster experiment with pep pills and goof balls than with the fatally addictive narcotics of the mainliner—heroin, cocaine and opium.

But Senator Dodd had a clincher for his argument to establish another spy web in America. The use of the drugs, he said, is increasingly "identified as a cause of sexual crime and violence."

It would appear that the senator had learned a few things about dealing with legislators from his old boss, FBI Chief J. Edgar Hoover, who never fails in his appearance before Congress to come prepared with frightening figures on rising crime and the menace of Communism.

Helping to enlist public support for the measure (and at the same time improve their Trendex rating), CBS television network produced a sensational three-part exposé, showing how easy it was for one of their men to get big shipments of barbiturates and amphetamines from drug houses by posing as a legitimate distributor.

The President's Commission on Narcotic and Drug Abuse had urged in their report that responsibility for curbing the sale and illicit use of dangerous drugs be transferred from the Department of Health, Education and Welfare to the Department of Justice. Other advisers on Capitol Hill suggested handing the job over to The Narcotics Bureau.

But both the FBI and the Bureau of Narcotics quietly let it be known that they wanted no part of the task of policing somnolent truck drivers and thrill-seeking teenagers.

The American Medical Association opposed Dodd's bill, but did not risk sending a representative to testify at the hearing because of the delicate matter of public image. Instead, the association sent a letter to the committee, in which it was pointed out that "although the characteristics of either habituation or addiction may occur with any drug capable of modifying behavior, the need for special measures of control should depend on the problem. *In the United States at this time, complusive use of amphetamines and barbitu-*

rates constitutes such a small problem that additional legislation to control such abuse does not seem necessary." [Emphasis added.][6]

The AMA went on to suggest that the best answer to the problem would be appropriate state and local laws, rather than federal legislation.

As in the past, however, public anxiety coupled with a bureaucratic grab for power won out. What lawmaker dared go on record as opposing a measure that would help retard juvenile delinquency?

The new FDA bureau was established in February, 1966, and training of a new corps of secret agents began. The first class was graduated and given guns three months later.

A further extension of police power seemed an easier way of meeting the issue of pep pills and LSD than a penetrating, realistic inquiry into the conditions of American life that cause young and old alike to seek escape, something better or just peace of mind in drugs.

Another factor which helped to beef up the already formidable enforcement arm of FDA was the appointment of a new commissioner to head up the agency.

He was Dr. James Lee Goddard, a career public jobholder who, prior to his FDA appointment, was chief of the Communicable Disease Center in Atlanta, Georgia.

The new commissioner, it was soon obvious, was hardly the man to halt the agency's encroachments upon individual privacy and freedom.

Perhaps the best clue to what might be expected from Dr. Goddard's tenure was one of his own statements about himself, quoted in a laudatory profile published in *Life* magazine:

"My nature is such that I can't be in a factory or store or hotel 10 minutes before I see all sorts of things wrong and start trying to reorganize the whole place." [7]

This reformatory outlook became evident the moment Commissioner Goddard took over. Using the big stick that Congress had just handed him, he struck out in all directions. Scores of drug firms were ordered to mend their marketing ways or to stop selling their products. One edict alone, issued on March 8, 1966, directed seventy companies to halt the sale of anti-histamine throat lozenges. Nine days later, he announced that *all* drugs approved by his predecessors prior to 1962—an estimated three thousand compounds—would now be screened for effectiveness.

The latter provision is one requiring the pharmaceutical industry not only to prove that its products are safe, but also that they meet FDA's ideas of effectiveness. Burden of proof that a given product is "effective" rests with the maker.

This regulation allows bureaucrats to keep off the market something that is harmless and which the public may deem to be efficacious, simply because it does not conform to arbitrary criteria set up by the government agency.

Not satisfied with the far-reaching, interventionist authority he had inherited, Dr. Goddard appeared before a House committee with a prepared statement outlining plans for further expansion of his prerogatives.

One of the agency's most important objectives, he later announced, is that of installing a large-scale computer system for handling information. Presumably this new data bank would also establish secret electronic dossiers.

The scope and intensity of the new Commissioner's crash program not only set off a wave of uneasiness among drug makers, but stirred up opposition from FDA's erstwhile allies, members of the medical profession.

Even within the agency itself, his intemperate policies reportedly led to the resignation of Dr. Joseph F. Sadusk, Jr., medical director, and of Dr. Joseph M. Pisani, ranking assistant.

Capitol Hill observers dubbed the new drug boss Go-Go Goddard, and one critic mused aloud, "I wonder when he will finally come out and drop the last four letters of his surname."

The nation's doctors, who had long been content with FDA's flagrant disinclination for the American citizen to decide his own diet and to determine for himself the nutritive value of the food he eats, now cried foul when Dr. Goddard arrogated to himself the exclusive right to say what new drugs they could administer.

Is the government going to become Big Brother, they now asked, leaning over the shoulder of every physician to control his medication?

Dr. Chauncey D. Leake, past president of the American Association for the Advancement of Science, firmly rejected the premise that Washington bureaucrats knew more about medicine than the country's practicing physicians.

Doctors, he declared, are dedicated members of a sophisticated society. They are fully qualified to decide whether a given drug should be administered to one of their own patients.

Every case, Dr. Leake pointed out, is different, involving as it does an individual with his own idiosyncrasies and medical history. Rigid rules should not be set by government, but the kind and extent of medication should be left up to each practitioner.

Dr. Goddard immediately challenged this view. During an interview in Washington, he flatly declared that doctors should be permitted to use only drugs that his agency had decided they might use. He said most practicing physicians are not qualified to use new medication that has not been approved by FDA.[8]

It is worthy of notice that, while thus implying that the medical profession was reckless or inept in administering new drugs, but that the FDA was more cautious, just the opposite situation came to light.

The drug in question was amantadine hydrochlorise, made by DuPont and marketed under the trade name, Symmetrel. It had been approved by FDA for use in preventing viral infections such as Asian-A influenza. The adult dose was 200 mg. a day.

But doctors who were using Symmetrel discovered that a tiny fraction more than the prescribed dose was dangerous. Even young adults in good health suffered severe side effects when given 300 to 400 mg.

Dr. George Gee Jackson, of the University of Illinois, who had studied reactions to the drug among medical students taking an overdose, reported alteration of the emotional state and of cerebration. The students experienced anxiety, depression and inability to concentrate. Some of them told of sensations of depersonalization and altered body image.

Dr. Albert B. Sabin, developer of oral polio vaccine, was quoted as saying: "There is great concern about the large-scale use of this drug because its margin of safety is very, very narrow."

But Dr. Goddard imperiously swept aside these opinions that conflicted with his own. He told a reporter for the *Medical Tribune:* "The risks involved in using the drug were weighed against possible benefits." [9]

It was not the first instance in which the medical profession had urged caution upon FDA with respect to dangerous side effects of a drug. The previous year, four doctors at Johns Hopkins University had reported a joint study of a drug called Investigational Drug 760. Although effective in lowering the cholesterol level of the blood, it was found to have hazardous side effects.

Nevertheless, it was more than a year after the FDA had received the adverse report before that agency finally ordered a halt to the drug's experimental use on humans. When confronted by a congressional committee with this dangerous dereliction of duty, FDA officials pleaded that they were short of personnel.

It will be recalled that FDA agents were at that time active throughout the country on such high-priority assignments as bugging school teachers and health lecturers, harassing "food faddists," raiding a church and waging a full-scale war on vitamins.

If the agency has been short-handed, it is not because a ready Congress has not responded enthusiastically to their requests for a bigger staff and a bigger club. FDA has been, in fact, one of the fastest growing organizations in the over-all regulatory apparatus of the government.

In 1954, the agency employed only seven hundred persons, most of them honestly and properly concerned with the safety and sanitation of the nation's foods, drugs and cosmetics. Today, the Food and Drug Administration staff numbers an estimated fifty-five hundred persons. Its budget in the same period has increased tenfold.

Commissioner Goddard apparently feels that, in addition to being incompetent to prescribe new drugs as they are available, the country's physicians are also helplessly naive when it comes to evaluating what they read in their medical journals.

He cannot—yet—directly censor the editorial content of such professional periodicals, but he can cool down those seductive, full-color advertisements; blue-pencil that enticing, direct-mail literature; and pass upon the acceptability of convention exhibits.

He has left no doubt that he intends to do so. "We *are* watching," he said, "and we are acting, too." [10]

There were also signs that the new drug czar intended to continue another familiar FDA tactic, used in the past to silence controversial opinion with which the government officials are not in sympathy.

On November 17, 1966, Associated Press—the largest wire service in the United States—carried a news story out of Washington based upon a notification sent by FDA Chief Goddard to a pharmaceutical firm.

The story reported that Dr. Robert A. Wilson, a prominent gynecologist and author of the controversial book, *Feminine Forever,* had been ruled "unsuitable to test drugs in humans."

While this was presumably an order from FDA to the drug house, it was turned over to the press by the agency. Released nationwide, it was greatly damaging to the reputation of Dr. Wilson, whose theories of ovarian function grew out of more than forty years of practice and research.

It was not until February 11, 1967—almost three months after the original story appeared—that the *New York Times* published what newsmen call a "skinback," that is, a correction and apology, which usually discourages a threatened libel suit.

The original statement about Dr. Wilson had been erroneous, the *Times* said, adding that the Associated Press also had voiced its regrets over the release. The facts were that Dr. Goddard had informed G. D. Searle & Company, the concern which makes an oral contraceptive called Enovid, that the Brooklyn gynecologist was unacceptable as an investigator of possible uses for Enovid in menopause. Searle had retained Dr. Wilson as one of its researchers of the drug.

Commissioner Goddard's directive to the pharmaceutical firm had declared that Dr. Wilson (despite his undeniable professional qualifications) could not be used in the research because he had publicized the use of Enovid in unnamed lay publications, stating that it was effective in preventing the symptoms of menopause.

The medical and scientific communities have suggested various alternatives to the commissar system of policing drugs and cosmetics. One proposal, made in 1964, which appeared to have strong endorsement of the drug industry as well as support by the medical profession and academic circles, called for establishing a scientific review board to which appeals could be made from decisions by FDA.

Appearing before the House subcommittee on government operations, a representative of the drug industry pointed out that on purely legal matters the FDA can be challenged in court, but in questions of scientific judgment there is no appeal from bureaucratic fiat. If the government agency makes a ruling or offers its own verdict concerning a scientific issue, such a pronouncement is almost certain to stand, even if it is considered unsound in the opinion of competent scientists.

One of the problems of trying to set up such an independent "drug court" would be finding an impartial review board to evaluate disputed compounds. Most qualified pharmacologists who might serve are already closely allied with the drug industry in one way or another.

Another complication is the fear of manufacturers that their closely guarded formulas and trade secrets might fall into the hands of their competitors.

Recently, a medical organization proposed the creation of a corps of accredited drug testers. Such a professional roster would include a broad range of specialists, and would be self-policing in much the same way as certified public accountants.

While the responsibility of protecting the general public from harmful drugs and against fraud is the most important function of the FDA, it by no means receives the agency's major attention.

By its own estimate, about 70 per cent of FDA's efforts concern the food we eat.

This means that virtually everyone in America is affected by the agency's policy decisions and scientific judgments concerning nutrition. Yet, like most experimental areas in medicine, there is scarcely a question of any consequence in the field of nutrition on which experts do not differ.

FDA's exercise of tight control, not only of the medicine cabinet, but of the dining table as well, has not always been easy.

Manufacturers can be brought to heel by a combination of legal harassment and attacks in the mass media which, without dropping a comma, publish heart-stirring accounts of the government's all-out war against unscrupulous food and drug makers who are ready to prey upon the ignorant and sometimes frightened public.

Doctors can be intimidated by a threat to their professional standing. Here, too, the slow-witted press is a willing accomplice, even at the cost of sacrificing what little claim to objectivity it has left.

But when FDA swings its club directly over the heads of the general public, it often meets a resolute and highly vocal protest.

Thus, Commissioner Goddard found his big stick had struck a hornet's nest when he proposed sweeping regulations that would empower his agency to decide what diet supplements and vitamins could be sold to the public.

Speaking from on high, Dr. Goddard had declared that Americans get all the vitamins and minerals they need from an ordinary, varied diet. Food supplements, he said, are just a waste of money.

Although this pronouncement was delivered with the certainty of a voice from Mt. Sinai, it did not reflect a consensus of the country's scientists.

For example, Dr. George M. Briggs, chairman of the department of nutritional sciences at the University of California at Berkeley, was quoted during a university explorer broadcast over CBS as saying that "as many as 20 to 30 percent of the people in this country have lower than the recommended allowances of vitamins. School children and teenage girls in particular appear to be very lax in their nutritional habits."

The California scientist—one of the country's top biochemists, who did outstanding early research that led to the isolation of Vitamin B12—said studies among selected populations of the country have shown that nearly 50 per cent of teenage girls are not consuming recommended daily allowances of such important vitamins as Vitamin C and Vitamin A. This, he added, is one of the many statistics which indicate that the public still has a long way to go in learning about nutrition.

Dr. Briggs also reminded his interviewer that vitamin research is "a comparatively new field, and all the answers aren't in yet. . . . There are still unidentified factors which remain to be discovered. These factors may not be too important, but we know that they exist for experimental animals."

"Many people," said Dr. Briggs, "take a multivitamin pill for the day's minimum requirements—not the therapeutic formula.

"I see no harm in this even though it is not prescribed by a physician." [11]

Ignoring this and similar opinions of other scientists, Commissioner Goddard published in the Federal Register of June 18, 1966, new regulations which, among other things, would require all multivitamin and mineral products to carry in a prominent place on their labels the following notice:

"Vitamins and minerals are supplied in abundant amounts by the foods we eat. The food and nutrition board of the National Research Council recommends that dietary needs be satisfied by foods. Except for persons with special medical needs, there is no scientific basis for recommending routine use of dietary supplements."

The new ruling would also forbid the sale of many vitamins in amounts greater than 70 mg. to the tablet or capsule, except with a doctor's prescription, which could only be filled by registered pharmacists. According to the federal law, any drug that requires a prescription is classified as dangerous.

The FDA did not argue that vitamins in larger amounts are harmful. The agency held merely that they were unnecessary and therefore a waste of the consumer's money. This role of economic watchdog clearly represented an extended, and unauthorized, exercise of administrative power.

To many, the reasoning itself seemed contradictory, in view of the fact that countless Americans who are convinced they need the vitamins would either have to buy many more to get the same potency they were accustomed to taking; or they would have to buy them by prescription, adding substantially to their cost.

The FDA also served notice in the published canons that the government intended to regulate the amount of added nutrients that could be used in fortified foods such as enriched bread, dairy products and cereals.

In this bid to become overseer of the marketplace as well as the laboratory and factory, Commissioner Goddard was seemingly undeterred by an earlier federal court ruling which clearly stated:

"The basic flaw in the Government's case against the product is that it is seeking, under the guise of misbranding charges, to prohibit the sale of a food in the marketplace simply because it is not in sympathy with its use. But the Government's position is clearly untenable. The provisions of the Federal Food, Drug and Cosmetic Act did not vest in the Food and Drug Administration or any other Federal agency the power to determine what foods should be included in the American diet; this is the function of the marketplace."

The court cited a Supreme Court opinion (*U.S. v. 62 Cases, Etc.*) which warned that "in our anxiety to effectuate the congressional purpose of protecting the public, we must take care not to extend the scope of the statute beyond the point where Congress indicated it should stop."

Applying this view to the fortified sugar case, the court concluded that "Plainly, only Congress can or should regulate the use of vitamins *and then only to prevent public injury.*" [Italics supplied.]

FDA, however, like other federal agencies, considers legal decisions binding only in the case at bar. Agency officials know that not every individual or firm can afford long and costly litigation to defend their rights. Therefore, for each instance in which the government's illegal acts are challenged in court, there are countless others in the same category that stand by default.

The new dietary and vitamin regulations were to become effective on December 15, 1966. But the wave of protest which ensued when the public became aware of their scope and meaning was too great to be ignored, even by a federal agency that enjoys a unique concentration of power.

Part of the dissent was in the form of a nationwide campaign organized by makers and distributors of dietary foods and supplements. This call to arms also had the support of many who never bought vitamins or food supplements. The latter group opposed the extension of police power because they recognized it as being based upon the stupid and untenable notion that one man or one federal bureau had either the qualifications or the right to restrict the sale of harmless nutrients.

On December 14, 1966, the day before the regulations were to be implemented, the FDA ordered an indefinite delay in the effective date.

No thinking person will deny the need for adequate laws to protect the public from dangerous or harmful food and drugs. Nor is it necessary to argue that manufacturers and merchants are all above fraudulent practices.

But the crucial question is: Should a federal agency be allowed, under the guise of providing this protection, to control the marketplace and scientific forum, employing such techniques of spy government as electronic eavesdropping, intimidation, censorship and punishment by publicity?

Senator Long reported that one characteristic of the FDA stood out clearly all through the Senate subcommittee's investigation of its activities. This was its rejection of any suggestion that an improvement in its procedures was called for. Unlike other agencies which—ostensibly at least—were willing to examine abusive practices, the FDA regarded itself as above reproach.[12]

During the Senate hearings, a New York attorney pointed to the fact that other regulatory agencies—the Federal Trade Commission, the Federal Power Commission, Federal Communications Commission, etc.—are staffed by more than a single commissioner. The commissioners have fixed terms of office; and they represent divergent and competing interests in all segments of our society. Their decisions, he said, are based upon a balance of these interests for the good of the nation as a whole.

FDA, on the other hand, with its one-man rule, seeks to enforce conformity to its own arbitrary dogma.

In its desire to impose uniform obedience to bureaucratic edict, the FDA is not alone. The practice represents a disturbing trend that is spreading throughout government on all levels.

The Department of Agriculture, for example, prosecuted a New

York dairy farmer because he transported cream in a single twenty-quart container instead of ten two-quart cans, as specified in government regulations.

Here, clearly, we are not dealing with general welfare, but with insistence upon conformity and obedience to arbitrary government criteria.

Plutarch, writing of the ancient Lacedaemonians, tells of that kind of law enforcement. The despotic ephors or overseers deprived Terpander, a prominent musician, of his harp because he added one string to it in violation of established custom.

And what was the legacy that Lacedaemonia left mankind?

While in neighboring free Athens, the creativity of spiritual youth exploded in a cultural sunburst that has illumined men's minds for three thousand years, Sparta dwindled and disappeared into the darkness of history, leaving not a single intellectual memorial.

7

Publicity as punishment

The circumstances in some of these cases strongly suggest
that the FDA has used its power of press release, not just
to inform or warn the public, but to suppress an un-
friendly or unacceptable point of view.

U. S. REPRESENTATIVE DAVID S. KING

Government agencies sometimes prefer to prosecute an accused citizen in the press rather than in the courtroom.

The great advantage of this smear-and-scare technique is that it
eliminates the annoyances of due process—witnesses, cross-
examination and judicial opinion.

Too, by substituting unfavorable publicity for litigation, administrative officials can continue to harass an individual almost indefinitely.

Consider, for example, the case of Dr. Carlton Fredericks,
whose unorthodox opinions on nutrition, as expressed on broadcasts and in printed works, have made him the most "unwanted"
man on the U. S. Food and Drug Administration's blacklist. For
more than fifteen years, the federal agency has sought to muzzle
both Dr. Fredericks' radio programs and his publications.

We are not here concerned with the merits of Dr. Fredericks'
opinions on diet and health, but with the tactics used by the government in trying to suppress them.

In sworn testimony before a Senate committee, Dr. Fredericks said FDA efforts to gag him began back in 1949, when he criticized over the air the agency's proposed standards for white bread.

The day following the broadcast, Dr. Fredericks said, the *New York Times* carried a release by FDA declaring that food faddists had a terrible hold on the American public, a situation that must be cleaned up immediately.

"This was the beginning of a relentless, unmitigated, uninterrupted effort by the U. S. Food and Drug Administration to silence my radio broadcasts by the use of every device—legal or tangentially legal—that has occurred to the mind, the fertile mind, behind the mimeograph machines in that department."

Dr. Fredericks told the senators that an FDA agent appeared at New York University, where he was then studying for a doctorate in public health education, and informed the dean of the school of education that the FDA took a very dim view of Fredericks' fitness to receive a Ph.D. degree.

During the ensuing years, Dr. Fredericks charged, the FDA has issued countless press releases and public letters attacking him by name. The publicity material denounced him as a food faddist, cultist, crackpot and dispenser of nutritional nonsense.

These handouts were duly picked up and published throughout the country in major newspapers and magazines, as well as in professional journals.

In an attempt to silence Fredericks' broadcasts, FDA enlisted the help of the Federal Communications Commission.

After a meeting by an FCC official with the Food and Drug director of information, the president of the American Institute of Baking and an official of the American Medical Association, the FCC sent a letter to all radio stations carrying Fredericks' program, "Living Should Be Fun." It reminded licensees that under FCC regulations, they were supposed to play a positive role "in bringing about balanced presentation of opposing viewpoints."

It further hinted that there was a tie-in between Dr. Fredericks and advertisers who had commercials adjacent to his program. In view of this, the stations were asked to submit to the FCC within fifteen days a statement setting forth (1) past performance and future intentions with respect to presenting viewpoints opposed to those of Dr. Fredericks; and (2) the inquiry, if any, they had made with respect to announcing sponsorship of the program.

A copy of the letter was also sent to two FDA officials for their information.[1]

Thus threatened, even if indirectly, with loss of their broadcast licenses, many stations immediately dropped Dr. Fredericks' program. In reply to a listener's letter complaining about the cancellation, one radio station (WJOY, Burlington, Vermont), said they had reluctantly suspended the broadcasts after FCC had indicated concern over the program.

"As you may know," the letter declared, "we are a licensed medium and are bound by many rules and regulations. Our first concern must be to protect that license. . . . Our legal counsel agreed that it would be best to suspend broadcasts until Dr. Fredericks can prove that charges made against him and the program are groundless."

Dr. Fredericks could not, of course, disprove the charges, since, as he told the Senate committee, "I have never been the target for any legal charge which would allow me to go into a courtroom and defend myself." [2]

Meanwhile, radio stations across the country continue to tiptoe around Dr. Fredericks' program "Living Should Be Fun," in the fear that, as the publication *Advertising Age* put it, "their own living might not be so much fun at renewal time."

In addition to censoring controversial opinion on the air, there are indications that the FDA (and other federal regulatory agencies) would also like to prevent the sale of books that challenge official dogma. But standing squarely in the way of this kind of suppression is the constitutional guarantee of free speech and a free press.

To get around this legal roadblock, when a book contains what

FDA considers scientific heresy, the agency resorts to a game of semantics. Claiming that such books (or other printed material) are used as labeling for drugs and food banned by the government, FDA seizes them under its authority to confiscate anything which misbrands a product.

Actually, the courts have supported this claim only when it can be shown that there is a definite promotional tie-in between a book and a food, drug or cosmetic.

Addressing a meeting of the Institute of Food Technologists in Berkeley, California, an enforcement official of FDA boasted that his agency had seized large stocks of the best-selling book, *Folk Medicine,* by C. D. Jarvis, M.D., because it was used to promote the sale of honey and vinegar.

The truth is that in November, 1964 the U. S. Court of Appeals (in *U.S. vs. Balanced Foods*) struck down the government's attempt to censor the book on the ground that it was labeling for honey and vinegar products. The court held the seizure to be improper and not within the scope of the agency's powers. In his decision, the judge pointed out that under its labeling theory, FDA could seize the Bible, since it recommends honey for therapeutic use.

(Isaiah VII:15 declares, "Butter and honey shall he eat, that he may know to refuse the evil, and choose the good.")

In another case (*U.S. vs. 8 Cartons, More or Less, Molasses,* 97 F. Supp. 313 [W.D. N.Y. 1951]), the FDA had seized a book, alleging that it had been shipped with some blackstrap molasses. The publication was labeling, said FDA, because it recommended molasses.

The court thought otherwise. In discussing the allegation against the book, the judicial opinion noted that "the book discusses the merits and the uses of many foods, drugs and cosmetics generally, including blackstrap molasses. It does not mention 'Plantation' blackstrap molasses (the offending brand) or any other food, drug, device or cosmetic by trademark or brand name. It advertises no products."

When it came to suppressing the best-seller, *Calories Don't Count,* by Dr. Herman Taller, FDA officials felt they at least had one legal leg to stand on. In the book as originally published, the reader was told where he could obtain safflower .oil capsules to be used in the diet regimen recommended by the text. The reference cited the capsule source by name: Cove Vitamin and Pharmaceutical, Inc.

Agents from the enforcement arm of FDA seized copies of the book, together with Cove's safflower oil capsules, and a false-labeling charge was made against the publication.

The federal agency then took depositions from everyone concerned with the preparation and publishing of the book.

With these events to provide the basis for a news story (the publisher was one of the oldest and best known in New York), FDA Commissioner George P. Larrick issued a long press release, attacking both the book and its publisher, Simon & Schuster.

In his statement, which was given nationwide coverage by newspapers, radio and television, Commissioner Larrick charged that:

1. *Calories Don't Count* was deliberately created and used to promote and sell "worthless safflower oil capsules."

2. The book had been rewritten and the "catchy title" devised by a freelance sportswriter.

3. The references to Cove Vitamin were inserted when the manuscript "went to the office of General Development Corporation, apparently for that purpose."

4. Cove then created the CDC (Calories Don't Count) Corporation to produce the capsules. Financial interest in the new corporation was held by, among others, Dr. Taller and two vice presidents of Simon & Schuster.

The full truth, as later disclosed, did not completely coincide with these "facts," as released to the news media by FDA.

There was no evidence to support the claim that one of the main purposes in writing the book was to promote the sale of CDC capsules. Dr. Taller sincerely believed (and still does) in the theory advanced in his book. He had originally recommended safflower oil; the idea of capsules occured to him as an afterthought—he believed that would be an easier form in which to take the oil.

It was true that a freelance writer named Roger Kahn—provided by Dr. Taller's agent, Herb Jaffe—had rewritten the manuscript, converting Dr. Taller's "jungle of medical jargon" into what the book trade calls "a mail-order, inspirational style."

Such a practice is common among New York publishers, and it is doubtful whether any popular book on a medical theme now on the market was written by the doctor-author without assistance. Kahn also provided the "catchy title," which FDA found offensive.

As for a financial deal between publisher and capsule-maker, Simon & Schuster categorically denied ever having had any interest in Cove Vitamin. Richard Grossman, then vice president of the publishing firm, who was in charge of producing the book, was offered an opportunity to acquire an interest in CDC Corporation, but rejected it. Another Simon & Schuster vice president, who had no connection with the editing, production or promotion of the book, did—after publication—buy some shares in the capsule corporation as a personal investment.

The publisher insisted that the FDA knew from sworn testimony that neither Simon & Schuster nor rewrite man Kahn ever sent the manuscript to General Development Corporation for the purpose of adding any reference to Cove, as stated in the government press release.

There is no way of assessing how much damage was done to sales of the book and to the publisher's reputation. A veteran newsman assigned to cover the story for *Saturday Review* reported that in areas where the FDA release was given the widest publicity, sales of the book fell to almost nothing. In areas where it had received less prominence, they held up well.

The issue again is not whether the book in question was a good or bad book. It is not a question of whether it was "nutritional nonsense," or even whether it promoted the sale of safflower oil capsules. The overriding issue is whether an agency of the federal government, using its prestige and tax-supported facilities, has the right to silence theories and opinions of which it does not approve. Put in the simplest terms, has it the right to substitute the news columns for the courthouse?

Answering the critics, M. Lincoln Schuster, then president and editor-in-chief of the publishing firm, put the matter in its proper perspective, perhaps, when he said, "We have been book publishers for thirty-eight years, and have always believed that a free market place is incontestably essential for an open society and a democratic culture. Unless a publisher has the right, and indeed the duty and the obligation, to publish controversial and nonconformist and dissenting ideas and books, on subjects on which the experts and doctors themselves disagree, these principles become hollow slogans and meaningless cliches."

The restraining effect of such government attacks by press release, against even courageous publishers like Simon & Schuster, is evident in a reporter's account of an interview with Peter Schwed, Essandess vice president and editor.

The newsman asked about a manuscript called *Fallout In Foods* which, it was rumored, had been submitted to Simon & Schuster some weeks before.

The editor's reply, according to the reporter, was: "Eighteen weeks ago, before *Calories Don't Count,* we would have a contract signed by this stage. But we don't. I've sent the book around to a lot of people who are interested in fallout. Some of them are pretty unenthusiastic, and I'm not sure we'll do the book. I'd like to, because I think it is interesting, but I'm not sure. . . ." [3]

Senators Everett M. Dirksen and Long have introduced a bill (S. 1336) which will curb the seemingly irresistible impulse of bureaucrats to inflict punishment by publicity.

Section 9, paragraph (b) of the act states that publicity which a reviewing court finds was issued by the agency or any of its officers or employees to discredit or disparage a person who is under investigation, or a party to any agency proceeding, "may be held to be a prejudicial prejudging of the issue in controversy." Therefore, the court may set aside any action taken by the agency against such a person.

At this writing, the bill is still in committee. If passed by Congress, it will severely restrict, if not completely eliminate, the trial-by-press procedures now prevalent.

Unfortunately, it will apply only to administrative agencies of the federal government. In the past, some of the most flagrant abuses of the press release have been by national, state and local law-enforcement officials.

Even Congress itself, in conducting its investigative hearings, has too often established an unpopular figure as a criminal in the public mind, then subsequently allowed his testimony to be used against him as a basis for legal prosecution.

Aside from seriously undermining a man's reputation before he is found guilty in a court of competent jurisdiction, pretrial statements by prosecutors and government agencies sometimes make it difficult or impossible to select an impartial jury to hear his case. Once impaneled, of course, the jurors are carefully shielded from outside contacts and information that might prejudice or influence their unbiased judgment.

But by that time, irreparable damage may have been done. What of the sensational stories they have already read in the press, seen on TV or heard over the air? Can the average individual erase from his unconscious mind and memory, as he is asked to do, the blazing headlines, the opinions of the police, the highly emotional outbursts of adversaries in the case?

In instances where the accused is implicated in a charge that has come before a congressional committee, he may already have been virtually convicted by hostile and often inflammatory lawmakers in a nationally televised forum.

The long and bitter fight between Jimmy Hoffa and the government provides many examples of this strange kind of justice in the land of the free.

From the outset, few Americans had a very high regard or much sympathy for the cynical teamster czar, who bossed the nation's biggest union. He had helped create the image of himself as a ruthless and bullying tyrant whose philosophy of life was based upon the premise that "every man has his price."

But over the seven years that it took the U. S. Department of Justice to get a final conviction, upheld by the Supreme Court, that image was extensively elaborated by federal officials using extralegal means—an image fixed forever in the public mind.

Sidney Zagri, the late legislative counsel for the Teamsters Union, testified before a Senate hearing that Hoffa had been called as a witness before the McClellan committee on forty-eight different occasions over a two-year period. During the same time, Hoffa was also a defendant in two criminal cases, and indictments were under consideration by one or more of twenty-seven grand juries investigating him at the time.

The impact on millions of viewers of these searching interrogations under the glare of TV lights, said Zagri, compromised Hoffa's position in the minds of the American people, including prospective or actual members of grand juries.

During these appearances before the admittedly hostile committee, Hoffa was, of course, not given an opportunity to cross-examine his accusers, some of whom, according to the Center for the Study of Democratic Institutions, were anti-union employers; nor to offer evidence to refute their testimony.

Zagri also charged that after Robert Kennedy, who was counsel for the McClellan committee, resigned to manage his brother's campaign for the presidency, his "pursuit of Hoffa" continued.

Appearing on the TV program, *Meet The Press,* at a time when a grand jury was convened to consider the government's charges against Hoffa, Robert Kennedy was asked to comment on a campaign statement reportedly made by his brother, to the effect that he (JFK) was not happy about Hoffa's still being at liberty. "I wonder," said the panelist, "if you feel the same way about Hoffa?"

Kennedy replied that he thought "it is an extremely dangerous situation at the present time; this man who has a background of corruption and dishonesty, has misused hundreds of thousands of dollars in union funds, betrayed the union membership, sold out the membership, put gangsters and racketeers in positions of power, and still heads the Teamsters Union."

After Kennedy became attorney general, his efforts to put Hoffa behind bars apparently were continued with renewed vigor. Such efforts were proper and wholly in keeping with his job as the country's chief prosecutor. His tactics in accomplishing that end were something else again.

In testimony before the Long committee on March 2, 1965, Attorney Thomas A. Bolan told how he had stumbled upon a memorandum concerning Hoffa in the files of *Life* magazine, while checking the files in connection with an article about his own client, Roy Cohn.

The memo, dated March 6, 1961, had been written by Hank Suydam of the Time-Life Washington bureau, addressed to E. K. Thompson, his New York editor. It was written on *Time* magazine stationery, and was marked *Personal and Confidential.*

"Last Saturday," it read, "I got a phone call from Bob Kennedy asking if I could drop whatever I was doing and come to his office. I did, and when I got there, he closed the door and told me the following: in a back room was a high official of the Teamsters, a man who had been privy to the inner workings of the organization since 1953. He was particularly knowledgeable about Hoffa. This official is honest, said Kennedy, and also quite an idealist. The man had been working directly with Kennedy and in secret for the last 2 years. He was now so disillusioned and disgusted with the corruption he saw around him, particularly as concerns Hoffa, that he has just about decided to make a public break with the union. Kennedy said *he had suggested to this man* that he make his break via an article in *Life* in the form of a personal exposé of Hoffa. Kennedy asked my personal word that for the moment only you and I would know of this matter. Kennedy feels, perhaps melodramatically, perhaps not, that the man's life would be in danger if word leaked out of his intentions." [Italics mine.]

The informer in question turned out to be Sam Baron, a teamster official who secretly hated Hoffa. The *Life* writer heard his story, the memorandum says, "after a cloak-and-dagger shift of scenery, involving Kennedy slipping us out through back corridors, a drive by roundabout route to the guy's home in Virginia, and the assigning to me of the code name 'Brown.' " [4]

On the day following the public disclosure of the *Life* memo, Robert Kennedy appeared before the same Senate committe, and angrily denied that he had "handled myself in some improper or shocking way while I was attorney general."

Kennedy asserted that it was Baron's idea to tell his story to *Life* and that he had merely put the teamster official in touch with the magazine's editors. "I made that arrangement. I did nothing else. It was my understand that if anything was published, it was going to be published if something happened to him. If he was killed or in some way beaten."

Asked whether the *Life* memo was genuine, Kennedy said he had read it and had no reason to believe it was made up. "It is a true document."

Committee Counsel Bernard Fensterwald observed that "there is no implication in that document that I can find that this article was to be done only on Mr. Baron's demise. Do you have some independent evidence on that point?"

Kennedy replied: "I will say that my testimony, No. 1, and the fact that the article was never published."

Then the following lively exchange between Kennedy and Fensterwald took place:

FENSTERWALD: The article at that stage had not been written. This was an arrangement whereby, as I understand it, you were putting what would normally be described as a "fink" in touch with Time-Life to write a magazine article.

KENNEDY: Normally described as what?

FENSTERWALD: Fink, f-i-n-k.

KENNEDY: I never heard that.

FENSTERWALD: A "stool pigeon." Does that word strike a chord?

KENNEDY: I thought it was a citizen who was reporting information and evidence in connection with illegal activities.

FENSTERWALD: That is correct. That would be a very good definition.

KENNEDY: That is your definition of a "fink."

FENSTERWALD: Wait.

KENNEDY: Let me say, I am shocked to hear that. There have been a lot of loyal people, if I may say, Mr. Counsel, who have provided information to the U. S. Government in connection with Communist activities, underworld activities and narcotics activities at great risk to their own lives, and I think that has been very, very helpful to the United States.

FENSTERWALD: And is it also your position, sir, that it is proper for the Attorney General to take such people, even when a case is under investigation and indictment, and attempt to see that their testimony is printed in the public press rather than taken into court? [5]

While Robert Kennedy believed in the public's right to know all about Hoffa, he evidently did not extend that share-the-information attitude to the Justice Department's star witness against the teamster boss.

The witness in question, upon whose testimony Hoffa's eventual conviction was largely based, was a man named Edward Partin, former teamster official and trusted confidant of Hoffa.

At the time Partin agreed to "cooperate" with the government, he was lodged in a Louisiana jail facing a number of charges that included embezzling, kidnapping and manslaughter. According to the union counsel's estimate, the total maximum jail sentences hanging over Partin's head at the time amounted to two hundred and eleven years.

The Justice Department freed him, then sent him as a bugged informer to Nashville, Tennesse, with instructions to get the goods on Hoffa.

Later, according to a story released by columnists Robert S. Allen and Paul Scott, Robert Kennedy—using the full power of his office as the nation's chief legal officer—interceded to prevent Senate investigators from questioning Partin.

The Senate internal security subcommittee had wanted to ask Partin about allegations that he was involved in an arms deal with Fidel Castro. However, the attorney general called the committee's acting chairman, Senator Thomas Dodd, and arranged to have the hearing called off.

Although thus protected against having to talk to a Senate executive committee, Partin was allowed to blab freely to *Life* magazine, which published a feature story, *Inside Hoffa's Ugly World,* based upon the informer's sensational revelations.

On another occasion, Attorney General Kennedy was publicity-shy when the *Nashville Banner* proposed to run a story about someone posing as one of the paper's reporters in order to get reaction quotes from prospective jurors in Hoffa's 1962 trial.

The Nashville newspaper offered a reward of $5,000 for information leading to the arrest and conviction of the person who had posed as a *Banner* reporter.

Soon afterward, Hoffa announced that he had a transcript of a telephone conversation between Robert Kennedy and *Banner* publisher James G. Stahlman, in which Kennedy was trying to suppress a detailed story of the phony reporter incident.

Hoffa would not reveal how he had come by the transcript, but it was well known that he had employed the country's leading wiretap expert, Bernard Spindel, ostensibly to protect him against FBI bugging and wiretapping.

Hoffa's widely quoted charge obviously required some explanation or denial. To defend his paper's position, Publisher Stahlman admitted that the transcript Hoffa held was a true recording; and he published it in full in the *Nashville Banner*.

The telephone conversation revealed that Robert Kennedy had sought to dissuade Stahlman from publishing details of the jury-poll occurrence because the story might help Hoffa to obtain a mistrial.

Stahlman replied that "we are just as anxious to see a successful case against this fellow as you are." But the publisher added that a gross injustice had been done to him, to his newspaper and his staff, and he felt it was necessary to make their position clear.

Kennedy's answer to that was: "These matters require sacrifice by many people."

Clearly piqued, the newspaper publisher told the attorney general, "I have made as many sacrifices for the Department of Justice as any man in middle Tennessee. . . . I am suggesting to you that what has happened has made it necessary for me to defend the reputation of my newspaper, which has existed for 86 years, and I don't intend to have it sacrificed for Jimmy Hoffa, the Federal Government or anybody else."

During the entire course of Hoffa's legal troubles, the seamy side of his life was laid bare in countless newspapers and magazines.

Americans who rejoiced to see him held up to ridicule and extra-legal condemnation in such mass-circulation periodicals as *Life* and *Look* did not stop to realize that such practices go to the very heart of justice as we have known it in this country since the birth of our nation. They were unaware that they had embraced the cardinal premise of Marxists and Communists, namely, that the end justified the means.

Also, they did not identify with a man they considered to be evil and corrupt, a dishonest union boss and racketeer, who at last was "getting what he had coming to him."

It has been reported that under Kuomintang rule in China, a condemned prisoner was sometimes dressed in the most bizarre way possible. Red and white paint was splattered on his cheeks, and he was drawn through the streets, squatting absurdly in a cart.

By thus making him ridiculous, says the writer, the police removed him from the sympathy of the crowd, the common humanness of mankind itself. Because he was not one of them, the sentence meted out to him was of little concern.[6]

This same formula of isolation plays a significant role in the disfiguring, pretrial profiles of unpopular figures such as Hoffa.

But the procedures thus adopted and legally approved become precedents at law. Once they are fully established, prosecutors can feel justified in using them in the same way against any American citizen, good or bad.

The Department of Justice eventually "got Hoffa." The U. S. Supreme Court upheld his conviction by a vote of six to one. Yet, in the government's inglorious handling of the case, they employed all the familiar, ugly tactics of a police state: wiretapping, bugging, smears, planting of coerced informers and secret payoffs.

Chief Justice Earl Warren noted sadly that "the Government paid an enormous price" for Hoffa. Planting a spy in the accused's quarters and councils and prevailing upon friendship with the victim "is no less proscribed than an invasion accomplished by force." Here, he said, the government reaches into the jailhouse to hire a man (Partin) facing more serious charges than those against Hoffa, makes him the equivalent of a bugging device.

"In the four years since he first volunteered to be an informer against Hoffa," the chief justice noted, "he has not been prosecuted on any of the serious Federal charges for which he was at that time jailed, and the state charges have apparently vanished into thin air."

For his services to the government, then, he was well paid, "both through devious and secret alimony payments to his divorced wife and, it may be inferred, by executed promises not to pursue the indictments under which he was charged at the time he became an informer."

No conviction based heavily upon his testimony should be allowed to stand, Warren added.

It was not even necessary to raise the question of constitutional rights—"for the affront to the quality and fairness of Federal law enforcement which this case presents is sufficient to require an exercise of our supervisory powers."

The dissenting opinion recalled that in another case (*Mesarosh v. United States,* 352 U.S. 1, 14 [1956] a new trial had been ordered because of the testimony of an unsavory informer who, the government admitted, had committed perjury in other cases. "The government of a strong and free nation does not need convictions based upon such testimony. It cannot afford to abide with them."

If the tables had been turned and Hoffa had insinuated his informer into the prosecution's camp, said Chief Justice Warren, he would be guilty of obstructing justice.

Justice William O. Douglas, while voting with the majority to uphold Hoffa's conviction on other technical grounds, nevertheless took the occasion to denounce the government's reprehensible handling of the case and to comment upon what is happening in America.

"We are rapidly entering the age of no privacy," said he, "where everyone is open to surveillance at all times; where there are no secrets from Government. The aggressive breaches of privacy by the Government increase with geometric proportion. Wire tapping and bugging run rampant, without effective judicial or legislative control.

"The dossiers on all citizens mount in number and increase in size. Now they are being put on computers so that by pressing one button all the miserable, the sick, the suspect, the unpopular, the off-beat people of the Nation can be instantly identified."

But returning to the subject of this chapter—punishment by publicity—it is encouraging to note that at least partial relief may be in sight by way of remedial legislation.

Concerned about the adverse effect of widespread, pretrial publicity on the conduct of a trial, a Senate subcommittee launched an inquiry into the question of free press and fair trial.

A bill (S.290), introduced by Senator Wayne Morse of Oregon, would make it contempt of court for any federal employee, or for any defendant or his attorney, to make available for publication any information not already filed with the court, if such information might affect pending criminal litigation.

Significantly, the bill does not seek to restrict newsmen in using information that they manage to ferret out in other ways. Nor, under guarantees of a free press, could it be so.

Media spokesmen say they fear that, if the bill is passed, it might provide a legal veil of secrecy that could shield law enforcement agencies against public criticism. It might even place in jeopardy the rights of the defendant, if authorities are thus legally empowered to conceal records and to withhold information about investigative procedures such as polygraphs, psychological tests and so on.

This sudden concern for the defendant seems rather pharisaical in view of the reckless disregard the press has shown for the rights of accused persons in the past.

In academic circles, and among publishers attending conventions far from their base of operations, there have been high-flown discussions about responsibility of the press. But in more than fifteen years as a newsman, I have never known the topic to be raised in the haunts of the working press.

As the city editor of a metropolitan daily once told me, "There are just two important questions to be answered in evaluating a news story—if you get it before the opposition does—namely: Is it libelous? Will it sell newspapers? If the answer to the first question is no and to the second, yes, you've got it made."

The notion, widely propagated by B-movies and by the newsmen themselves that every story is carefully "checked out" in order fairly to present all sides is also donkey-dust blown from the Fourth Estate corral.

When a reporter or rewrite man checks an individual's file (if any) in the newspaper morgue, he does so for two reasons. One, he wants to make certain of identity in order to avoid a libel suit if there are two persons of the same name. Two, there may be a juicy tidbit from the past—marital row, nightclub brawl, sex offense, etc. —that can be used to sweeten up the current story.

As for making an honest and diligent effort to get "the other side of the picture" in the case of a person charged by the police, indicted by a grand jury or defamed by a federal agency, reporters rarely extend themselves very far in that direction.

If a defense attorney provides them with material that makes good copy, they will use it. But they are not eager to "blow down" a hot story by citing extenuating circumstances or reporting possible false arrests.

Police and prosecutors are well aware of this trait, and sometimes exploit it for their own ends. Law-enforcement officials are often quoted as to the guilt or innocence of the arrestee before he is even arraigned. Or they will volunteer prejudicial information about a prisoner's behavior in jail, or unproved data about his family background. If he has a prior record of arrest, that also will be mentioned.

Prosecutors, too, often lay the groundwork for their courtroom contests by "leaking" damaging or inflammatory details concerning a case about to be tried. Sometimes they lead the press to expect more than they finally deliver. Such was true in the sensational Jelke case involving the heir to an oleomargarine fortune, charged with pandering.

The editor of one of New York's dailies told a lawyers' conference that some of the stories about the case, vouchsafed by the prosecution, were more thrilling as originally whispered to newsmen than they turned out to be in the actual trial.

There is no evidence to suggest that any of the newspapers made an effort to pin down the hard facts. Any official statement is regarded as sufficient justification for a story.

The author of a book on nutrition, which had been attacked (along with the author) and its contents falsely described by the Food and Drug Administration, asked the science writer of a major New York newspaper, "Why did you permit publication under your name of the FDA release attributing to me a diet for cancer, when all you had to do was pick up the telephone and order a copy of my book, which was printed right here in New York City, to find out for yourself that what I have said is directly the opposite?"

The newsman was reported as replying that "when it comes in under a Washington dateline, with a Government agency's imprint, we do not check the accuracy." [7]

Another man, whose difficulties with the FDA had been presented to the public only by quoting the agency's "news" handout, not only complained of unfairness, but sent in documentary proof that the FDA release had misrepresented the facts.

In an answering letter, the editor said: "The story which appeared . . . is based upon an FDA report. I would suggest that any argument you may have with this report should be directed toward the agency." [8]

Perhaps it was this kind of responsibility of the press that H. L. Mencken—himself a veteran of the Fourth Estate—had in mind when he commented that "journalistic codes of ethics are all moonshine. Essentially, they are as absurd as would be codes of streetcar conductors, barbers or public jobholders."

8

Programing our youth for bondage

██

New generations appear, each temperamentally adjusted
—or as I believe our American glossary now has it, "conditioned"—to new increments of State power.

ALBERT J. NOCK

Is it fanciful to say that many signs point to the emergence of a new
type of American: the Transparent Man?

He is the citizen of the future—fully structured and intimately
programed down to what Gestapo chief Reinhard Heydrich once
called "the smallest egotistical longing."

He stands before us like the glass model of man recently built for
neurological research: his brain visible, his nerves unsheathed, his
viscera shown, his heart laid bare.

A man of no secrets. Nor does he believe in such a thing as
privacy. An old-fashioned idea, an outgrown need of older generations.

Since almost half the nation's population is under twenty-five
years of age, it might be helpful to examine the dominant outlook
of this burgeoning society of tomorrow.

Over a period of fifteen years, Purdue University's division of
educational reference made a continuing study of teenage opinion
in America. The poll's findings showed that 83 per cent of the
young people approved of wiretapping; 58 per cent accepted the

third degree as sometimes necessary in police procedure; 60 per cent endorsed outright or favored censorship of books, newspapers and magazines; and 25 per cent thought it proper for law officers to search homes without first obtaining a search warrant.[1]

It is hardly surprising that young people today take for granted a monitored and controlled society, if we examine the environment into which they have been born and reared. The games and toys of their earliest childhood have included battery-powered tape recorders with a remote microphone hookup for eavesdropping on friends and other members of their family; junior-size lie detectors ("watch the fibber squirm"); spy cameras; a parabolic microphone ("aim it at friends a block away and hear every word"); and Secret Agent outfits of spy disguises.

Some of their favorite television programs feature the exploits of undercover operatives equipped with fantastic intrusion devices—and tough cops who kick in doors and wouldn't recognize a search warrant if they ever saw one.

At school, the student is under the microscope from the time he enters kindergarten until he emerges more than a decade and a half later with a degree and a pedigree behind him—a bulging dossier that contains all the intimate details of his life to that point.

The drastic changes that have taken place in "school days, school days, good old Golden Rule days," were graphically pointed up in a cover-story on teenagers which appeared in *Newsweek* magazine.

The report noted that even relatively small, rural schools feel obliged, because of demands for information made on them, to adopt the methods of massive educational bureaucracy practiced in the cities.

As a telling example, the article cited the case of a junior-senior high school in Iowa. Records at the school in the 1890's listed the student's name, grades, and the number of times tardy. Today, at the same school, student dossiers contain the following: grades, attendance record, birthplace, parents' background, phone number,

Social Security number, various kinds of achievement-test scores, IQ scores, extra-curricular activities, rank in class, grade average, personality and mental maturity tests, insurance claims, pupil-profile charts, health records, immunization record, reams of conduct records and the residual import of those intimate discussions with guidance counselors.[2]

Such is the beginning of a comet's tail of data that will follow the individual throughout his life. Both private and governmental investigators will be dipping into these files for basic material to add to other files.

On the college level, the vexing problem of how much information about a student should be given out has now become quite acute in some areas. Committees have been appointed to study the question and to provide guidelines for faculty members who are increasingly called upon to answer questions put to them by federal agents, military intelligence, the FBI and private investigators.

Yale Professor Charles E. Reich recently cited an example of the kind of questions about a student asked by government agencies. In an inquiry from the Department of Health, Education and Welfare concerning Student X, he said, was the following:

"How do you rate the applicant's relationships with other people? Consider such things as ability to work and get along with superiors and subordinates."

Then, having asked the question, said Professor Reich, his interrogator proceeded to give him a choice of certain answers: "Mediocre. Wants to do thing his own way more often than is desirable. Disliked by some associates. Somewhat lacking in tact. Becomes sullen when criticized. Tends to react negatively to suggestions."

Asked Professor Reich: "Do I really know what I'm talking about when I check these things off?

"It seems to me if I were a psychiatrist, maybe I would be qualified to answer questions like this; but as a professor of law, I do not really know anything about the personal adjustment of my students. I do not really know anything at all about their relationships to other people. I see them in a very special situation in the class, and I am asked to say all kinds of things, good and bad, about subjects that I know nothing whatever about."

The Yale educator added that if he were to refuse to fill out such detailed questionnaires, somebody in Washington would say, "There must be something to hide. This professor is unwilling to answer these questions." [3]

Meanwhile, back at school—on elementary and intermediate levels—a growing number of procedures are conditioning the student to accept without question the right of the government to make such haphazard incursions into his private life.

In California, at least one high school—and perhaps several—has equipped both boys' and girls' toilets with one-way mirrors. The reason offered for these peepholes is that they allow school authorities to keep the youngsters under surveillance to prevent vandalism and cigarette smoking while classes are in session.

Countless other schools, coast to coast, are now equipped with loudspeaker boxes in each classroom. This system is used not only for its ostensible purpose—that of paging teachers or making general announcements—but also as a feedback which the principal can switch on silently to monitor activities in the classroom.

The argument has been made that such an arrangement is less obtrusive than the old practice of principals making their observations through glass panels in the doors or visiting the classroom in person.

But as Dr. Alan Westin pointed out, in a paper presented at a Civil Liberties Union biennial conference, the effect of a silent sentinel, on both teachers and students, is quite different from that of the physical presence of the principal.

Researchers who have studied the problem of visibility and conformity have found that such electronic eavesdropping devices have a devastating effect on morale and academic freedom.

Dr. Westin suggested that perhaps one way to change the view of school administrators who advocate such a listening apparatus would be to urge the school board and city council to place similar monitors in the principal's office. That would insure that *his* standard of performance in relation to teachers, pupils and parents was also up to par.

In New York, the executive director of the Board of Education disclosed that school intercom systems in that city, installed as a protection against vandalism, could also be used to eavesdrop on classrooms and corridors.

As disturbing as such practices are, the federal government has embarked upon a surveillance program in public schools that is far more unsettling in its scope and possible effects on the nation's youth.

Known officially as the School Resource Officer (SRO) program, its chief feature is the stationing of police officers in public schools to keep students under constant surveillance.

At the opening of the 1966 fall term, the U. S. Department of Justice announced that its Office of Law Enforcement Assistance had assigned a grant of $63,377 to the Tucson (Arizona) police department to help expand the project, which had been in operation there for two years. That amount represented one half the total allotment the government is providing for a two-year pilot program in the Arizona city.

Government spokesmen referred to the move as a "crime control" program. To allay the fears of those who had misgivings about police officers in the school buildings, federal officials said similar projects would not be set up in other cities until results of the Tucson experiment could be evaluated.

The Civil Liberties Union, which is opposing the scheme, reported that the Justice Department is not, in fact, waiting to examine results of the Tucson pilot program. Instead, it has handed the Minneapolis police department $70,400 to start a similar operation in the Minnesota city.[4]

The next cities to receive federal money may very likely be Flint,

Michigan, and Atlanta, Georgia, where SRO programs are already under way, financed by private funds.

The Law Enforcement Assistance Act of 1965, under which the government made the grants, requires that in each case the federal allotment be matched by more than equal local funds.

In the Tucson project, each policeman assigned to an SRO beat was given jurisdiction over the school, the school area and the elementary feeder schools.

A report issued by the Tucson police department, covering various aspects of the SRO program, declared: "Contacts were made with various business establishments frequented by the area students. . . . A request was made for notification of the School Resource Officer of even minor violations and improper demeanor on the part of the students." [5]

Among the things that deeply disturb this kind of Big Brother operation in the schools is the fact that, no matter how friendly the cop in the corridor, he is still a cop. At a public meeting in Tucson, an SRO assured the townspeople that he was first of all a policeman and would fulfill his role as a policeman at all times.

How, ask critics of the program, can students speak and act freely in the ubiquitous presence of the policeman?

Warned a civil libertarian: "The officer may become a hero or friend to many children, but he may at a later date, use their confidence to obtain evidence against the child, his friends, or family." [6]

Prior to 1966, SRO police could interrogate students privately, without a parent or school official being present. It was easier, declared one SRO, to get the truth out of a kid when a parent was not on the scene.

Even more significant, perhaps, was his assertion that, if such questioning turned up some reason to take the child to Juvenile Court, "the interest of the State preempts the interest of the parent."

As the result of strong protests made in Washington, the government agreed to approve SRO grants to police departments only if they consented to conduct interrogations in the presence of parents or teacher, or both; and to obtain prior consent of the student's parents to proceed with such interviews.

Under the new SRO regulations, police are also required to notify the parents of any child in serious trouble as soon as it has been determined that the pupil is in what the law officers call "accusatory position."

Another major concern about the federally financed pupil watchers is that the police might use their authority to pry out of children information concerning family activities at home. Such snooping, say SRO opponents, invades the privacy of the home as well as that of the school.

In addition to what he may learn from the children, who may talk too freely, the SRO has access to all those confidential files that have been accumulating in the school office.

The 1964-65 Tucson report noted that vast quantities of information had been accumulated during the course of police surveillance in the schools.

Commenting on this statement, *Civil Liberties* said: "In his zeal to prevent crime, the SRO is tempted to over-research his subjects."

In another type of undercover operation, spies and junior informers have infiltrated teenage clubs and other gathering places. There they are encouraged to keep a secret watch on their peers and to report to the authorities any activities that appear suspicious or might be illegal.

A major record company is exploiting the growing interest in privacy invasion among the young people. It has put on sale a fifty-minute recording that eavesdrops on parties at which teenagers went on LSD "trips."

A company executive said that episodes in the album were culled from more than forty hours of tape recordings, most of them obtained by planting secret microphones in places where LSD parties were to be held.

The record company spokesman said piously that it was not the aim of the firm to sensationalize the subject, but "to illuminate it."

He said that heavy advance orders for the album indicated that it might become a best seller among the Now Generation. The company is considering similar "documentary reports" on such subjects as homosexuality and venereal disease.

It is almost impossible for the youth of today to do anything anywhere with full confidence that they are not being spied upon or monitored.

Take, for instance, the San Diego (California) public library, frequented by high school and college students in great numbers to do reference work. A young man wearing a badge is assigned the job of keeping a close watch on everybody. He prowls tirelessly and continuously among the tables and stacks. Nothing escapes his notice—what books are being read, what whispered confidences are passed, what items girls take out of their purses and so on.

Observing him on one occasion, squatting between the stacks and peering through the books at a group of students seated at a table, I asked a youth who had just picked his way around him: "What is he checking on?"

The student shrugged indifferently. He did not appear to be resentful nor even much interested in the watcher. Replying to my question, he said flippantly: "Maybe he's hooked on that miniskirt."

Recently added to an unknown number of political informers and other spies on campus was a squad of secret agents from the Food and Drug Administration. Dr. James L. Goddard, the fast-moving FDA commissioner, disclosed in February, 1967, that undercover operatives from his agency, posing as students, are invading colleges across the country in an attempt to break up the sale of LSD, amphetamines and "goof balls."

"We're not interested in making criminals out of our college students," he intoned sanctimoniously, "but we're trying to get at the illegal sources of supply, trying to take the profit out of the sale of these items."

When newsmen sought more information concerning the scope of the government's clandestine activity, officials of the Bureau of Drug Abuse Control, the new FDA division which runs the program, put them off by saying that the data they sought were scattered among the bureau's nine field offices.

A deputy director of the bureau's investigation division told the Associated Press that the "point of diversion" at which legally produced drugs are turned to illicit users is almost invariably off campus.

"We find that if the student is involved as a distributor, he is usually just a small operator. They usually don't have the funds it takes to operate at a wholesale level." [7]

If the students are small fish, why the campus spy web? One answer to that question might well be that, when the FDA agents ferret out a student user of LSD or other drugs, he will not be arrested, but will be pressed into service as an informer or a decoy. With a possible jail sentence facing him, he will not be in a position to refuse to "cooperate."

To advocates of more police power as a solution to the rising crime rate, introduction of the spy system among our youth may show promising results. Under the visible restraint of the policeman and the invisible restraint of the hidden informer, youthful wrongdoing seems to decline.

But as all history proves, such an improvement is temporary and illusory. The substitution of vigilant authority for individual conscience weakens the whole fabric of society.

The individual is no longer governed by a sense of right and wrong; he responds only to the whereabouts of the policeman. He exercises no moral judgment—only an animal sense of caution.

R. H. Towner put the problem in its proper perspective when he wrote that "Future generations learn to be eye servants, fearing only corporeal punishment. They do not see with spiritual eyes, hear the spirit's voice, fear spiritual punishment, or obey spiritual commands. As this change takes place, society is deformed. The church loses her usefulness, irreligion grows, worship is limited to ceremony and formalism; worldiness grips those who fear worldly punishments and hope for worldly rewards.

"Distinctions between right and wrong become entirely earthly, corporeal and visible, enforced by government as part of its general undertaking to compel uniform obedience to governmental will. The populace remains good while the spy system is effective, and while the spies themselves are good. There is no spiritual stamina, and every relaxation of espionage leads to frightful excesses.

"A spy system once begun, therefore, must be retained and augmented. The number of spies and their inquisitorial powers must be continuously increased. [Emphasis added.]

"But the spies themselves are recruited from the remainder of the population, and after a few generations, moral deterioration has attacked the spies. As they are born to ancestors who were continuously spied upon, the habit of espionage is inherited. The spies themselves must be spied upon." [8]

Involving students in the dark art of espionage is apparently nothing new in the academic life of the country. Nor is the practice wanting for ardent supporters.

A nationwide furor was sparked in February, 1967, by disclosure that for fourteen years or more, the Central Intelligence Agency had been paying a secret subsidy to the largest college student organization in America. Purpose of the covert aid was to finance the group's overseas activities.

After the exposé, advertised by a monthly magazine in a full-page ad in the *New York Times,* the government admitted that the CIA had funneled unaudited funds through real and dummy foundations to the three hundred chapters of the National Student Association. The NSA embraced the student governments of virtually every major college or university in the United States.

An NSA spokesman in Washington reported, after intensive investigation by his organization's board members, that during some years since 1952, as much as 80 per cent of the association's annual budget was agency money. The budget had sometimes been as large as $800,000.

Sam Brown, twenty-three-year-old divinity student, who headed the NSA national policy board, charged that the government spy agency had trapped American students who were officers of the group, by placing them under "fantastic pressures" not to reveal their ties with the CIA. "People were duped into this relationship with CIA, a relationship from which there was no way out," Brown said.

He then told how it had been done. NSA staff members who were selected by the intelligence agency for overseas missions at international student gatherings were first given a full security check without their knowledge or consent.

Those who passed muster were then interviewed, either by officials of the student association, by staff members previously recruited by the CIA or directly by agency employees.

Each prospective student-agent was told that there were certain things about the National Student Association of which he was not aware. Some of the information to be given to him to help him in his work as a representative at international student rallies would be from classified sources.

For that reason, he was asked to sign an oath under the National Security Act that he would not divulge anything he learned from these sources.

Only after he had signed the official secrets oath was he informed that he had in fact been employed by the CIA.

"The agony of these people who were trapped and were unable to break this relationship was awful," the NSA spokesman declared.

He revealed that information secured by the agency recruits overseas included dossiers on foreign student leaders, and written assessments of the policies and objectives of foreign student organizations.

Some of the data were passed directly to CIA agents, Brown said, and some went into the files of the National Student Association. However, the government agency also had access to the student organization files through its undercover operatives within the association.

The NSA leader confirmed earlier reports that the federal spy agency had intervened to obtain draft deferments for students in its employ.

Other inducements were lots of money to spend, a sense of doing important work and overseas travel.

When reporters asked the NSA policy board chairman whether the CIA had sought to silence association officers or staff members by intimidation, he replied that there had been no physical threats, but it seemed apparent that under the National Security Act—considering the statement the students had signed— there would be the probability of prosecution by the government if they disclosed anything.

If you would interpret that as intimidation or pressure, he added, then yes, there was considerable pressure. "A 20-year jail sentence [provided by the security act for violations] to maintain your integrity is a very high price to pay." [9]

Lawrence R. Houston, the CIA's general counsel, said the government did not prosecute the students who had revealed their clandestine link with the spy agency because "these boys were pushed into a corner" by the magazine that broke the story.

But, lest some of the student pawns should get the idea that public confession was good for the soul, he added that the students did not "have it carte blanche" to tell everything about their subterranean relationship with the government's secret agents.

That this was no idle threat was evident in the report of some of the student association's board members, who said they had been threatened with jail sentences for breach of their security oaths if they talked about their activities.

In the nationwide controversy that followed the NSA disclosures, the CIA was not without its staunch defenders. Robert F. Kennedy, for one, who had been fully cognizant of all intelligence operations during his tenure as attorney general, was quoted by news media as saying, "It was money well spent." The secret funneling of funds through foundations, he said, was an act "of the Government itself, acting through a representative of the President."

A later interim report by a committee appointed by President Johnson to review the CIA operation corroborated Senator Kennedy's point of view.

As a matter of fact, said the report, "When the CIA lent financial support to the work of certain American private organizations, it did not act on its own initiative, but in accordance with national policies established by the National Security Council in 1952 through 1954."

Throughout, said the president's apologists, CIA had acted with the approval of the secretaries of state and defense, or their representatives. "These policies have, therefore, been in effect under four Presidents."

Noting that President Johnson had appointed only his own representatives, including CIA Director Richard Helms, to investigate their own boss, the government, student spokesmen dismissed the inquiry as "a whitewash."

Senator John Stennis of Mississippi called the uproar a "tempest in a teapot," and warned that by discussing the CIA's actions publicly, "you destroy the CIA."

Representative Samuel S. Stratton of New York offered the same rationale as other defenders of the CIA operation: The Communists do it, so why shouldn't we?

"Everybody knows," he told a Wahington newspaper correspondent, "that youth organizations in Communist countries, and in most foreign countries for that matter, are official spokesmen for their own national point of view and are not only directly subsidized, but also organized and controlled by their country's leadership."

The honorable gentlemen all seemed to have missed the point. No one was objecting to American students being subsidized to attend international youth gatherings for the purpose of countering Communist propaganda with American facts and figures.

What critics—including most of the academic community—were objecting to was the typically spy-government way the program was undertaken.

Government spokesmen who cited the effectiveness of the Communist students—whom everybody knew to be subsidized openly by their governments—argued that open support of American youth would have made them appear as United States agents and therefore they would have been less influential.

Even this specious reasoning hardly excused the deceptive manner in which the students were recruited, and the intimidation that followed when they had been trapped into signing the security oath. As Senator Gaylord Nelson of Wisconsin observed, "We cannot conquer communism or crime by adopting Communist or criminal tactics."

Even worse, the eventual and inevitable disclosure of the CIA infiltration of the country's largest student association merely undermined the integrity of America scholars in the eyes of the world.

The full story of CIA involvement with student groups and others will probably never be known because of the tight security walls surrounding the spy organization.

A number of colleges and professional associations have carefully considered the dangers inherent in having government agencies involved in academic programs. In every case they arrived at the same conclusion: Except in time of declared war, academic institutions should not undertake research projects that are subject to security restrictions.

On November 17, 1966—several months before the CIA-NSA flap—one of the country's leading anthropologists warned that secrecy and pressures by U.S. intelligence agencies were eroding the prestige of American scholarly research abroad.

In a paper delivered at the American Anthropological Association's annual meeting in Pittsburgh, Dr. Ralph L. Beals of the University of California at Los Angeles criticized what he described as attempts by some government agencies to disguise intelligence activities by hiding them under the cloak of scholarly research.

He cited instances in which young scholars had been offered generous government aid for academic work abroad, only to be questioned later by intelligence agents seeking to solicit political information.

Dr. Beals said he had seen reports that some regular intelligence agents were themselves posing as anthropologists in foreign countries.

Such impostors, said the professor, were soon detected because they lacked the scientific knowledge and academic references to carry out the deception.

In fact, he went on, some foreign governments—notably those of the Middle East—welcome phony scholars as spies because they are so naive and can be fed all sorts of incorrect information.

Dr. Beals' report was based on a year-long study in the Middle East and Latin America following cancellation of Operation Camelot, an army-financed investigation of social changes in Chile.

The Camelot project, which was being carried out by the American University of Washington, was discontinued by the State Department in 1965, after the government of Chile had made a formal protest.

Dr. Beals called attention to the real danger of government involvement in the academic world when he noted that constraint, deception and secrecy have no place in the universal fellowship of learning.

Actions which compromise the intellectual integrity and autonomy of research scholars, Dr. Beals said, not only weaken those international understandings essential to the advance of knowledge, but in so doing they also threaten any contribution new discoveries might make to our own society and to the general interests of human welfare.[10]

9
The partners in anti-crime

> Himmler used to go about asking visiting foreigners why
> it was that the Gestapo had got such a bad name for
> itself.
>
> EDWARD CRANKSHAW
Gestapo: Instrument of Tyranny

A distinguishing feature of the police state is that those who implement its tyranny are not aware of wrongdoing.

Members of Hitler's Gestapo regarded themselves as patriotic Germans. They justified their acts of espionage and terror with the claim that these were necessary to rid the Fatherland of "the internationalist, capitalist, Jewish conspiracy."

The Soviet secret police and mass executioners who carried out Stalin's bloody purges were, in their own eyes, performing a necessary service to their country in eliminating vile "enemies of the State." Stalin himself always spoke of his Soviet dictatorship as "the perfect democracy."

Mussolini's blackshirt bullies shared the same sense of high calling and heroic service when they beat up innocent people throughout Italy.

Like Caesar's assassins, they were "good men all."

It might be well to keep in mind these extreme examples of public-spirited dedication when we are asked to excuse abuses of police power on the ground that they are necessary to thwart criminals and subversives.

It was just such an argument that Supreme Court Justice Louis D. Brandeis had in mind, no doubt, when he remarked that "the greatest dangers to liberty lurk in insidious encroachments by men of zeal, well-meaning but without understanding."

Such "well-meaning men," deeply convinced of their own important mission and the necessity of their methods, often regard any criticism as little short of treason.

The United States today is swarming with informers, spies and undercover agents of one kind or another, each convinced that he is a selfless and devoted public servant.

When laws stand in the way of carrying out their messianic mandate as they interpret it, the statutes are deliberately misread or ignored. That has been, and is, the practice not only of rank-and-file law officers and bureaucrats, but of the nation's highest legal authorities.

There is no better example of this kind of lawless law enforcement than the history of wiretapping in the United States.

More than a quarter century ago, Congress enacted a law—the Federal Communications Act—which makes it a crime to tap wires and for the tapper to divulge or to use "for his own benefit or for the benefit of another" any information obtained in that way.

Yet court cases, congressional investigations, sworn statements and official admissions within recent time have all revealed wiretapping on a colossal scale.

As Washington Attorney Edward Bennett Williams told a Senate subcommittee in 1959, the anti-tap statute has received less compliance than the Volstead Act, outlawing liquor.

The reason, said Williams, has been that law-enforcement agents themselves have been breaking the criminal statute. In the case of prohibition, at least, "We didn't have law-enforcement agents selling whiskey. They might have drunk it, but I don't recall instances where there was widespread sale of alcoholic beverages by agencies of the Government." [1]

Williams noted, however, that for twenty-five years the FBI has been tapping wires. "I don't say this to impugn their motivations. . . . They have done it, I believe, in good faith and with a laudable objective. But nevertheless, I think it is clear that they have been violating the criminal statutes of the United States."

This charge of wiretapping, recently admitted by both the FBI and the Department of Justice, is sharply at odds with public utterances of FBI Chief J. Edgar Hoover over the years. At various times, he has strongly criticized wiretapping as unethical and an "archaic and inefficient" method of investigation. The practice has proved to be, he said, "a definite handicap or barrier in the development of ethical, scientific and sound investigative techniques."

Handicap or not, the public record reveals a gradually increasing number of cases in which federal agencies, including the FBI, have been involved in wiretapping activities.

In his testimony before the House subcommittee referred to earlier, Edward Bennett Williams said that as a lawyer he had been disturbed when the Director of the FBI had told a television audience on May 18, 1958, that at that time his agency was monitoring ninety wiretaps. Hoover's statement was particularly ironic, said Williams, because on that very day a Justice Department prosecutor was asking a jury in New York to return a verdict of guilty against a defendant who was charged with having tapped one wire.

Williams commented on this situation in a lecture which he made soon afterward at Georgetown University, "because I believe . . . that laws are just as applicable to agents of the Government as they are to private citizens. . . . Ours is a Government where the policemen are *under* law, instead of a Government where they *are* the law."

Later on, Williams received a letter from Louis B. Nichols, assistant to J. Edgar Hoover. It read:

"Dear Ed:

"I read with considerable interest the story in Tuesday's *Evening Star* of your lecture at Georgetown. I wish I could have heard it. You did a great disservice, however, to the FBI in your comment that 'the FBI and New York State continue to tap wires in spite of the fact that the Federal courts have ruled them illegal.'

"I, of course, would presume to speak only for the FBI and I am unaware of any court decision which has ruled that wiretaps are illegal per se. What the courts have done is to ban evidence secured from wiretaps, and this whole matter was explored rather fully in the attached statement of the late Mr. Justice Robert H. Jackson, when he was Attorney General. In the FBI, all taps are utilized only with the written approval of the Attorney General in cases involving internal security or those involved in kidnaping.

"I know that you would want to keep this in mind in the future because it is manifestly unfair to attribute crime to an act that has been upheld time and time again.

Sincerely yours,
Louis B. Nichols"

To the letter was attached a copy of the opinion of former Attorney General Robert Jackson, who thought he had found a loophole in the law, which would permit wiretapping by federal agents. In the memorandum, dated March 9, 1941, and addressed to the House Judiciary Committee, Jackson set forth for the first time the dubious legal theory on which government law officers have ever since based their authority to tap wires.

Jackson wrote: "There is no legal statute that prohibits or punishes wiretapping alone. The only offense under the present law is to intercept any communication and divulge or publish the same."

The fact is, of course, that Section 605 of Title 47 of the U. S. Code (to which Jackson referred) forbids "any person having received an intercepted communication or having become acquainted with the contents, substance, purport, effect or meaning of the same or any part thereof, knowing such information was so obtained, to use for his own benefit or for the benefit of another, that information."

But for the Department of Justice, the FBI and law officers on all levels, the statute becomes a little blurred at its end.

To a literal mind, it is perfectly clear that when the FBI (or anyone else) taps a telephone line and then uses that information for investigative leads, or passes it on to another agency or official, a crime has been committed.

But by a twisted logic known only to mental contortionists, the government has said over and over again that when federal agents tap and tell each other, they are not divulging.

As far back as 1937, however, the Supreme Court (in *Nardone v. U.S.*, 302 U.S. 379) rejected that argument, finding that "the plain words of 605 forbid anyone, unless authorized by the sender, to intercept a telephone message, and direct in equally clear language that '*no person*' shall divulge or publish the message or its substance to 'any person.' "

To recite the intercepted message before a court, said the supreme tribunal, is to divulge the message.

The ruling also took note of the argument, still being advanced by advocates of police wiretapping, that it is necessary to combat crime. "It is urged that a construction be given to the Section which would exclude Federal agents, since it is improbable Congress intended to hamper and impede the activities of the government in the detection and punishment of crime."

The answer to that reasoning, said the court, is one of policy. "Congress may have thought it less important that some offenders should go unwhipped of justice than that officers should resort to methods deemed inconsistent with ethical standards and destructive of personal liberty. The same consideration may well have moved Congress to adopt Section 605 as evoked the guaranty against practices and procedures violative of privacy, embodied in the Fourth and Fifth Amendments of the Constitution."

From that time on, evidence known to be the result, direct or indirect, of wiretapping has been inadmissible in federal courts.

It has not, however, discouraged the tappers. Said Robert Kennedy in June, 1962 when, as attorney general, he was asking Congress to legalize wiretapping: "Almost no one believes this law . . . to be satisfactory. Indeed, bills to change it—Section 605 of the Federal Communications Act—have been introduced in virtually every session of Congress since it was passed in 1934." [2]

So they have. And to see what the aim of such legislation has been, we have only to examine Kennedy's own proposed bill.

It provided that:

1. The Department of Justice could, upon securing a court order, authorize wiretaps in the investigation of crimes involving murder, kidnaping, extortion, narcotics, bribery, transmission of gambling information and travel or transportation in aid of "racketeering" enterprises.

As we have already seen in the case of the Organized Crime Drive as carried out by the Internal Revenue Service, some of these categories can be given a broad enough interpretation for law-enforcement agents to tap anybody's telephone.

There are today thirty thousand federal investigators at large in the land, any or all of whom could conceivably tap wires under the racketeering provision of the act.

2. The attorney general could, *at his sole discretion* and without a court order, grant federal agents permission to wiretap in suspected crimes involving espionage, sabotage, treason, sedition and subversive activities.

Under the pretext of investigating "subversive activities," the FBI or other government undercover men could have made a probe of almost anybody's activities. The "FBI Reports," revealed during the Judith Coplon trial and on court order, pointed to just such taps. There has been persuasive evidence to suggest that the government has tapped wires of many innocent and loyal citizens to build dossiers on persons believed to be disloyal to the United States.[3] Such a procedure is one of the salient features of a police state.

3. On the state level, wiretapping would be permitted upon obtaining an order from a state court of competent jurisdiction in cases dealing with murder, kidnaping, extortion, bribery or drug traffic, including marijuana.

The bill was not passed. Congress apparently did not share the view of Robert Kennedy, who said, in urging passage of his wire interception act: "I cannot agree with those who say wiretapping should not be permitted in any circumstances and that the right of privacy outweighs other considerations." [4]

Attorney General Kennedy had good reason to expect that his wiretap bill would receive favorable attention in Congress. The lawmakers had previously pushed through an anti-crime package of five bills sent to them by his office.

One of the bills makes it a federal felony, punishable by imprisonment up to five years and a fine of $10,000 to cross a state line with *intent* to promote extortion, bribery, gambling, liquor, narcotics and prostitution.

As Senator Samuel J. Ervin, Jr., of North Carolina noted at the time the measure was being passed, under its provisions the government can punish a man for criminal "intent," even if he "got religion and got right with the law" before ever doing anything illegal.[5]

Senator Ervin said he considered it dangerous to write federal laws that would penalize "thoughts in the mind, or words that vanish into thin air" without any requirement for showing that some criminal act had been committed. Nevertheless, the bill was passed and is now the law of the land.

Punishing the citizen for his "intentions" is another familiar police-state practice, as is the restriction of free movement by the citizen from one part of his country to another.

While neither Mr. Kennedy nor any of his predecessors in the

Justice Department was ever successful in getting a bill through Congress to legalize wiretapping, proponents of the practice are still trying.

With other forms of eavesdropping, there has been no real problem. There is no federal law which prohibits bugging—that is, the use of concealed microphones to pick up conversations in a room and transmit them to monitors or recording devices outside the surveillance area.

The Supreme Court, however, has ruled that any evidence resulting from a listening device that was planted by physical intrusion into the bugged premises is "tainted" and therefore inadmissible in federal courts. Since physical penetration or illegal entry is used in virtually all cases of bugging, legal use of the information thus obtained would seem to be nil.

That would certainly be the case if the court or the defendant in a given litigation knew that electronic eavesdropping had taken place. But only rarely do they learn of it.

Recent public disclosures, resulting from a Supreme Court inquiry, indicate clearly that FBI agents, operating either on their own authority or with Justice Department approval—or both—have engaged in the sinister art of bugging quite often.

The first official admission of the government that G-men had been using electronic devices to eavesdrop was made on July 13, 1966. On that date, the Justice Department's solicitor general, Thurgood Marshall, told the Supreme Court that the FBI had used the snooping gear in what he called "major criminal investigation."

Under departmental practice which had been in effect for several years, Marshall said, the Director of the FBI was given authority to approve the installation of surveillance devices for intelligence purposes, but not to gather evidence. That authorization applied to cases involving internal security or national safety, "including organized crime, kidnapings and matters wherein human life might be at stake."

The solicitor general admitted that information which FBI

agents had obtained by electronic eavesdropping had been passed along to government attorneys who prosecuted Fred Black, Jr., a businessman convicted of income-tax evasion.

According to the memorandum submitted by Marshall, on February 7, 1963, FBI agents had drilled into the wall of Black's suite from an adjoining room in Washington's Sheraton-Carlton hotel, and had installed a tubular microphone. From the following day through April 25, 1963, the G-men had made summaries and tape recordings of conversations that took place in the rooms.

As it has done in other cases, the government maintained that the material gathered in all those weeks of monitoring was not used against Black. Were the FBI agents just listening for their own entertainment? Why did they share their stolen confidences with the Internal Revenue Service, which brought the charge against Black?

After receiving the Justice Department's memorandum which admitted the FBI microphone surveillance, the Supreme Court overturned Black's conviction and ordered a new trial.

Earlier, a bitter controversy erupted between FBI Director J. Edgar Hoover and the governor of Nevada, when FBI agents testified in a Denver court that they had planted a microphone in offices of the Desert Inn hotel in Las Vegas. The federal agents were investigating allegations of underworld rakeoffs and hidden gambling interests. For over a year, sixteen agents had eavesdropped and kept logs on every conversation that had taken place in the bugged area.

This—and other suspected electronic intrusions by G-men—violated Nevada's anti-bugging statute.

Edward Levinson, an executive of the Fremont Hotel in Las Vegas, promptly filed a six-million-dollar damage suit against the Central Telephone Company of Nevada, alleging a conspiracy with the FBI to illegally bug his office.

Telephone officials reluctantly admitted that from 1961 to 1963 they had leased twenty-five lines to the FBI. These lines led from the local FBI office to concealed bugs in various Las Vegas hotels, including the Desert Inn, Stardust, Fremont, Sands, Dunes and

Riviera. The FBI had the telephone company bill the agency in the name of the Henderson Novelty Company, a bogus musical rental service.

The then-Governor Grant Sawyer asked FBI Chief Hoover to explain why the federal lawmen cynically flouted the laws of Nevada. In his outspoken criticism of the FBI, Governor Sawyer said their eavesdropping technique "reminds me of all I have heard and read about Nazism."

In a two-page letter to J. Edgar Hoover, the governor demanded that the FBI make public any knowledge it had of crime in Nevada.

"I once again insist that if there is a violation of the law—prosecute. We will be the first to join forces with you, if you have any evidence to support your claims. You must not, however, violate Federal or State law, and you must conduct your agency in such a way that this nation remains one of laws, not of men."

Governor Sawyer's demand that Hoover explain why his Bureau did not feel itself bound by the criminal laws of the state was backed by the *San Francisco Chronicle*. In a strongly worded editorial, the *Chronicle* said Sawyer's question "clearly deserves a direct and unequivocal answer."

The editorial observed that Hoover had confirmed the widespread and systematic use of listening devices in Las Vegas, saying that his Bureau "had full authority of the Justice Department to install these microphones."

Such vindication of the practice, the newspaper continued, "compounds rather than excuses the grave offense; it alarmingly suggests that police-state methods of the FBI have the sanction of a Federal department which calls itself the Department of Justice."

The *Chronicle* concluded: "This was not the first time the FBI has been caught in the disgraceful act of breaking the law to obtain evidence of lawbreaking. It is time that its director, who has long enjoyed a curious immunity from official censure or criticism, should be restrained from further trampling upon the law that his bureau is intended to enforce."

J. Edgar Hoover did not condescend to reply directly to Governor Sawyer. But in a letter he wrote to a Las Vegas newspaper publisher, he made his familiar charge that any attack on the Federal Bureau of Investigation constituted an attack on him personally.

"The gambling industry in your state," wrote Hoover, "occupies a position of major importance in the scheme of organized crime and racketeering. Funds illegally skimmed from certain Nevada casinos have been used for a multitude of nefarious purposes."

So have the main profits, most likely. But this hardly answers the question of whether the FBI is above the law.

Only a short time previously, Mr. Hoover had declared during a Chicago address: "If we short-cut the law, we play a dangerous game, which can only result in total defeat for all of us because, if we destroy our system of government by law, we destroy our only means of achieving a stable society."

Edward Bennett Williams, whose career as an attorney involved defending unpopular clients against the questionable tactics of the federal government, called the FBI's wholesale bugging operation in Nevada "a studied, well-organized, amply financed legal conspiracy."

And William Turner, a former FBI agent who had once served as one of the Bureau's eavesdropping specialists, said the G-men were probably still engaged in bugging in Las Vegas, in violation of President Johnson's order that it was to cease.

"As former Senator Kefauver told me once," said Turner, "Hoover is more powerful than the President."

The ex-FBI agent said at a press conference that the FBI director has often dodged executive orders and has done as he pleased.

Turner expressed doubt that Hoover himself knew the full extent of electronic eavesdropping by FBI personnel. "Hoover conditions his agents to believe eavesdropping isn't evil, and then tries to control it from Washington."

But, he added, under pressure to obtain convictions, field agents will often install a "suicide tap" on their own. Those trained in such practices are given incentive awards of $500 to $1,000 in cash for the risks they take.

Sometimes when there is a concerted drive to make arrests, the FBI has on occasion subcontracted its electronic espionage out to private detectives.

Turner's prediction that the FBI's bugging activities in Los Vegas would probably contaminate gambling-connected prosecutions for some time to come proved accurate.

At the end of November, 1966, the Justice Department announced that it had begun a review of thousands of criminal cases —past and present—in which evidence may have been gathered by means of electronic eavesdropping.

A government spokesman said that not only the FBI, but all federal agencies with investigative arms, would be covered by the review. This would include, among others, the Internal Revenue Service and the Bureau of Narcotics, both of which have made extensive use of snooping gear. The review was to go back five years.

The Justice Department made this unprecedented announcement in a memorandum similar to that of July 13, advising the Supreme Court on the second occasion that the income-tax conviction of a Brooklyn man, Joseph Schipani, had been tainted by evidence obtained through bugging.

The court earlier had declined to give Schipani, who had been sentenced to three years in jail, a hearing. After the new disclosure made by the solicitor general, it sent the case back to the U. S. District Court "for a new trial should the Government seek to prosecute the petitioner anew."

The Justice Department pointedly informed the court that the FBI reports to the attorney general's office had not disclosed how the information had been obtained. The implication was clear: The government attorneys had been ignorant of the bugging when they prosecuted Schipani.

In its court memorandum, the Justice Department also disclosed that three weeks earlier then-acting Attorney General Ramsey Clark had sent a directive to all U. S. Attorneys, cautioning them that "this Department must never proceed with any investigation or case which includes evidence illegally obtained, or the fruits of that evidence."

Throughout the bugging disclosures, Justice Department officials maintained that they were surprised to learn of the FBI's use of electronic intrusion devices in Las Vegas and in the Fred Black, Jr., Bobby Baker and Joesph Schipani cases.

The director of the FBI, who has always carefully nurtured the image of the G-man as a clean-cut, fearless—but strictly ethical—gangbuster, was said to be deeply embarrassed by the action of the attorney general's office.

Smarting under the implication that the bugging had been carried out on his orders alone, without the knowledge or approval of the attorney general, Hoover responded with a flat denial that such was the case.

Replying to a convenient letter from Representative H. R. Gross of Iowa, J. Edgar Hoover said: "Your impression that the FBI engaged in the usage of wiretaps and microphones only upon the authority of the Attorney General of the United States is absolutely correct."

Hoover added that "full documentation exists as proof of such authorization."

The veteran G-man attached to the letter a communication dated August 17, 1961, signed by former Attorney General Robert Kennedy, in which the FBI informed the Justice Department that in connection with the use of microphone surveillance, it was frequently necessary to lease a special telephone line in order to monitor the bug (as was done in Las Vegas).

"If we are permitted to use leased telephone lines, as an adjunct to our microphone surveillances, this type of coverage can be materially extended both in security and major criminal cases."

The document went on to state that in the New York area, the telphone company insisted that the FBI furnish a written request on each occasion such a leased wire was installed. The telephone officials also required the approval of the attorney general. "Accordingly, your approval of our utilizing this leased line arrangement is requested."

At the bottom of the document, opposite the word "Approved:" was Robert Kennedy's signature.

Mr. Hoover's letter to Representative Gross continued: "Mr. Kennedy, during his term of office, exhibited great interest in pursuing such matters and, while in different metropolitan areas, not only listened to the results of microphone surveillances, but raised questions relative to obtaining better equipment. He was briefed frequently by an FBI official regarding such matters."

When Representative Gross made the Hoover letter public, Robert Kennedy—himself an image-maker whose new-found liberal supporters were too young to remember his connection with and admiration for, Senator McCarthy—immediately replied: "Mr. Hoover has been misinformed."

Senator Kennedy then produced a document of his own. It was a letter to him from Courtney A. Evans, a former FBI agent who, he said, had acted as a liaison officer between the attorney general and the Bureau.

According to Robert Kennedy, Evans had been present on each occasion "when any matter was discussed with any representative of the FBI, including matters referred to in Mr. Hoover's statement."

The Evans letter, dated February 17, 1966, said that since prior attorneys general had allowed the FBI to use microphones, as contrasted with wiretaps, without specific approval of the attorney general, "I did not discuss the use of these devices with you in national security or other cases, nor do I know of any written material that was sent to you at any time concerning this procedure, or concerning the use, specific location or other details as to installation of any such device in Las Vegas, Nevada, or anywhere else."

In a riposte, FBI Director Hoover produced a memorandum written by the same Courtney A. Evans, which appeared to be an outright contradiction of his later (and evidently solicited) letter to Senator Kennedy. It was dated July 7, 1961, and was addressed to Evans' superior, Alan H. Belmont, then assistant to J. Edgar Hoover. It said:

"In line with the Director's approval, the Attorney General was contacted this morning, July 7, 1961, relative to his observation as to the possibility of utilizing 'electronic devices' in organized crime investigations.

"It was pointed out to the Attorney General that we had taken action with regard to the use of microphone surveillances in these cases and while they represented an expensive investigative step, we were nevertheless utilizing them in all instances where this was technically feasible and where valuable information might be expected.

"The strong objections to the utilization of telephone taps as contrasted to microphone surveillance were stressed.

"The Attorney General stated he recognized the reasons why telephone taps should be restricted to national defense-type cases, and he was pleased we had been using microphone surveillances where these objections do not apply whenever possible in organized crime matters."

Replying to Hoover's counter demonstration in the document duel, Robert Kennedy said, "I believe Mr. Evans was telling the truth in his letter to me."

Rarely had the American public witnessed a confrontation of two national figures of the prominence of J. Edgar Hoover and Robert F. Kennedy, who were, in effect, accusing each other of being liars.

Who was telling the truth?

Senator Edward V. Long, chairman of the subcommittee then investigating privacy invasion by the government, said he would invite both Kennedy and Hoover to testify at a public hearing as to what did go on at the Justice Department when, as one newspaper columnist put it, "these two men were partners in anti-crime."

At the time of this writing, no such showdown under oath has occurred. Nor is it likely to take place. Neither of the principals in the controversy seems eager to be questioned in an open hearing.

During the Long committee's probe of snooping by other government agencies, it was reportedly planned to ask the FBI to explain some rather olid practices uncovered by the Senate investigators.

Such plans were quietly dropped, however, following a visit to Senator Long at his home in Missouri by then-Attorney General Nicholas deB. Katzenbach. A magazine article later asserted that Katzenbach had carried a message from the president, asking Senator Long to lay off the FBI.[6]

Well-informed sources in Washington say there is little doubt that the FBI engaged in a great deal of bugging without Attorney General Kennedy's knowledge or specific approval.

But in view of the indisputable fact that wiretapping, bugging and other privacy-invading practices by various government agencies were all greatly intensified when Mr. Kennedy took over as attorney general, his professed surprise at the FBI bugging in Las Vegas is a bit much.

"The first time I became aware of these eavesdropping practices," he insisted, "was when they were described in the press in connection with the Las Vegas investigation."

Said a Kennedy critic:

"Let all who believe that stand on their heads."

10

Little bugs have big ears

I have learned from long experience that the mouthpiece
of the standard telephone is one of the most effective,
most unsuspected eavesdropping mikes ever invented.

BERNARD SPINDEL
(Noted Wiretap Expert)

Few Americans today are ignorant of the fact that a man's home is
no longer his castle. They are even dimly aware that there are no
longer solid walls outside the home either. The office, the cafe, the
place where they shop—even their church—are all vulnerable to
the penetration of hidden intruders.

They have read of the tiny microphone disguised as an olive in
the martini, which can carry their unguarded remarks to a third
party eavesdropping in another room. They have heard accounts of
the innocent-looking cigarette package that conceals a radio transmitter, and of the lamp bulb that harbors an electronic bug to pur-
loin their confidences. Bugged hotel rooms, hidden tape recorders,
concealed cameras, laser beams—these techniques of the unseen
spy are as familiar as the plot of a James Bond movie.

Such glamour devices of the space age have led most people to
regard wiretapping as somewhat old-fashioned and out of date.
After all, it is known that the police in New York were actively
wire spying (as it was then called) as far back as 1895.

And a story published fifty-one years ago—on May 17, 1916—in the *New York Times* has the familiar ring of an oft-told tale:

"The Thompson Committee investigating public utilities," it reads, "heard yesterday that the police of New York had been tapping telephone wires by wholesale, and the Committee will begin today an investigation of the entire subject. An official of the New York Telephone Company told Senator Thompson that in the past two years, 350 telephone wires have been officially tapped by the police.

"According to information furnished to the Committee, telephone wire tapping was begun back in 1895, when William L. Strong was mayor. Through succeeding city administrations, the practice has prevailed and grown. . . ."

At this point of the story, another stock feature of the wiretap dilemma emerges:

"In each instance, he [Senator Thompson] said, the police demanded the right to listen in on the wires on the ground that they could prevent or detect crime."

The committee was assured that the wires of no prominent persons had been tapped, "a majority of them being those of dives, saloons, or meeting places of criminals."

Just one week later, however, the mayor of New York City went before the same state legislative committee and, over protests of the members, read into the record a transcription of conversations which the police had heard when they tapped the telephones of Father William H. Farrell, a Catholic priest, and Dr. Daniel C. Potter. The eavesdropping was done in connection with a current political scandal involving the city's department of charities.

The mayor read thirty-five different conversations that had been taken down during the tap, and told the committee these were only a small part of the number he had in his possession.

At the same session, another event occurred that will also strike present-day readers as a familiar procedure at legislative hearings.

"The mayor's appearance before the legislative committee precipitated scenes of great disorder. His reading of the conversations was interrupted by hissing, handclapping and cheering."

However, the newspaper accounting goes on to inform us that the head of the New York City detective bureau and twenty-five of his plain-clothes men were scattered through the crowd in the committee room. At a given signal, they arose and identified themselves by pinning their badges to the lapels of their jackets.

No one apparently was carried bodily from the hearing, although one dissenter left voluntarily after shouting his opposition to the reading of the priest's stolen confidences.

While these proceedings—and those of more than a score of federal and state wiretap probes since then—may seem like late-movie reruns of the same melodrama, there is one important difference, and it is this:

In 1916, the number of telephones in use in New York made the three hundred and fifty wiretaps admitted by the police seem "tapping telephone wires by wholesale."

By contrast, as mentioned earlier, one fact-finding study several years ago revealed that plain-clothes officers alone in New York City are responsible for making 26,000 wiretaps a year.

America now has 88,785,000 telephones—as many as existed in the entire world in 1955—and more than one half (53.1 per cent) of the world's supply today.

To eavesdroppers of all stripes, this means that there are more than eighty-eight million built-in devices for penetrating the nation's walls of privacy. Latest census figures show that 81 per cent of all households in the United States include at least one telephone, often equipped with extensions that can carry the secret auricle into any room of the house.

No other country on earth offers that kind of potential for national surveillance.

In Communist Russia, for example, where spy government is an

officially accepted way of life, Soviet secret police have to make do
with a mere seven million telephones. Even these are used far less
frequently than those in the United States. Perhaps Ivan Ivanovich
has learned to be more cautious than his opposite number in the
West.

Here, despite a growing awareness that there is always likely to
be an unseen third party on the line, Americans continue to bare
their intimate affairs in social intercourse via the humming wires.
During the year 1964, U.S. residents held more than thirteen and a
half billion telephone conversations. Even allowing for the tireless
activity of the teenager (that hated nemesis of the sonic nark),
such a vast flow of words must have provided full employment for
unknown legions of silent listeners.

The practice of tap-and-tell has become so widespread and now
utilizes such sophisticated equipment and expert technicians that
the scope of the activity can only be guessed at.

In the nation's capital, which sets the pace and provides the example, a government employee told me:

"I wouldn't say anything on the phone that I wouldn't say in a
broadcast over the air."

A business executive on the West Coast conducts his affairs with
the same sense of caution. He said that recently, while cleaning out
some old files, he found several placards that had been used during
World War II to remind personnel of wartime security. They read:
THE ENEMY IS LISTENING.

"I have installed one near every telephone in our executive
offices," he said.

In 1962, a House committee reported that 5,317 telephones in
federal offices were bugged, not by foreign spies seeking information vital to our national security, but by bureaucrats prying into
the affairs of the public and spying upon each other.

A Washington, D.C., police lieutenant, who had been engaging
in the common practice of tapping wires, said during a congres-

sional hearing that he finally had to give up in one of his attempts to tap a certain telephone because of line failure caused by the fact that so many other tappers were at work on the same line.

If telephone company officials have any idea as to the extent of these sonic snares, they are not talking—at least, not on the telephone. For many years, the mere mention of wiretapping has evoked from them long and pious harangues about the sanctity of private communication. They have sworn to protect with full vigor their subscribers' right to be secure against secret intrusions.

As proof of how seriously they regard eavesdropping on the line, telephone companies almost always dispatch a technician at once in response to a subscriber's complaint that he thinks someone is tapping his telephone.

Company spokesmen point out, too, that routine checks are made from hour to hour around the clock to detect unauthorized tampering with the lines.

Actually, these capacitance tests catch only the unskilled or uninformed tapper. The experts know how to make a tap without being detected. Bernard Spindel who, by his own admission, has tapped thousands of telephones for the past two decades, declared:

"I have tapped telephone wires with new techniques so undetectable that I have recordings of telephone company officials checking the lines and phoning the tapee to tell him that tests had revealed no interception." [1]

Like government and police wiretappers, Spindel often is mistaken for a telephone repairman because he dresses and looks like one. He carries the same equipment and tools dangling from his belt.

On several occasions, Spindel says proudly, he has installed taps on telephone poles while conversing affably with a policeman lounging in the street just below him.

Some government agencies go even further. They sometimes purchase (and perhaps, in the case of the FBI, even borrow) the familiar telephone repair trucks in which to carry their gear and to allay suspicion during their clandestine operations.

John J. Hanselman, assistant vice president of the American Telephone and Telegraph Company, told a Senate subcommittee several years ago that the strictest security regulations were observed to keep unauthorized persons from gaining access to telephone installations or equipment. He said that operating buildings are closely guarded and that outside persons are not permitted to enter until they have been properly identified and cleared. Such visitors are required to wear a badge to distinguish them from employees, and are escorted by a telephone company supervisor.

Senator Olin Jonhston, who was conducting the hearings, asked:

"What procedure has the telephone company followed to prevent its own employees from listening in on private telephone conversations?"

The telephone executive replied that only a small proportion of the total company personnel have access to equipment that would permit them to listen in on telephone conversations. These are primarily the operators and the maintenance people. He solemnly assured the committee that traffic personnel are carefully screened and that they are given a copy of Section 605 of the Communications Act, which tells what the requirements are with regard to maintaining the secrecy of telephone conversations, and setting forth the prohibition against divulging any information that they may overhear.

"Supervisory people continuously watch the people [i.e., operators, etc.] to make sure there is no listening in," Mr. Hanselman declared.

"Perhaps more importantly, as far as our traffic people are concerned, there is no reason why they would listen in on calls. They are instructed and trained, the minute the connection is up, to cut out of the connection."

To understand just how trustworthy the telephone companies are in their protection of subscriber privacy, these reassuring words must be placed alongside some facts recently brought to light by another congressional committee, investigating the problem in greater depth.

On September 14, 1966, testimony before the Senate Subcommittee on Administrative Practice and Procedure revealed that the telephone companies themselves were the biggest tappers of all.

Hubert Kertz, vice president of the American Telephone and Telegraph Company, admitted that in 2,200 locked "listening rooms" across the United States during the past year alone, Bell System employees had listened in on thirty-six million long-distance calls.

Although Mr. Kertz called the monitoring "random sampling," Senator Edward V. Long, who chaired the committee, said no telephones were exempt. Governors and other elected officials were subject to taps, as well as ordinary householders.

The AT&T vice president insisted that the monitoring had been done merely to improve the quality of telephone service and that, anyway, the practice had been discontinued three months before "because of technological improvements."

However, Senator Long suggested that the eavesdropping was stopped when officials of the Bell System learned that the Senate committee was looking into the matter as a possible invasion of privacy.

The most serious aspect of the case was information indicating that federal agents had been admitted to the locked listening rooms to eavesdrop on calls.

When the committee's investigator sought to interview some of the operators who had worked in one of the listening rooms, the company refused to allow him to talk privately with them.

Such a lack of cooperation has never characterized the company's relationship with government agents and law-enforcement officers. There is mounting evidence to show that law officers bent on tapping subscribers' lines have, time after time, received assistance from telephone companies.

In Kansas City, for example, Chief of Detectives James R. Newman admitted under questioning that, in order to tap anyone's telephone line, it was first necessary to have the pair cable numbers and appearances of the telephone to be tapped.

These numbers are supposed to be a closely guarded secret, which the telephone company will not reveal to anyone except their own repairmen and authorized personnel.

Nevertheless, Detective Chief Newman said that when he wished to tap a telephone, "I would make a request to the security officer of the telephone company, who would supply me with this information."

Chief Newman said he, in turn, would furnish this information to one of his men and instruct him to make the installation.

Lieutenant Hitchcock, the detective who actually made the taps, then told how it was done.

"After receiving the pair information and the exact locations, all of these locations, sometimes it is necessary to get away from the person's home. Like I say, if it is an extortion, he probably has the house under surveillance, so you would want to move a block away or so, wherever the pair showed, and then you would find the exact location and the pair number and the box where the tap shows, and merely tap into it."

Once the tap is made, said Detective Hitchcock, the police either record conversations directly from the line or install a battery-operated line transmitter, hung on the wire somewhere away from the telephone pole.

The tapes on which the police record these stolen conversations are secured in the police station in a file cabinet.

The disturbing question about these permanent records of unguarded conversations—the words not only of criminal suspects but of many innocent people as well—is what future use may be made of them.

H. Gordon Homme, who interrogated Detective Chief Newman for a Senate committee, was also troubled about this problem, as is shown by the following colloquy:

MR. HOMME: And it is not an uncommon practice that a detective from the Kansas City police detectives might be friendly to some other federal agency?

MR. NEWMAN: We hope he will be.

MR. HOMME: His duty as a good law-enforcement officer is to cooperate with his counterpart in other agencies?

MR. NEWMAN: Yes, sir.

MR. HOMME: In the course of that harmonious arrangement, information is passed back and forth between the lower level and you have a record of it?

MR. NEWMAN: Yes.

MR. HOMME: In other words, a detective assigned to a case where maybe they had a wiretap surveillance could, over a cup of coffee in the morning, pass information along to someone in another agency?

MR. NEWMAN: He could.

MR. HOMME: And probably would if he thought it would help the other agency?

MR. NEWMAN: Probably would, yes.

MR. HOMME: You have no way of knowing whether or not he passed such information or whether or not such information might be contaminated with illegal wiretaps and divulgence?

MR. NEWMAN: No, I would have no way of knowing that.[2]

Thus, by a devious route, information ordinarily inadmissible in court because it was derived from wiretaps (and therefore "fruit of a tainted tree") can be used by the prosecutor who can, in good conscience, state that he was not aware of its real source.

Just how much listening the police may do in a given case, provided they think it worthwhile, can be seen in the Tarrantino case. Referring to the tapes made of the defendant's telephone calls, the California state supreme court's majority opinion observed:

"The recordings, totaling 198 reels of tape or approximately 500 hours of listening time, were edited by the district attorney and the police, arranged according to subject matter, and recorded in part on composite tapes. The district attorney introduced 60 selected excerpts [that] . . . constituted corroborative evidence of the testimony of the prosecution's witnesses." [3]

Another service which telephone companies render secretly to law enforcement officers and government agents is the use of a device known as a pen register. This piece of equipment records every number dialed by the tapped telephone. When a call is made, each digit that is dialed sends out a sharp electrical impulse that goes through the automated equipment at the central telephone office. These impulses are so closely spaced that it is impossible to count them just by listening. But the pen register identifies the signals and records on tape the numbers called by the tapped subscriber.

Although the telephone company often provides the register to agencies requesting it, one government agency (the Internal Revenue Service), and doubtless others, now include in their inventory of spy equipment a number of their own registers. Records show that between November, 1962, and November, 1963, the IRS purchased or had assembled thirty-three pen registers at a total cost of $9,680. These were assigned to regional offices all across the country, and to the national office in Washington, D.C. Of the three registers allotted to the national office, one was reported in 1965 to be on loan "to another Federal agency."

Special Agent Edward J. Zelick of the IRS Pittsburgh office, responding to questions put to him under oath, reported that after he delivered one of the IRS registers to the telephone office, when he wanted it taken off one subscriber's telephone and placed on another, all he had to do was to call the telephone company and they provided the service.[4] In none of these cases did Special Agent Zelick present a warrant or any other kind of legal authority to the telephone company. And apparently they asked for none.

While being used to record numbers dialed, the pen register can also provide a point at which to place a tap on the line being monitored.

The liaison between the FBI and telephone officials is even cozier than that enjoyed by local police or government agencies. The G-men do not have to resort to the crude form of tapping outside the central telephone office, where their furtive work might be discovered by accident.

Instead, the FBI tap is usually made within the closely guarded premises of the telephone company, from where leased wires run to FBI listening posts, called "Clubs" by the G-men among themselves.

Access to these Technical Surveillance Rooms, according to former FBI Agent Jack Levine, is limited to the Special Agent in Charge, his assistant, and to those agents who have been assigned to the monitoring.

Little wonder that on June 7, 1965, Federal Communications Commissioner Lee Loevinger stated that "information that I have obtained, both from the engineering staff of the FCC and from AT&T, is that it is possible to detect some of the more crude telephone recording devices and wiretapping devices, but that the more sophisticated of such devices are beyond detection by present electronic techniques." [5] It is hard to conceive a more "sophisticated" or satisfactory way to wiretap than to bridge the subscriber's wires behind locked doors of the central telephone office.

Another former FBI agent, who served with the Bureau for a full decade (1951 to 1961), reported that one of the foremost responsibilities of a "sound man" was to develop close ties with telephone company special agents and operating personnel.

"The cozier the arrangement, the easier it was to get confidential data on subscribers' lines and to lease lines without question. In most locales—New York City is the most notable exception—this was no problem. For example, on one occasion, an agent handling a prostitution investigation importuned me to place a temporary 'suicide tap' [an unauthorized tap]. When a telephone lineman accidentally discovered it, I received a call from one of the telco special agents. 'Know anything about some wires in the Ballard area?' he inquired. 'Guess I do,' I replied. 'O.K., forget I called,' he said. The tap stayed in." [6]

Since wiretap evidence is not admissible in court, information recorded from the taps is attributed by the FBI to confidential informers, who are designated only by symbols and numbers.[7]

Although the cases of wiretapping so far uncovered by accident or by congressional subpoena have been confined to local areas, there is no reason to believe that they will continue to be. Recent advances in electronics, plus the rapid increase in telephone service abroad, now make wire spying possible on a global basis.

All that is necessary is a device called an Infinity Transmitter. This mechanism—which is a miniaturized combination microphone, amplifier, switching device and transmitter—will pick up conversations within a forty-foot radius and transmit them over telephone lines for unlimited distances.

Descriptive literature put out by a company in New York, which sells them to anyone willing to pay the price ($1,000), leads off with the following "teaser" in boldface type:

"How close do you have to be to eavesdrop on a conversation in San Diego? Try Newfoundland."

The brochure adds that the Infinity Transmitter now makes coast-to-coast surveillance a reality. "If you can reach a telephone, you can hear what's happening any place that you can dial direct, whenever and as often as you wish."

The small device, which can be concealed in the telephone itself, requires no batteries or separate power supply.

The insidious feature of the gadget is that it does not interfere in any way with normal use of the telephone so that its presence is undetectable except by accidental discovery or direct search.

Let us suppose you have taken an apartment in Paris and that someone in Washington, D.C., wanted to eavesdrop on your conversations there. An accomplice in France would install the Infinity Transmitter in your telephone. The Washington spy could then dial your number and the telephone would not ring. Yet from the moment the number was dialed, the eavesdropper in America could hear everything said within forty feet of the telephone.

Since 97 per cent of the world's telephones can be reached from any telephone in America, and since worldwide direct dialing will eventually connect most of them, the possibility of anyone escaping Big Brother's constant vigil over their lives grows less each year.

Electronic snoopers are proud of their ability to keep pace with advances made in related scientific fields. Bernard Spindel, the freelance expert, recently told an interviewer for *Life* magazine that he has already worked out a method for tapping the new video-phone soon to be made available to the public. By jumping the circuitry, he said, he will be able to see right into the subscriber's home. Comments *Life:*

"The subscriber, as usual, won't be able to see Bernie."

Wiretappers who do not enjoy the sanctuary of telephone company facilities understandably prefer wireless taps. These give no clue to their presence and, if discovered, will provide no wires leading to the hidden snooper's listening post.

Technological advances in recent years have provided the cautious eavesdropper with several types of miniature transmitters that can carry both ends of a telephone conversation to a remote FM receiver, where it can be recorded without arousing the slightest suspicion.

One of the most widely used of these inventions is a transistorized transmitter that fits snugly behind the mouthpiece of any standard telephone. Energized by the telephone's own power, it will operate indefinitely as an unsuspected "bug," and will pick up conversations in a room even when the telephone is in the cradle or on the hook.

An East Coast supplier of this sonic cat's-paw points out that it can be installed in a matter of seconds, "as easily as screwing in a light bulb."

Another spy device offered by the same dealer is a highly sensitive unit only slightly larger than a thimble, which he calls the 009 Line Tap Transmitter. According to the sales literature, it "will receive and send signals from any telephone line into any present FM receiver at distances now unheard-of in this field." The price is $179.

Still another aid available to all who deal in pilfered information is a vest-pocket-size wireless pickup called the Byphone. Its operation is very simple. Just place it near the telephone (say the directions) and you will "get back on the good old party line." The device needs no external power supply and will continue to operate indefinitely. It is recommended for agents in situations "where telephonic eavesdropping is needed."

In cases where the eavesdropper cannot conveniently gain access to the premises where the target telephone is installed, he often makes use of a tap system especially designed for locating the correct pair of wires in the circuitry outside.

Ralph V. Ward, vice president of Mosler Research Products, Inc., makers of the equipment, had this to say about its use:

"Now, very frequently people tend to say, 'Oh, well, that isn't going to happen because nobody can find my pair of wires unless they are working for the phone company.' But this isn't true.

"The way to find your pair of wires is simply to know you are in your office and go to any junction box where your telephone circuit appears. In this country, we do everything very methodically; and on every floor or every corridor there is going to be a terminal box, and that reappears on every floor. And it appears in the master terminal box in the basement, and then goes out in an underground cable.

"To check these terminal boxes to find your circuit, if you are on the phone, all we have to do is to take this induction coil and go down over the terminals with this rubber-insulated probe, not actually connecting to them, but as we bring this adjacent to every terminal, we will hear the conversation, and we will just keep going until we hear your familiar voice, and wait until you hang up and then connect right across the terminals, and we have a direct tap. We don't know what pair number it is or what cable number it is, but that isn't important. We have got the pair of wires we want. So, the equipment goes much further than just having the capability of listening; it also has the capability of picking out whatever pair of wires you use." [8]

Any user of the telephone today would do well to ponder the words of a memorandum recently issued by the American Telephone and Telegraph Company itself. It said:

"The art of wiretapping has become so sophisticated that there is no known equipment that will detect all possible cases. It is our experience that as soon as one method of detection becomes available to us, the illegal devices are modified or new ones introduced to overcome the new detection method." [9]

If the telephone has become the most undetectable and far-reaching of intrusion devices, it has many close rivals in the field of electronics. Many of the newer inventions are perfect instruments for helping to establish a watched society. They would have gladdened the heart of any dictator who has swaggered across the stage of world history.

As students of the past well know, spy governments have always been eager to set up total surveillance over the people. But it remained for the electronic marvels of our day to make that dream (or nightmare, depending upon your situation) come true.

Babylonian and Persian tyrants had to depend upon dancing girls, prostitutes and paid informers to penetrate the privacy of their subjects' lives. In ancient India, a secret legion of spies called "reporters" swarmed over the land, disguised as holy men, idiots, commercial travelers, buffoons, thieves and lunatics. In addition to providing information regarding criminal activity, they kept close watch on the populace to detect any sign of disloyalty to the Crown. Their job was also to keep government officials under surveillance and to report any misconduct to the palace.

By contrast, the government that wishes to follow this Asiatic spy system today has at its disposal a frightening array of scientific wonders with which to lay snares for the unwary. Some of these have been widely publicized; others are known only to small coteries of scientists and government officials. Their secrecy is insured by the fact that they are part of highly classified defense and space research.

The two chief contributions of science to the delicate art of snooping are the transistor and the printed circuit.

The transistor is an electronic device consisting of a small block of semi-conductor material such as germanium, on which are set three tiny electrodes. Unlike the larger and less dependable vacuum tubes they replace, transistors require no heater current, and operate at very low voltages. This means they have eliminated much of the bulk that formerly added weight and size to electronic equipment.

The printed circuit, which did away with complex wiring, further decreased the size of microphones and transmitters. During the past ten years, these vital elements of surveillance gear have grown smaller and smaller.

The vast sums spent to produce such Lilliputian auricles were not originally earmarked for development of monitoring tools. Instead, the budgets were voted by Congress for space research and for the defense program. Severe weight restrictions on spacecraft made it urgently necessary to have devices that would occupy the smallest possible niche, and yet be powerful enough to send back information from vehicles voyaging thousands and even millions of miles from earth.

The fruits of this huge scientific effort include micro-miniaturized radio transmitters so tiny that they can be disguised as sugar cubes on your luncheon table, or encased in your guest's cuff link. If the diner sitting across from you is a woman, she may be carrying one of the miniature transmitters in her purse, lipstick, earring or brooch.

Other common places of concealment for the social "bug" are tie clasp, fountain pen, wristwatch, cigarette lighter, cigarette pack, the now-famous martini olive—even in the cavity of a tooth.

There are bugs so small that microphone, transmitter and battery are all contained in a tiny box the size of a postage stamp and only a quarter inch thick. One of these, called the Model 007 Spy Transmitter, will pick up a whisper across a large room and transmit it with excellent fidelity to any good FM radio set or tape recorder.

Power is supplied by a 1.5-volt hearing-aid battery that will operate continuously for a period up to one hundred hours. Some of the more ingenious bugs are equipped with what is called a free-power circuit, which enables them to draw their power from the signal of any high-potency local broadcasting station. This means they will remain operational as long as the station is broadcasting.

To increase the little transmitter's range, it is sometimes concealed where it can be connected to metal objects in the room— conduits, radiators, file cabinets or bedsprings. These act as antennae, supplementing the necessarily minute one installed in the bug itself.

With slight chance of detection, an experienced information thief can hide the 007, or any of several similar devices, in the folds of drapes, air ducts, lighting fixtures, behind pictures or beneath carpets (where they fit snugly into holes cut out of the padding). If by some outside chance, the bug should be discovered, there is no way of identifying the person who put it there.

Of course, with bugging in the hands of amateurs or inexperienced agents, the risk of discovery is always present. A few years ago, an inadequately trained spy was caught like an eavesdropping maid at the keyhole when he shoved a bug under the door of a room where a conference was in progress.

One of the farsighted conferees observed the movement of the tiny transmitter and, signaling his companions to continue their discussion, he tiptoed across the room and threw open the door to reveal the greatly embarrassed snooper retreating down the corridor.

In another instance, a man in Washington, D.C., who was walking down a hotel corridor, heard a conversation coming from one of the rooms he was passing. The voices sounded familiar and he paused to listen. To his surprise, it was a discussion in progress in the room he had just left. The agent who was secretly monitoring the conference down the hall had the volume of his FM receiving set turned too high.

Commenting on this incident, a surveillance expert who instructs would-be wireless sleuths on use of the equipment, cautioned:

"An investigator has to use discretion. You don't want to broadcast it; just monitor it." [10]

When an eavesdropper gains access to premises he plans to bug (usually by illegal entry), and wishes to install a transmitter that will operate over a long period, he often places it behind an electrical outlet along the baseboard. Here it will escape detection and can draw power from the regular house current for its operation.

Ralph V. Ward, whose firm makes this type of transmitter, said: "I know of one case where this was put in and remained in constant operation for eighteen months. When we took it out, it was still working perfectly."

Parasite transmitters of this kind are also secreted in table lamps, radios, electric clocks and television sets, where they will not be noticed and yet will have a continuous source of power.

If security measures are tight enough to keep a word-trapper from entering a home or office to set his snare, he sometimes resorts to a time-honored subterfuge to accomplish his purpose.

He will either send a gift in which the transmitter has been implanted; or he will intercept some object the victim is expecting, and bug it before it is delivered.

A now-celebrated instance of this Trojan-horse technique attests to its effectiveness. In the summer of 1960, Ambassador Henry Cabot Lodge displayed before the United Nations in New York two halves of a carved wooden plaque of the Great Seal of the United States. He said the Soviet government had presented it to U.S. Ambassador W. Averell Harriman back in 1945.

The interesting thing about the two pieces was that they revealed a hollowed out cavity inside the seal, where the Russians had hidden a vibrator of spring steel. That simple device had enabled them to monitor conversations in the ambassador's office.

The story was this: When Soviet diplomats had bestowed the gift—with finely turned phrases of friendship—Ambassador Harriman, without suspecting its sinister purpose, obligingly hung it behind his desk. From a radar set across the street from the embassy, Russian intelligence agents then beamed a powerful, continuous wave on the vibrator encased in the seal. By picking up the vibrations set in motion by voices and translating them again into speech, the Soviet agents were able to listen to every conversation held in the ambassador's private office.

For seven years the clandestine device remained there, undetected by American security technicians who, time after time, "swept" the office in search of hidden microphones and eavesdropping equipment.

When the seal's scandalous secret was eventually laid bare, it touched off a frantic search through other U.S. embassies in Iron

Curtain countries. The effort was rewarded by the discovery of a hundred more intrusion devices in various buildings of the American foreign service.

In cases which permit Big Brother to approach a room or building, but not to enter it, he has at his service several tools that permit him to listen through walls.

For this purpose, most experts favor a powerful, audio-electronic stethoscope called the Medetron. A completely transistorized instrument, it is so sensitive that it will pick up voices and sounds through thick walls. An auxiliary output is provided for plugging into a tape recorder.

Like many of the eavesdropper's tools, the Medetron was not developed originally for the nefarious purposes for which it is now used. Instead, it was designed to aid doctors and researchers in the medical profession. Because of its great sensitivity and selective tuning controls, it is ideal for hearing the subtlest variations of heart action, allowing doctors to make a faster and more accurate diagnosis of cardiac function. It is also legitimately used to listen to the fetal heartbeat to determine the sex of an unborn child.

But by far the widest application of the invention today is that of snooping.

Another, less expensive, instrument, used to listen to conversations or activity in an adjoining room is known as the Audio Wall Probe, selling for $65. It is fitted with a suction-cup amplifier which, when placed against a wall, will pick up sounds and amplify them for tape recording or monitoring through stethoscopic earphones.

In a legal opinion referring to an earlier version of this equipment (*Goldman v. United States*), Justice Frank Murphy of the U. S. Supreme Court said:

"There was no physical entry in this case. But the search of one's home or office no longer requires physical entry, for science has brought forth far more effective devices for the invasion of a person's privacy than the direct and obvious methods of oppression which were detested by our forebears and which inspired the Fourth Amendment. Surely the spirit motivating the framers of that Amendment would abhor these new devices no less. Physical entry may be wholly immaterial. Whether the search of private quarters is accomplished by placing on the outer walls of the sanctum a detectaphone that transmits to the outside listener the intimate details of a private conversation, or by new methods of photography that penetrate walls or overcome distances, the privacy of the citizen is equally invaded by agents of the Government, and intimate personal matters are laid bare to view."

Another piece of basic equipment for penetrating walls (and privacy) is a form of contact microphone called the spike mike. It is a slender, metal rod about one foot in length. It is driven through the partition separating two rooms until the point rests against the inner surface of the wall of the target room. It then uses the entire wall as a sounding board.

With the vulgar contempt that undercover agents often show for those they spy upon, the snoopers among themselves refer to the use of the spike mike as "giving them the shaft."

Several years ago, in a case involving privacy invasion by means of the spike mike, the U.S. Supreme Court unanimously condemned the action as "an actual intrusion into a Constitutionally protected area."

The court reversed the convictions of three men charged with operating a gambling operation across the street from the State Department in Washington, D.C. The defendants had been sentenced to serve twenty months to five years in prison and to pay a fine of $1,000 each.

At their trial, both in district court and later in the court of appeals, the prosecution was allowed to admit evidence obtained by metropolitan police and Internal Revenue agents who had used a spike mike driven into the wall until it had contacted a heating duct which acted as a sounding board capable of transmitting conversations from any place in the house.

Writing the court's unanimous opinion, Justice Potter Stewart declared:

"Eavesdropping accomplished by means of such a physical intrusion is beyond the pale of even those decisions in which a closely-divided Court has held that eavesdropping accomplished by other electronic means did not amount to an invasion of Fourth Amendment rights."

The earlier decisions to which Justice Stewart referred were those of *Olmstead v. U.S.* in 1928; and *Goldman v. U.S.* in 1940.

In the Goldman case, a detectaphone had been placed against an office wall to listen to conversations taking place inside. The court at that time upheld the intrusion by a vote of five to three.

In the Olmstead case, involving a Seattle bootlegger whose telephone had been tapped by federal officers, the court decided by a one-vote majority (five to four) that the Fourth Amendment, which protects Americans against unreasonable searches and seizures, referred to material things, "not to evidence secured by sense of hearing."

In 1928, when this close decision was made, the subtle and all-pervasive electronic tools of today's snooper were unknown. For that reason, the court has been urged repeatedly to reconsider the Olmstead and Goldman rulings in the light of present-day needs.

It seems clear from more recent findings that the court is now moving away from its earlier view that privacy (including confidential conversations) is not protected by the Constitution.

"At the very core [of the Fourth Amendment] stands the right of a man to retreat into his own home and there be free from unreasonable governmental intrusion. This Court has never held that a Federal officer may, without warrant and without consent, physically entrench into a man's office or home, there to secretly observe or listen, and relate at the man's subsequent trial what was seen or heard." [11]

Spy novels and cloak-and-dagger movies that depict secret agents meeting in some open place such as a park or in a boat on a lake are now completely out of date. Anyone trained in espionage is familiar with the so-called shotgun mike that will overhear conversations up to a quarter mile away. No Russian spy worth his rubles would ever be caught by it.

But since the general public is slow to become aware of such instruments of interception, the device is still used by police and nonsecurity agents of the federal government to invade the ordinary citizen's privacy.

The shotgun mike is a long bundle of aluminum tubes about one-fourth inch in diameter and varying in length from six inches to four or five feet. These are connected at the rear or "breach" to a large round microphone. Highly sensitive and directional, the strange-looking invention will pick up only those sounds at which the tubes are pointed. It is often used in conjunction with a motion-picture camera, equipped with a telephoto lens.

One of the better-known surveillance experts in California told me he has used the shotgun mike in the back end of a truck with the tailgate down. The tube ends were covered with a light black gauze, making the truck appear empty.

Another intrusion specialist said proudly that, in over fifteen years of surveillance work, not a single subject of his scrutiny ever became aware that his conversations were being listened to, or that the recordings of these private exchanges now form part of a permanent file in some official archive.

"In this state [California]" he said, "I doubt that anybody who isn't a hermit can spend his whole life without coming under investigation at least once. Some people have been monitored so often that they just don't have any secrets left. Their lives may not be an open book, but they're sure a few hundred miles of magnetic tape."

My informant said that at various times in the past he had made his services and equipment available to private investigators, divorce attorneys, insurance companies and personnel offices. But the majority of his steady clients are law officers and government agencies. These have included police departments in virtually every large city of the state, as well as district attorneys, county sheriffs, the Narcotics Bureau, the State Pharmaceutical Board, the Board of Medical Examiners and others.

His basic equipment, which he carries in an ordinary-looking station wagon (panel trucks have begun to arouse suspicion) includes all the customary paraphernalia of the electronic termite, plus a few devices he has invented for himself. He identified for me a microcircuit radio transmitter, bugs in various forms, miniature microphones (disguised as everything from a briar pipe to a pocket knife); ash trays and other office furnishings with transmitter bases; tape recorders, both pocket and standard sizes; an ultra-sensitive FM receiver; a gimlet for boring holes so small they cannot be detected by the naked eye; a small, battery-operated vacuum cleaner for cleaning up any telltale plaster particles or insulation fuzz; spools of extremely fine wire in all colors (to match any decor); induction coils and wiretapping instruments, one of which permits monitoring six telephones at one time; reels of magnetic tape; special solder that leaves a dot so small it is easily mistaken for a fly speck; various accessories and batteries of all sizes, from the midget pack to twelve-volt storage batteries concealed under the hood of the station wagon.

Even with such a vast array of insidious tools, this journeyman eavesdropper felt short-handed.

"There are devices and techniques available only to the government," he said, "that makes a lot of this stuff obsolete."

Just what these new inventions are or how many are already in use is strictly classified information. But all intrusion specialists with whom I talked agreed that extensive research is under way in a dozen secret laboratories, aimed at development of new components and systems easily adaptable to more effective surveillance.

As frightening as some of these new privacy-penetrating devices may be as portents of our future, an immediate cause for anxiety is the growing trend toward built-in monitoring equipment, which could change our national life into a watched society.

More and more police stations, jails, hospitals, schools, hotels—even apartment houses—are being fitted at the time of construction with permanent viewing and listening devices. In other cases, existing systems such as intercoms, doorbells and piped music circuits are being adapted for use with spying gear.

As with all intolerable encroachments upon our traditional freedoms, the idea of a permanently installed surveillance system was first used with an unpopular victim. The public learned over sixteen years ago that secret bugging devices had been built into the new home of racketeer Mickey Cohen in California. The popular reaction was one of amusement. After all, Cohen was a well-known hoodlum. What right did he have to privacy from police intrusion? Americans had not, and have not, learned that liberty and justice are indivisible. If our laws and our Constitution do not protect those in disfavor with society, neither do they protect the upright citizen.

Today no American can be certain that his intimate conversations with his lawyer, accountant, priest, wife or even his doctor are not listened to and/or observed.

Not long ago, for example, it was discovered that the Internal Revenue Service had installed hidden microphones, two-way mirrors and secret recording devices in IRS conference rooms in various cities across the country. There they could spy and eavesdrop upon taxpayers while they were holding supposedly privileged conversations with their attorneys or discussing tax matters with their accountants.

Some of the cities in which IRS agents admitted using surveillance were New York City, Brooklyn, Baltimore, Detroit, Montgomery, Alexandria and Kansas City.

In one instance, apparently taking as their mentors the Soviet intelligence agents, IRS men concealed a camera in the seal of the Internal Revenue Service that hung on the wall of one conference room.

Since the application of the transistor and integrated circuits to opto-electronic devices, minature television cameras no larger than a lady's evening purse (6" x 4" x ½") have come into use.

In the newest model, the vidicon tube has been eliminated altogether, and the camera requires only four watts of power, which can be supplied by a hearing-aid battery.

These tiny, but penetrating, visual "bugs" can be hidden in a great number of places in an office, home or hotel room. Some are concealed behind mirors; others peer from lighting fixtures or recesses in ceilings and walls. They may even look around corners by means of newly developed optical fibers—a bundle of flexible glass rods, called light pipes.

Nor will darkness hide you from the scrutiny of some of these all-seeing eyes. It is now possible to equip the TV camera with an added device which captures the infra-red heat waves emanating from the human body (or any other warm object in view). This radiation is converted into visible light and transmitted into a magnifying telescope.

In total darkness, such a camera can clearly identify persons a hundred feet away; and can provide a recognizable image of moving objects at a distance of five hundred feet.

Aware of growing uneasiness among many Americans, who are beginning to sense the implications of this universal assault on privacy, legislators are promising new safeguards.

But to deal with the problem merely by passing more laws is unlikely to prove any more effective than the same solution has in the past.

A good example of the futility of these paper barriers as a deterrent to eavesdroppers is the 1966 ruling of the Federal Communications Commission banning the use of radio devices to transmit or record conversations without the consent of all parties concerned. The regulation specifically exempts law enforcement agencies which (as the manufacturers have testified) are the chief users of the devices. Moreover, as a former FBI agent pointed out, planting of the bug almost always involves illegal trespass or breaking and entering, a fact which does not seem of any great concern to law officers and government functionaries.

Too, it is most unlikely that the ordinary citizen will be prosecuted for a practice that enforcement agencies are indulging in themselves. As Justice Robert H. Jackson said of wiretapping, when he was attorney general:

"I do not feel that the Department of Justice can in good conscience, prosecute persons for a practice engaged in by the Department itself, and regarded as legal by the Department."

The fact is that the sale of eavesdropping devices is booming, as never before. One of the largest makers of such equipment—the Fargo Company—has such a backlog of orders that, at last report, they are no longer soliciting business.

Another manufacturer, speaking of the FCC regulation, said:

"What effect will a $500 fine have on someone who is determined to use them [the transmitters]? It seems to me it would be like a parking ticket. No one wants to get one, but they go right on parking illegally." [12]

To thoughtful Americans, the most ominous significance of today's widespread espionage is that it provides the indispensable prerequisite for a police state—national surveillance.

A corollary factor is the existence throughout the country of an elaborate network of secret agents and official busybodies who are not themselves subject to enforceable law.

Such was the case in Hitler's Third Reich. "The Gestapo and security forces," says the Encyclopedia Britannica, "had been placed above the law."

The same was true of the Fascist OVRA, and of the various Russian secret police organizations, such as the OGPU, NKVD and the MVD.

Indeed, it has been the hallmark of every spy government since the reign of Thutmose II, 3,500 years ago.

11

The command of our heritage

Looking for a microphone is pretty much a hit or miss job. The agent has to spend a lot of time and when he is finished, the best thing he can tell you is that he didn't find any. He really can't say there isn't anything there.

RALPH V. WARD
(Electronics Executive)

What can we do to protect ourselves against the intruders who today assail our privacy (and therefore our freedom) from all sides?

Two main lines of defense come to mind—one legal, the other technical. At present, neither offers a very satisfactory barrier to intrusion.

Of the two, the legal safeguard is the weaker. The phrase, "right to privacy," is heard with increasing frequency these days, and most Americans feel that it is a right assured to them by law.

Certainly, it was meant to be. But in actual practice, it isn't. There is no specific mention of privacy as such in the Constitution or Bill of Rights, although to any mind unclouded by the sophistry of lawyers' arguments, the Fourth Amendment means that.

Nevertheless, the Supreme Court, as well as lesser tribunals, have interpreted the Fourth Amendment to mean that the citizen is protected against only those snooping devices which require physical penetration of the constitutionally protected area.

This leaves governement agents, police and even private eaves-droppers free to use an extensive arsenal of peek-and-pry equipment.

Only a few states have recognized the urgent need for legislation to ban bugging practices altogether, and even some of those permit law-enforcement officers (the worst intruders of all) to make use of electronic surveillance.

On the federal level, Congress has not taken any action regarding privacy since 1934, except the negative one in 1954, when the lawmakers reduced the crime of wiretapping from a felony to a misdemeanor charge. There was little or no debate over this legislation-in-reverse, and it was passed amid a rush of other matters.

Meanwhile, the freedom of communication and the secure privacy of the home sanctuary supposedly guaranteed by the Fourth Amendment have been repeatedly violated by federal and local governments alike.

Yet the very fact that most Americans still believe they are protected by law against such odious intrusions is a cogent argument that specific legislation is long overdue.

In the words of a New York legislative committee that examined the problem, "the law at its best is the embodiment of human customs and the common opinion of men." [1]

The committee observed that the mere fact that we have so generally assumed that eavesdropping is an invasion of a right of privacy is perhaps the best evidence that the law should be expanded to include recognition of it.

The most encouraging sign that more and more people are beginning to recognize the pressing need for a comprehensive law to guard our traditional privilege of confidential relations with each other came early in 1967.

In his message to Congress on the State of the Union, President Lyndon B. Johnson declared:

"We should protect what Justice Brandeis called the 'right most valued by civilized men—the right to privacy.' We should outlaw all wiretapping—public and private—wherever and whenever it occurs, except when the security of the Nation itself is at stake, and only then with the strictest safeguards. We should exercise the full reach of our Constitutional powers to outlaw electronic bugging and snooping."

By issuing a call for action at that time, the president achieved two important ends.

First, and most important, he lent to the supporters of a growing demand for congressional action the enormous prestige of his office.

Second, he forestalled an action by his own crime commission, a majority of whom were widely understood to be preparing a recommendation that a law be passed to *permit* legalized eavesdropping.

At a meeting of the commission on November 11, 1966, Acting Attorney General Ramsey Clark made an impassioned plea for the commission to stay out of the issue.

According to reports circulating in Washington, Cartha D. De Loach, assistant to J. Edgar Hoover, interrupted Attorney General Clark and stated that the FBI's bugging operations had helped to gain valuable information about criminal activity. He reportedly said the Bureau would be handicapped in fighting organized crime unless eavesdropping was legalized.

According to a published account of the meeting, when Commission Chairman Nicholas deB. Katzenbach called for a show of hands by those who wished to drop the eavesdrop recommendation, only two of the nineteen-member commission voted with Mr. Clark. These were Judge Luther W. Youngdahl of the District of Columbia; and Mrs. Robert J. Stuart, president of the League of Women Voters.[2]

Later, in President Johnson's crime control message to Congress, the Chief Executive reiterated his request for legislation to protect citizens against electronic eavesdropping.

In the forthright manner of a man who knows from personal

experience how serious an offense wiretapping and bugging is, the president said:

"I recommend that the Congress enact the Right of Privacy Act of 1967."

Again, he told the Congress why:

"Justice Brandeis called the right of privacy the 'right most valued by civilized men.' It is the first right denied by a totalitarian system. It is associated in the minds of most Americans with the right to be free of unlawful searches and forced self-incrimination. It is a hallmark of a free society.

"I believe we should protect that right against invasion by wiretapping and electronic devices.

"We would indeed be indifferent to the command of our heritage if we failed to take effective action to preserve the dignity and privacy of each among us. A new Federal law banning wiretapping and electronic bugging and snooping is essential.

"Present laws are clearly inadequate. They create serious uncertainties in their application and leave large loopholes in their coverage. In short, they invite abuse.

"I recommend that Congress enact the Right of Privacy Act of 1967.

"Within the full reach of the constitutional powers possessed by the Federal Government, this law would:

"Outlaw all wiretapping, public and private, wherever and whenever it occurs, as well as all willful invasions of privacy by electronic devices such as radio transmitters and concealed microphones. The only exceptions would cover those instances where the security of the Nation itself is at stake—and then only under the strictest safeguards.

"Prohibit the advertisement, manufacture or distribution in interstate commerce of wiretapping and eavesdropping devices."

The president's requested legislation, if passed by Congress (and there are powerful forces opposing it), might accomplish on a wider front and in a more successful way what Mr. Johnson intended to accomplish when he ordered all federal departments to cease the practice in 1965.

Those written instructions, although referred to afterward as an Executive Order, were actually in the form of a confidential memorandum. It was accompanied by a curious letter signed by White House aide Lee White, which cautioned:

"The President is anxious that the attached memorandum, which is designated 'Administratively Confidential,' be regarded as such and that special efforts be made to respect the designation.

"In compiling the inventory requested in the final paragraph, there is no reason to indicate this information has been requested by the President, and a memorandum under your signature to operating personnel need not indicate this is a Government-wide survey."

Why the secrecy about an order that was so obviously in the national interest? One inference is that, at the time it was issued, a confidential, government-wide investigation of snooping was under way and might be hampered by an open attack on the practice by the president.

Furthermore, a high-level source in the White House indicated to me that President Johnson had good reason to believe that his own office might be bugged. There were also rumors that telephone conversations by members of the president's immediate family had been monitored.

About the same time, engineers from the Federal Communications Commission discovered that the offices of two U.S. senators had been bugged.

The strong language of President Johnson's confidential instructions to agency heads left no doubt about where he stood on the subject of eavesdropping. He wrote:

"I am strongly opposed to the interception of telephone conversations as a general investigative technique. I recognize that mechanical and electronic devices may sometimes be essential in protecting our national security.

"Nevertheless, it is clear that indiscriminate use of these investigative devices to overhear telephone conversations without the knowledge or consent of any persons involved could result in serious abuses and invasion of privacy.

"In my view, the invasion of privacy of communication is a highly offensive practice which should be engaged in only where the national security is at stake. To avoid any misunderstanding on this subject in the Federal Government, I am establishing the following basic guidelines to be followed by all Government agencies:

"1. No Federal personnel is to intercept telephone conversations within the United States by any mechanical or electronic devices without the consent of the parties involved (except in connection with investigations relating to the national security).

"2. No interceptions shall be undertaken or continued without first obtaining the approval of the Attorney General.

"3. All Federal agencies shall immediately conform their practices and procedures to the provision of this order."

In reference to the practice of bugging, the president's memorandum said: "Utilization of mechanical or electronic devices to overhear non-telephone conversations is an even more difficult problem, which raises substantial and unresolved questions of Constitutional interpretation.

"I desire that each agency conducting such investigations consult the Attorney General to ascertain whether the agency's practices are fully in accord with the law and with a decent regard for the rights of others.

"Every agency head shall submit to the Attorney General within 30 days a complete inventory of all mechanical and electronic equipment and devices used for or capable of intercepting telephone conversations.

"In addition, such reports shall contain a list of any interceptions currently authorized and the reasons for them."

As we have seen in the preceding chapters, this presidential order, unequivocal though it was, did not deter some federal agents from their determination to penetrate the citizen's "domestic repose."

While most of the members of the presidential crime commission were apparently police-oriented in their thinking, a panel of scientists also appointed by the White House to investigate primarily the threats to privacy posed by behavioral research reached a different conclusion.

The group, headed by Kenneth E. Clark of the University of Rochester, reported that they had been "dismayed to observe the disregard for human values" shown by those in government and industry who employ eavesdropping and lie detection devices without clear justification."

The right to privacy, the panel declared, is the right of the individual to decide for himself how far he wishes to go in sharing with others his thoughts, his feelings and the facts of his personal life. It is, they said, a right that is essential to insure dignity and freedom of self-determination.

It was to prevent further erosion of that right that President Johnson has asked Congress which, over the years has not been idle in taking away some of the people's rights, to restore this one.

Mr. Johnson's recommendation for such a law included only the broadest outline of what its provisions should be. He properly left the details up to the lawmakers themselves.

However, some members of the legal profession—like Dr. Alan Westin and his associates—have spent considerable time studying the issue, and have suggested some of the stipulations they think such a federal statute should contain. They say it should:

—Prohibit all wiretapping by making it a federal offense for anyone acting as a private individual, or any public official—state or federal—to listen to or record surreptitiously any telephone conversation unless *all* parties to the conversation give their consent.

—Make it unlawful for any federal official, or person hired or engaged by him, to use a device for the purpose of spying upon, eavesdropping on or recording the speech, acts or location of any other person without his knowledge or consent.

Under the terms of this statute, no person could be interviewed or examined by a government agent equipped with a recording device unless the person so interrogated was first informed in writing of the device and advised that he might refuse to answer questions without his attorney being present.

The protection of the act would apply to zones of privacy within the meaning of the Fourth Amendment.

While advocating that the exact definition of "private place" and "private conversation" be left to judicial judgment, Dr. Westin suggests that "this approach recognizes that people seek and society has an urgent interest in protecting certain important moments of privacy in places that our law regards as public." These include streets, parks, hotel lobbies, restaurant tables, etc. Rather than draw the line strictly between privately owned premises and public facilities which, Dr. Westin points out, would surrender far too much territory to the snooper, he believes privacy should be claimed for certain activities in public as well as private places. After all, most of our life today is spent outside the home.

The statute would, of course, exclude electronic devices used for lawful and ethical purposes, such as protection against trespass on private property, as hearing aids, etc.

—Outlaw the use of any device to obtain data stored in a computer memory, without the knowledge or consent of the legal custodian of such data.

—Authorize the restricted use of surveillance by device for the FBI and possibly military intelligence in crimes involving national security, kidnaping and those on which human life is clearly at stake.

The use of electronic gear in such cases would be allowed only when the head of the Bureau obtained an order from a panel of three federal judges in the district where the surveillance is to take place. Such orders would issue only when the court was certain that there was probable cause and that all other investigative means had been tried or were impossible.

The surveillance order would be valid for a specified period, with renewal possible if further need could be shown.

—Require that all information or material (tape recordings, logs, summaries, photographs, etc.) obtained during such an authorized surveillance be registered and preserved. Such material or its import would be disclosed only during litigation concerned with the specific case for which the intrusion was authorized.

—Ban the sale of eavesdropping and spying equipment to anyone other than the few officials presenting an approved order, bearing an authorized signature.

—Provide injunctive relief for persons who believe their privacy is being invaded by government agents, by allowing such persons to bring a show cause order against the officials in the federal district court.

And since, as an old legal maxim declares, "there is no right if there is no remedy," the federal statute ought to further provide that individuals who have been made the victims of unlawful surveillance by device, could bring damage suits against the responsible agents.

—Prohibit the use, by all federal employees, of polygraphs, psychological techniques such as hypnosis, mind-modifying drugs and personality inventories.

The foregoing by no means exhaust the situations that will have to be considered by the congressional lawmakers who respond to the president's call for a Right of Privacy Act. But they point to areas where over-all safeguards might be established by legislation.

The outlook for combating the snoopers by scientific countermeasures is not, and never has been, a very promising one.

There is no completely reliable technical defense against electronic spying. Until quite recently, the march of science has been in the direction of greater intrusion.

There are encouraging signs, however, that the tide is changing. As the snooper's scope of operations has expanded and more people have become aware of its implications, the demand for anti-bugging devices and detection equipment has steadily grown.

Important military and diplomatic sessions in government are now held in "floating" rooms set up inside the conference room itself. The inner structure sometimes has as many as four lead walls, as well as a protective ceiling and floor, all of which fit together to form a room within a room.

This portable security chamber has no windows, since voice vibrations against the panes could be picked up from outside and the words spoken could be "reconstructed."

If a given meeting is to include top-secret information, the conference table may be entirely of glass to expose any hidden recorders, or wires.

Other highly classified and very costly anti-intrusion equipment has been developed by the government to provide the diplomatic corps and the military establishment with immunity from espionage.

Such elaborate precautions, however, are far beyond both the need and the pocketbook of the ordinary citizen.

Following are some of the simpler counter-intrusion devices currently available from most commercial electronic supply houses. As the public demand grows, and new laws restrict the sale of pry-and-spy gear, many manufacturers will turn to making protective apparatus.

A telephone supply company in New York sells a device called the Privacy Sentry, which the maker claims will detect any foreign interception in a telephone line. A probe is held against the metal surface of the bottom of the telephone. A needle on the instrument's dial deflects if the phone is being tapped. Price: $250.

The commonly held idea that buzzes, clicks or other extraneous noises on a telephone line indicate that someone else is "tuned in," is not true. Such sounds usually indicate trouble in a terminal box or moisture on the line. Skilled wiretappers are silent as ghosts.

Expert practitioners of the eavesdropping art say that such devices as the Private Sentry are far from infallible. In the last analysis, the best way of finding a telephone tap is inspection of the premises and of each junction box between the two ends of the given line.

Unless the intruder has available to him highly sophisticated gear such as that used by the FBI, it is usually possible to detect a tape recorder when it is connected to the telephone line. This is done by using a piece of equipment which identifies an inaudible, high-frequency signal used in the mechanism of most tape recorders.

A Santa Monica (California) firm manufactures a pocket-size electronic jammer, slightly smaller than a cigarette pack. According to the company's literature, it will jam any signal within its immediate vicinity. It operates on a rechargeable battery, good for ten hours of continuous operation.

Another and even more refined anti-bug is the Pen Scrambler, deceptively packaged in the barrel of an ordinary fountain pen. The New York firm (on West 46th Street) which sells it, claims that it will jam any transmitted signal within a radius of forty feet.

An anti-snooping apparatus called simply the Bug Eliminator plugs into the regular electric outlet of house or office. It is designed to render harmless any FM bugging device. Cost: $250.

The Detecto F201 is a mechanism selling for the same price. It is used, however, to locate a hidden bug rather than to knock out its signal. When a concealed transmitter is present, the Detecto flashes a warning light.

A simple means of minimizing the threat of a hidden microphone is to provide "cover" for a conversation. The "cover" can be a TV or radio set with the volume turned up, or some household noise background such as a vacuum sweeper or shower. Then the two or more persons who wish to engage in a private conversation get very close to each other and speak in a low voice or whisper. The human ear filters out the noise; the bug doesn't.

An inexpensive and easy way to eliminate the most common types of listening devices is simply to disconnect the AC power supply and (if possible) to unplug or disconnect the telephone. If the telephone is not the plug-in type, it is better to hold confidential conversations in another room, especially a room such as the nursery or storeroom, where such a conversation would normally not take place.

Equipment used by professionally trained technicians in combating snoopers includes a variety of such instruments as line analyzers, scanners, tuned receivers, radio frequency probes, metal detectors, field-strength indicators and so on.

In an interview with the *New York Times,* surveillance expert Bernard Spindel said that during the past two decades or more, the technology of electronic spying has advanced by leaps and bounds. He said that twenty to twenty-five years ago, a man could make an adequate search for bugs with $1,500 worth of equipment and one or two years of experience.

Fifteen years ago, he needed at least $15,000 worth of gear and three years of experience to do the same job. Eight to ten years ago, he needed $25,000 to $35,000 worth of equipment and a minimum of five years' experience.

Today, said Spindel, "you cannot do a good job unless you have $100,000 worth of equipment and at least ten years of know-how."

Commenting on the present magnitude of the detection problem, Spindel noted that, in addition to searching the frequency spectrum from 10 kilocycles to 50,000 kilocycles in testing a telephone system, trying to find hidden bugs and transmitters is an even bigger job.

It is necessary, he said, to look for infra-red and ultra-violet light beams, cesium, sonics, subsonics, audio radio frequencies and single side-band transmission.

In his hunt for hidden bugs, a thorough security man will search every inch of wall space, the ceilings, clocks, electrical outlets, air ducts, doorbells, television sets, radios, phonographs, lamps; beneath carpets and furniture, behind bookshelves and so on.

Even with the best equipment, a bug hunter may overlook the hidden intruder. "In the end," admitted Spindel, "you've got to rely on the skill, talent and knowledge of the people operating the equipment."

Ultimately, of course, the solution to the problem rests not with technologists, lawmakers, courts or public administrators.

It rests with the American people themselves.

So long as a considerable or influential segment of the populace is willing to barter their liberties for the short-range gains of catching criminals or detecting traitors, the creeping death of freedom as we have known it will continue to spread.

For the mutual confidence and trust of its people—in one another and in the government—is the connective tissue of American freedom. When that is eaten away, the Republic will fall.

12
Paul Pry in Britain

Every despotism creates its own nemesis in the cumulative degradation of a people's character. The ways of a bully and the ways of a sneak are complementary; a Paul Pry in Whitehall breeds a spiv in every alley.

London Illustrated News

In England, Lord Erskine once said, the inquisition began and ended with the Star Chamber—that infamous and oppressive tribunal abolished by the Long Parliament in 1641.

The venerable laws of England never tolerated a Torquemada. "Her noble, dignified and humane policy soars above the little irregularities of our lives, and disdains to enter our closets without a warrant founded upon complaint.

"Constructed by man to regulate human infirmities, not by God to guard the purity of angels, it leaves us our thoughts, our opinions and our conversations. . . . It does not dog men into taverns and coffee houses, nor lurk after them at corners, nor watch them in their domestic enjoyments. It lays no snare for the thoughtless life, and takes no man by surprise."

That was England of another century, in the days of her greatness.

Today, I have before me a copy of *The Evening News* (London), dated June 28, 1966. Across the entire upper half of the page is an eight-column photograph of seven men, all of them with their backs turned, walking away from the camera. Says a caption underneath the picture: "It would not do, of course, for them to be recognized."

They are dressed in neat business suits and carry umbrellas, briefcase, folded newspaper. In the streets of the City (London's financial district) they are indistinguishable from any insurance, bank and brokerage employees, going about their daily affairs.

But there is an important difference. These men are not underwriters or members of clerical staffs. They are police constables—a newly created Undercover Squad, whose job is precisely to dog men into taverns and lurk after them at corners.

The British journalist, with the same myopia that afflicts his opposite number in America, has dubbed them "the magnificent seven," and rejoices that they "were out again today with their umbrellas and briefcases *looking for crime in the City's square mile*." [Italics mine.]

The news story informs us that this spy system, in operation for only two months, has been so successful that there is a possibility that new squads, based on other police stations throughout London, may be formed.

When I directed the attention of an English friend to this story, he said, "Well there are quite a lot of pickpockets and thieves at work in the City."

I reminded him that the cutpurse and highwayman seem to have been an important feature of the London scene in Shakespeare's day, too. But the only undercover squad in those times was the people themselves.

He seemed unconvinced and not greatly concerned. It struck me that the difference between Lord Erskine's time and the present was not a changed condition of society itself, but a transformation of character in the people who make up that society.

As Marshall McLuhan, in one of his more lucid moments, appraised the situation: "We are now in the age of the hunter. This is a James Bond world, a CIA world." [1]

If Britain trails far behind America in massive intrusion into individual privacy, the time lag is one of tools and technology, not of volition.

Everywhere in the island nation there are signs that this initially slow start towards spy government will jolly well be overcome. The groundwork is being laid, the necessary equipment is being made available.

As in America, the younger generation seems already conditioned to the procedure, and the youth of Britain have become willing participants.

A Harley Street doctor recently told his colleagues at an annual meeting of the British Medical Association that a big attempt is being made in London to set up a teenage undercover squad to help reduce sexual promiscuity and the drug traffic among the British capital's young people.

The physician explained that youngsters would dress in Carnaby Street clothes (mini-skirts and all that) and frequent coffee bars and other youth haunts, mainly in London's West End.

There the teenagers will act as spies and informers, keeping their contemporaries under surveillance and later reporting their activities to the police.

Also gaining wide acceptance and use in English life are the hidden microphone and tape recorder. Hardly any private detective agency that is "with it" does not have at least a small arsenal of electronic intrusion devices. These are used in marital cases, company espionage and in an increasing number of personnel checks.

A divorce court judge recently granted a London woman a divorce after listening to a tape recording of her husband in bed with a teenage girl, who had been acting as a governess for the couple's children. The wife informed the magistrate that a private detective had planted a bug behind the head of her husband's bed.

The judge agreed that the tape-recorded conversation between the husband and the girl certainly indicated adultery. At the same time, he expressed distaste for the manner in which the evidence was obtained.

Another Londoner, who was seeking to shed his mate because she talked too much, played for the court a tape recording he had secretly made of her nonstop chin music during the course of a single day.

The bugged conference room, too, is no longer an exclusively American phenomenon. In the summer of 1966, a major row was touched off among officials of the British Broadcasting Corporation (a government organization) when it was learned that a supersensitive, miniature microphone had been planted in a BBC board room to pick up and record every word spoken at a policy-making meeting.

It was later disclosed that the bug had been installed on a wall, alongside an electrical outlet a mere six feet from where the board chairman sat.

One of England's largest private detective agencies had made the installation a few days before the meeting was to be held.

Even private citizens seem to be suffering from the James Bond syndrome. Take, for example, the case of the man who said his chisel slipped when he was putting up shelves in a bedroom of his house. Result—a two-inch hole through the wall into a bedroom of the house next door. As a gentleman should, he apologized to the couple in the adjoining residence and offered to make good the damage.

That night when his neighbors prepared to retire, the wife said she felt a little uneasy about that hole in the wall, and decided to plug it up with paper before undressing. In the hole, much to her astonishment, she found a small microphone.

In court, the man with the wayward chisel admitted "conduct likely to cause a breach of the peace," but insisted that he had meant no harm.

He was bound over for twelve months in the sum of ten pounds.

While the English public is willing, apparently, to shrug off the use of bugs and tape recorders, when stories of their use occasionally come to light (perhaps because they do not yet realize their potential as a privacy-invading tool), wiretapping is a different matter.

In 1957, a nationwide storm of protest greeted the revelation that a wiretap had been placed on the telephone of a barrister and that a transcript of the intercepted conversations had been used in charging him with unprofessional conduct before the Bar Council.

To allay the public's widespread anxiety about official tapping of private telephones, the government appointed a commission of privy councillors, under the chairmanship of Lord Birkett, to look into the whole question of wiretapping in Britain.

The commission found that Crown authority for intercepting private telephone intercourse was "obscure and conflicting." It seemed to rest upon a Proclamation of 1663, which didn't, of course, refer to telephones at all because they were nonexistent at the time. All it did set forth was implied authority for the Crown to intercept and open mail.

The actual purpose of the Proclamation was to forbid the opening of letters or packets by anybody except upon issue of a warrant. Later statutes (the Act of 1710 which established the Government Post Office; and the present law) repeat substantially the same wording.

The privy councillors decided that, if the mail could be intercepted by obtaining a warrant from the Secretary of State, the law was broad enough that, by extension, it could cover telephone communication as well.

Critics of this point of view argued that the Proclamation of 1663 was meant to create a monopoly for the Crown, one not based upon prerogative right, but upon the premise that those who entrusted letters to the posts would thereby render them subject to inspection at the wish of the Crown.

If such a practice was a prerogative, they asked, why was there no mention of it in Chitty's *Prerogatives of the Crown,* issued in 1820?

In its report the Birkett commission stuck to the position that telephone interceptions were lawful, provided they were used as a last resort in cases of serious crime or national security, and then only under a warrant personally issued by the Home Secretary. Information obtained from such taps would be used only for investigative purposes and not as evidence to secure convictions.

Further, the use of information acquired in this way should be strictly confined to the purposes which had persuaded the Home Secretary that it was necessary in the first place.

The councillors recommended a tightening of warrant procedures and limiting the period of time for which they would remain valid.

At the same time, the commission assured the public that wiretapping by the government was rare. The year previously (1956) there had been only 159 warrants issued for telephone interceptions.

(If all this has a familiar sound, it is because we in America have heard the same assurances, pronounced solemnly and often by officials of our own government.)

Many Britons were not satisfied with recommendations of the Birkett report. The influential weekly *Economist* decried the fact that "it defends the system in principle, recommending that, subject to those safeguards, it be continued for its present purposes and, by implication, on its present scale. To abandon it, it is argued, would be to handicap the police and security services in their job of protecting the law-abiding majority from crime at home and espionage abroad."

Terming this a "pitiful argument," the editorial declared that it applied equally to habeas corpus, abolition of judicial torture and so on—all heavy handicaps to police action.

The dust had scarcely settled from the 1957 broil, when the scandal was repeated, with virtually the same script, but with different actors.

The new case, which brought cries of outrage from the press and set off a debate in Parliament, involved a doctor in Reading who, like the barrister in the first wiretap crisis, had been brought before the disciplining committee of his profession—the General Medical Council. The hearings were to determine whether the physician should be struck off its local register because of alleged adultery with a woman who was one of his patients.

The woman patient had committed suicide but, before taking her life with an overdose of sleeping pills, she had written a letter to the Medical Council, charging that the doctor was unfit to practice medicine.

The police entered the case when they launched an investigation to determine whether the doctor had provided the woman with the sleeping pills used in her suicide, and whether he was an accomplice to her death.

In the course of their inquiries, the Reading police secretly recorded the doctor's telephone conversation by eavesdropping from a private switchboard in the house from which the call was made.

On the basis of what they learned during their undercover work, the police concluded that there were no grounds for criminal prosecution of the doctor.

However, the medical board then instituted proceedings against him and subpoenaed the police investigators to give evidence, which included a transcript of the intercepted telephone call.

The problem of wiretapping by police was again brought to public attention. All shades of opinion expressed concern over the issue, and some editors bitterly denounced what they considered to be a repudiation of the Birkett commission's recommendations, which had been accepted by the government.

It was noted that every one of these recommendations had been flagrantly violated in the present case. The wiretap had *not been* authorized (a warrant had not even been applied for); it did *not* concern serious crime or national security; and the fruits of the interception *were* made available to a domestic tribunal.

One editor called for the immediate disciplining of the Reading police, whose arrogant action had made nonsense of the whole elaborate system of safeguards set forth by the Birkett commission. He concluded, "The time is now ripe for legislative action." [2]

Of course, the Reading police were not disciplined. The parliamentary debate of the issue, which followed, was inconclusive. Legislative action was not taken. Wiretapping and electronic intrusion are moving ahead just as relentlessly, if more discreetly, in England as in the United States.

In the use of concealed microphones and tape recordings, English law-enforcement agencies are given even more legal latitude than their counterparts in America. In the United States (at least, in federal courts) evidence obtained by illegal wiretap is not admissible. In English courts, on the other hand, the only test of admissibility is whether the evidence is relevant. In criminal cases, however, the judge may disallow such evidence if he chooses to do so.

For the most part, though, English jurists have tended to admit tape recordings as evidence, sometimes in cases where there are strong indications they were illegally obtained, and sometimes when they raise serious doubts that the defendant has been accorded his traditional right against self-incrimination.

The first litigation involving the use of tape recording to attract the attention of the British legal profession occurred little more than a decade ago. At Wiltshire Assizes, two men were charged with conspiracy to prevent the course of justice.

The prosecution offered in evidence a tape recording of a conversation between the two men, which had taken place at the Salisbury police station. Details of how the police obtained the tape are not disclosed by a review of the case appearing in the *Criminal Law Review* for July, 1956. The presumption is that the English constables followed a procedure common in American police stations today and placed the two men in a bugged room where their supposedly private conversation could be monitored.

The judge ruled the tape admissible on the ground that "it is a first-class mechanical reproduction and therefore might be said to be the best evidence, in the circumstances, of the conversation."

After the tape had been played, the judge ruled—over objections of defense counsel—that copies of the transcript should be given to the jury to assist them. The recording was also played a second time.

While admitting the bugged conversation in evidence, the jurist indicated his skepticism about the need for such police practices.

"I don't know why we have got to have these new departures," he said. "We have always got on very well, especially with police officers who make notes at times or immediately afterwards, of long conversations which are vital to the matter. I don't know why it is supposed we should now go in for tape recording."

One good reason *not* to adopt the practice was cited by the *Economist* several years later. Comparing the testimony of the man behind the badge and the tape-recorded conversation which can be permanently filed and falsely edited, the weekly noted that "one is the inarticulate or sketchy report of a gum shoe—the other a record to be bandied about and misused."

In defending the integrity of the police in their bugging procedures, an Oxford don who appeared on a BBC program series concerning the law in action, said the situation in England was not comparable to that in America. His implication was that the British police would not stoop to some of the tactics that have been revealed as commonplace in the United States.

This observation was true—up to a point. There are today increasing signs that the code of honor and high rectitude that once made the English police constable a law-enforcement model for the world is wearing a little thin.

There has been a steadily increasing number of complaints by citizens, who charge police with corruption and abuse.

Britons were greatly perturbed several years ago, for example, when two detectives in Sheffield were convicted on charges of using a "rhino-tail" whip to flail a confession out of a suspect.

Later, the Home Secretary ordered an investigation of allegations that police brutality had been largely responsible for the death of a sixty-year-old man picked up by London cops for questioning following an automobile accident in which he had been injured.

There was a case in Cheshire in which four detectives were accused of assaulting a nineteen-year-old youth. On the basis of published reports of the incident, most Britons seemed to feel that the charges were true.

During the turbulent visit of Queen Frederika of Greece to England, two of the demonstrators arrested in connection with the street disorders claimed that police had deliberately planted bricks on their persons in order to incriminate them.

Members of Parliament were shocked to hear that, in one case, local authorities had paid a man to drop his lawsuit against a police constable who, it was alleged, had thrown him over a hedge. But the police officer had not been disciplined, even though his guilt was clearly indicated by the city's willingness to settle the dispute out of court.

Such incidents, which Americans have unfortunately come to pass over as a routine part of the day's news, are deeply disturbing to the Englishman, who rightly believes that public confidence in law-enforcement officers is a prerequisite for order and justice.

The abrasive relationship between citizens and police has continued to grow as the rise in traffic violations and stresses of urban life bring the two oftener into confrontation.

The spreading hostility was clearly reflected several years ago in a Yuletide greeting widely heard in the London pubs. It was: "Cheers! And don't forget—kick a copper for Christmas!"

Concerned over the frequency of incidents involving local constables, Parliament decided to look into the issue. The members discovered that, with the exception of London's metropolitan police, the nation's cops were not answerable either to the central government or to Parliament.

As a result of this question being raised, the government appointed a royal commission to determine what, exactly, was the constitutional status of the police throughout Great Britain.

The commission was directed to study in particular:

1. The relationship of the police with the public; and means of insuring that complaints by citizens against the police are effectively dealt with.

2. The legal status and function of local police authorities.

No specific instructions were given on the subject of wiretapping, but a thorough study of the kind could hardly avoid it. Like law officers in America, British police claim they cannot cope with the rise in crime and violence without the aid of snooping devices.

The Oxford don, previously mentioned, quoted with approval during his BBC discourse a statement by a high-court justice, who had ruled that a secret tape recording made by police to gain a murder confession could be admitted in court. The judge had said: "A criminal does not act in accord with the Queensbury rules."

It is perhaps not too great a coincidence that one of the largest manufacturers of snooping devices in America, at about the same time, made exactly the same statement in testimony before a Senate hearing.

The fact is, however, that the Oxford law professor did not, in his broadcast, tell his listeners some very interesting and vital aspects of the case—information which would have certainly raised judicial eyebrows in America.

The case was of considerable interest to the English legal profession because for the first time (on April 9, 1965) in Great Britain, an appeal was based on the fact that a tape recording had been admitted as evidence in a criminal trial.

The court's ruling, therefore, set a precedent at law concerning a procedure that is being practiced to an ever greater degree in England.

Details of the case, as revealed in a transcript of the trial and in the carefully prepared decision of the three-judge appellate court, were these:

Maqsud Ali, twenty-eight years old, and Ashiq Hussain, twenty-seven—two natives of Pakistan residing in the city of Bradford—had been convicted by a jury on November 20, 1964, of murdering Hussain's wife, Nasim Akhtar.

The young woman had been found with her throat cut, in the cellar of a house occupied by both defendants.

Bradford police testified that the two Pakistanis had gone to the town hall (police station) "voluntarily" at the "request" of a police constable. There they were conducted into the surgery, where officers had previously concealed a microphone behind a waste basket, with a wire leading to a tape recorder in the police matron's lavatory.

The constable who had escorted the men to headquarters, and a Pakistani consular official who accompanied him, then left their two voluntary guests alone. The tape recorder was switched on (it was 6:20 P.M.), and for the next hour, police secretly recorded the conversation between the two suspects.

In the subsequent trial, the defendants' counsel sought to exclude the tape recording from evidence, and for good reason. The language that had been spoken by the two accused men during their monitored conversation was an obscure Punjabi dialect, limited to a particular area in Pakistan. It was established that there were other similar dialects in Pakistan, in which the words had different meanings at different times, depending upon the context in which they were used. The vocabulary was extremely limited, and there were no separate words representing pronouns.

Furthermore, the version of the tape presented to the jury had first been translated from the difficult Punjabi dialect into Urdu (another Indian tongue) and from Urdu into English.

Notwithstanding the confusion of this Oriental glossalia, the trial judge admitted a transcript of a transcript of a transcript in evidence.

Answering a defense objection also to the method used by police in obtaining the recording in the first place, Justice Stevenson (the trial judge) said: "Such a machine avoids the hazards of human memory." Then he added that "it is not for me to make any pronouncement about the propriety or otherwise of the use in general by police officers of tape-recording instruments, and I do not do so. . . . I can see no practical distinction between a police officer present at a window of a room in which two people are conversing and of which he later gives oral evidence, supplied by a note, and a tape recording proved to be a transmission through a microphone in a room to a machine recording on tape."

Chiefly on the basis of the "confession" made by the two defendants during what they thought was a private conversation in the surgery at police headquarters, a jury of three women and nine men reached a verdict of guilty after deliberating four and three-quarter hours. Ali and Hussain were both sentenced to life imprisonment (capital punishment has been abolished in Great Britain).

In their appeal, defense lawyers argued that the tape recording was thoroughly unsatisfactory as evidence, and the translations so tainted that neither the recording nor the translation should ever have been presented to the jury.

They also raised—for the first time in any British court of appeal—the following questions:

Was the tape recording admissible in evidence as purely a matter of law?

Was a transcript of the police recording admissible as a matter of law?

Answering the question of admissibility, the court noted that prints of photographs, which are reproduced by mechanical means, are admitted; and declared that it could see no difference between photographs and tape recordings. It would be wrong to deny the advantage to be gained from new techniques, provided the voices were properly identified.

Accordingly, the court said, the tape recording admitted in the discretion of the trial judge was rightly admitted.

The court declared that it did not feel it necessary to go into great detail regarding different passages in the various translations of the tape. Suffice it to say that *if* they were accurate, there were *phrases* on the recording in which *words* were said by both the appellants, which on their face value, amounted to or came very near to a confession of guilt of murder.

Since in England, as in the United States, the suspect legally enjoys the guarantee against self-incrimination and is supposed to be cautioned by arresting officers, the manner in which the police obtained their "confession" had to be considered.

That was easy. The court ruled that at the time the two Pakistanis had been conducted to the police station, and left alone for an hour in the police surgery, they were not really in custody, but had gone to the room voluntarily. The implication was that they were at liberty to leave if they wished, but they just remained in the surgery of the police station for more than an hour to have a friendly and self-incriminating chat.

Being thus at liberty, the appellants were not "subject to the judge's rules," that is, entitled to be cautioned against self-incrimination.

Consequently, the high court ruled, *there was nothing improper in the way the tape recording had been obtained.*

This finding is important because it has provided a dictum, a firm precedent at law on the basis of which other police throughout Britain can now feel free to bug their "voluntary" prisoners whenever the ignorance or helplessness of the suspect provides the opportunity.

There was not the slightest indication in the statements of either the trial judge or in the opinion handed down by the higher tribunal that any of the jurists understood some of the shortcomings of the "new" technique of recording on magnetic tape.

They ignored the fundamental fact that magnetic tape is the most untrustworthy kind of evidence conceivable.

Tests made by a team of technicians in connection with a sixteen-month study conducted by Samuel Dash proved that tape can be edited in such a way that the speaker's voice is made to say something directly opposite the original statement. By shifting syllables, an experienced tape editor can even form new words.

If the edited conversation or discourse is then transferred onto an entirely fresh tape, it is almost impossible to detect that the recording is rigged.

It is noteworthy that, as in similar legal precedents in America, an unpopular figure was the means of establishing electronic eavesdropping as an acceptable procedure.

The case was one of a particularly savage murder. The defendants were Pakistanis, members of a minority thoroughly disliked by many Bradford residents, from whom the jury was selected. Scarcely two years prior to the trial, the color bar excluding Pakistanis from Bradford's big Mecca ballroom had been lifted only after much pressure and threats of legal action.

A Pakistani bus conductor (the same job held by one of the murder defendants) had been fired from his job because he would not shave off his beard which, as a Moslem, was a religious requirement that he had worn since he was fifteen.

If the Ali-Hussain case can be taken to be representative of present legal attitudes towards individual rights in Britain, the U.S. Supreme Court ruling in the case of *Miranda v. Arizona* must seem incomprehensible to English jurists.

The U.S. court held that any criminal suspect must be warned "prior to any questioning, that he has the right to remain silent, that anything he says can be used against him in a court of law; that he has the right to the presence of an attorney, and that if he cannot afford an attorney, one will be appointed for him prior to any questioning, if he so desires."

Quite a different view was expressed not long ago on England's BBC program, *The War Against Crime.*

Lord Dilhorne, a prominent member of the British legal profession and former Lord Chancellor, said during the radio interview: "My personal view is that we really should get rid of all this cautioning business. I can see no reason why a police official interviewing someone should be required to caution him as a condition precedent to the admission in evidence of what that person says."

Supporting Lord Dilhorne in this opinion was Lord Shawcross, a former attorney general, who added: "I see no reason at all why these artificial rules about statements from the accused should be maintained. They arose at a time when there was a real danger that people might be forced to make untrue statements either by fear or by bribery. Well, that does not exist any more."

For their lordships, apparently, the "request" of a policeman does not inspire fear, even when it is made in the hostile environment of a police station. (In the case just cited, a hint of just how free of intimidation police interviews still are emerged when the defendants' attorney asked the police sergeant in the case if the men had not been struck during interrogation at headquarters. The police, of course, vigorously denied the charge.)

Nor do such things as entrapment by electronic bugging, deprivation of counsel, or right against self-incrimination seem to trouble a large section of the British legal conscience.

But perhaps the last word will not be that of the judge, prosecutor or policeman. In the English character, perhaps more than that of any other people in the world, there is a deeply ingrained, traditional sense of human decency and fair play. Indeed, it is largely upon this tradition of liberty, dating from the Magna Carta in 1215, that American constitutional freedom is based.

If the odious practices of spy government are spreading in Great Britain (and they are), it is because the people as a whole are not yet aware of them. When instances of abuse are exposed and fully understood, the ordinary Briton is outraged.

A case illustrative of this steadfast and almost instinctive resistance to despotism occurred in the summer of 1966. Just ten days before a Cheshire woman was to go into divorce court to charge her husband with cruelty, she was contacted by the Inland Revenue inquiry department (British equivalent of the U.S. Internal Revenue intelligence division).

The agents informed her that they were investigating her husband and stated that they had no objection to her attending the hearing.

The day chosen for the interview just happened to be the day after she received her divorce decree.

Indignant, she refused to attend. "I regard this as scandalous," she was later quoted as saying. "It seems clear they thought I would be very upset after the divorce, and angry with my husband. This sort of thing should be stopped. It smacks of the Gestapo."

When a newspaper reporter asked the Inland Revenue whether this kind of procedure was normal, he was told that revenue agents were not allowed to discuss activities of the inquiry branch.

Growled the Fleet Street watchdog:

"Watch it. That's my message to the private eyes of the Inland Revenue inquiry department. Let's admit they've got a tough job. Finding the fiddlers isn't easy. But how far can they reasonably go in pursuing their inquiries?" [3]

A great deal farther, if they follow in the footsteps of their American cousins—as they appear to be doing.

13
Death takes little bites

Unless there is a change in direction, the time is coming—
it may already be here for some—when the average person will have to pause to consider the implications of
every spoken word and every action in view of its possible interpretation.

SENATOR EDWARD V. LONG

In the preceding pages, we have examined in some detail the incu-
bus that haunts the American Dream.

We have witnessed unlawful breaches of privacy by agents of the
government whose duty it is to enforce the law. Wiretaps, hidden
microphones, lie detectors and personality tests are their tools; secret dossiers and computers are the depositories of their data for
controlling us.

Taken individually, each increment of police power may be of
little consequence. They are the misfortunes of the criminal suspect, the gambler, the weak, the unpopular.

But the process is insidious. Death takes little bites when devour-
ing our freedom.

In its first stages, spy government is almost indistinguishable
from democracy. That is because it is nothing more than a logical
extension of our industrialized society.

The movement of population into urbanized centers means the
setting up of controls formerly unknown. Likewise, the steady increase of federal legislation requires the rapid expansion of police

powers. These powers include not only traditional law enforcement, but also inspectional, licensing and regulatory agencies.

So the first burgeoning of autocratic rule is seen in the increasing jurisdiction of centralized government.

At the outset, this seems to be a good thing. Functioning within the concept of "ordered liberty," the bureaucratic watchdogs promise to stabilize the economy, collect taxes, safeguard the citizen from harmful drugs and false advertising claims, assist with providing his children an education, keep an eye on the enemy within (organized crime) and, in general, to oversee the individual's welfare from birth to burial.

At first, these self-appointed duties are carried out in a spirit of benevolence. But as the government's power becomes more firmly established, "initial patience and expediency give way to unbridled terror." [1]

The rational balance between regulation and creative freedom has shifted. The relationship between the government and the governed has changed. Where initiative once rested with the individual citizen, it now rests solely with the state.

A centralized power not only stabilizes the economy, it directs it. Taxes are indeed collected, but the means used to collect them now include spying, intimidation and blackmail. The citizen is not only protected against false labeling; he is forced to accept the judgment of government functionaries as to what food and drugs shall be available to him, or what he may read concerning them. His children are educated, but only within the ideological limits set by the regime. Academic freedom disappears.

The key to all these destructive changes is control through surveillance. The open society becomes a watched society. The hidden eyes of government are omnipresent.

Like Hitler, who claimed authority over every German, even when he resided or traveled in other countries, our government has begun to extend its surveillance and power to the high seas and to foreign lands.

For example, published reports show that agents of the Internal Revenue Service now operate in more than one hundred cities of fifty-five foreign countries. IRS officials in Washington say that the far-traveling corps just want to help Americans living and traveling abroad to cope with the complexities of their tax returns.

But as one IRS agent in the big London bureau told a correspondent for *Business Week,* the agents also keep an eye on the comings and goings of Americans. He said the agency wants them to know that IRS is there, "to destroy the myth that when you go overseas you are out of reach."

In November, 1966, when the Greek ship *Olympia* returned to New York from a cruise in international waters, FBI agents arrested twenty-four American passengers for alleged "crime on the high seas."

The government cited a little-known federal law (Sec. 1082, title 18, U.S. Code) which presumes to make it illegal for U.S. citizens to take part in operating gambling games, even when the ship is under a foreign flag and is in international waters outside the twelve-mile territorial limit of U.S. jurisdiction.

The FBI agents had gone along on the cruise and mingled anonymously with the passengers, spying on them and taking notes, and buying photographs from a commercial photographer aboard.

Reports later said that the FBI had been joined by the Bureau of Customs and the Post Office Department in the investigations and arrests. The part they played was not disclosed.

In another instance of global jurisdiction over American citizens, the government has forbidden Americans to buy or own gold abroad.

How can the federal authorities exercise police power over the acts of citizens while they are within the jurisdiction of another sovereign state?

Perhaps the rationale can be found in the legal codes of Communist Russia. The Kremlin rulers claim the same universal control over Soviet citizens.

Although direct censorship of books will not yet be tolerated in this country, the government has found more subtle, sophisticated ways of book control. This technique, based on secrecy and deception, came to light recently, during a congressional hearing on Appropriations. It was revealed that the U.S. Information Agency, as part of its "Book Development Program," had secretly produced manuscripts and had subsidized supposedly independent publishing firms to bring them out.

A USIA spokesman told the subcommittee that "We control the things from the very idea down to the final edited manuscript." [2]

The reader has never been aware in buying the books, which carry the imprint of established publishers, that he is, in fact, being sold a work that the government wants him to read to influence his opinions.

As Geoffrey Wolff, *Washington Post* book editor, pointed out in an article for the *World Journal Tribune,* the taxpayer who buys one of the government-generated books pays for it three times. First, it was his money that was paid to have it written. Second, he unknowingly pays for its publication. And finally, he pays the retail price at a bookstore to buy it.

The USIA also buys six million dollars worth of books for distribution, presumably abroad. According to the *World Journal Tribune* account, in 1965 the agency purchased 175,032 volumes, representing 1,500 titles.

As the publishing industry's biggest cash customer, there is little doubt that the government exercises an indirect censorship over the production of books in America.

Another recent development in the United States which has raised serious questions about infringements on privacy and freedom is Florida's privately financed secret police force.

The undercover service, headed by former FBI agent George R. Wackenhut, is of concern not only to Floridians, but to all Americans because, using the now familiar catch phrase, "organized crime," Florida's Governor Claude Kirk has been quoted as saying that, although based in Florida, the private agents would be active throughout the country. Kirk is known to have sought the cooperation of Governor Ronald Reagan of California, as well as that of officials in New York, Illinois and other states.

Governor Kirk has stated that conferences have also been held with FBI officials, the Treasury Department (Narcotics) and Internal Revenue agents. He said all have shown a desire to join "in a mutual effort to rid Florida of one of its greatest problems—organized crime."

In his Miami-based investigative firm (one of the largest in the United States), Florida's chief private eye boasts that he has over three million confidential files on individuals in the United States. He claims to add ten thousand new names each week.

Fears have been expressed in some quarters that the clandestine crusade being waged by the "Wackencops" could be turned against not only suspected gamblers and racketeers, but other segments of society such as organized labor or even the business competitors of the sponsors who are paying the private agents.

One consideration which cannot be overlooked is that secret police systems, not accountable to the electorate, are a striking trait of all totalitarian governments.

Whether officially or privately controlled, such spy webs pose this question for everyone who believes in freedom as envisaged by the Constitution:

Does the changed condition of our society really require the ever-spreading presence of these silent, faceless men, lurking in the shadows?

If it does, then we face a future no better than the Nazi, Communist and Fascist past.

For the ultimate definition of privacy is simply human dignity. It is that self-respect of the free man, that precious "island of separateness" that the police state must eradicate at all costs.

There are already signs that the growing espionage practiced throughout the country is beginning to take its toll on the mental health of the nation.

Dr. Alan F. Westin, professor of law at Columbia University, told members of the American Psychological Association at their annual convention in the fall of 1966, that Americans are being driven to suicide and nervous breakdown by the widespread invasion of privacy.

"If the growth of electronic eavesdropping continues," Dr. Westin warned, "it will leave the individual naked to ridicule and shame and put him under the control of those who know his secrets.

"The numerous instances of suicides and nervous breakdowns resulting from such exposures by government investigations, press stories and even published research constantly remind a free society that only grave social needs can ever justify destruction of the privacy which guards the individual's ultimate autonomy."

To realize fully what such complete destruction means, we have but to recall the cringing, brutalized creatures of police-state terror.

Does it seem a gross exaggeration to compare the bugged and monitored American with the naked and shorn Nazi victim, that "anxiety-ridden shadow," slumped against the bare wall of his cell, observed through a peephole by his captors?

The difference is only in degree, not in kind.

References and notes

CHAPTER 1—*Say privacy, say freedom*

1. *Hearings,* Senate Subcommittee on Administrative Practice and Procedure (Invasions of Privacy), p. 436.
2. *Hollywood Citizen-News,* April 15, 1965.
3. *Hearings, op. cit.,* p. 350.
4. *Ibid.,* p. 384.
5. Public Law 89-44, 89th Congress, H.R. 8371, June 21, 1965.
6. *Hearings, op. cit.,* p. 61.
7. *Hearings, op. cit.,* p. 381.
8. *Hearings, op. cit.,* p. 60.
9. Samuel Dash with Richard F. Schwartz and Robert E. Knowlton, *The Eavesdroppers* (New Brunswick: Rutgers University Press, 1959).
10. *Ibid.*
11. *Hearings, op. cit.*
12. *Hearings, op. cit.,* p. 389.
13. *Hearings, op. cit.,* pp. 424-50.

CHAPTER 2—*Tax and tyranny*

1. *U.S. v. Gase,* 66-1 USTC.
2. *U.S. v. Horwitz,* 66-1 USTC.

3. Sen. Edward V. Long.
4. *U.S. v. Cooper*, 63-2 USTC.
5. *Saturday Review*, October 1, 1966.
6. *Lord v. Kelley*, cited in Long Committee hearings, p. 1401.
7. *Hearings*, Senate Subcommittee on Administrative Practice and Procedure (Invasions of Privacy), pp. 258-59.
8. *Ibid.*, p. 1463.
9. *Ibid.*, pp. 1800, 1811.
10. *Ibid.*, p. 1823.
11. *Ibid.*, p. 1188.
12. *Ibid.*, p. 1920.
13. *Los Angeles Times*, November 6, 1966.
14. *Ibid.*, Bob Jackson article.
15. *Hearings, op. cit.*, p. 1921.
16. *Hearings, op. cit.*, p. 1659.
17. *Hearings, op. cit.*, pp. 1540-79.
18. *Hearings, op. cit.*, pp. 1165-66.
19. *Hearings, op. cit.*, p. 1486.
20. *Hearings, op. cit.*, pp. 1632-35.
21. *Hearings, op. cit.*, pp. 1816, 1535.
22. *Hearings, op. cit.*, p. 1160.
23. *Hearings, op. cit.*, p. 1928.
24. *Hearings, op. cit.*, pp. 1928, 1932.
25. *Hearings, op. cit.*, p. 1159.

CHAPTER 3—*The right to know . . . everything*

1. *American Psychologist*, November, 1965, p. 861.
2. *Ibid.*, pp. 878-89.
3. *Saturday Review*, February 5, 1966.
4. *Hypnosis in Criminal Investigation*, by Harry Arons (Charles C Thomas, 1967).
5. *New York Times*, January 11, 1967, 1:3.
6. *Saturday Review*, February 5, 1966, pp. 65, 66.

CHAPTER 4—*Filed—for eternity*

1. Other congressional committees which examined individual federal income-tax returns were: Senate Committee on Government Operations, for the years 1947 through 1963; Senate Committee on Foreign Relations, for the years 1950 to 1962; Senate Committee on Rules and Administration, for the years 1959 to 1963; House Committee on

Public Works, for the years 1956 to 1963; House Committee on Un-American Activities, for the years 1947 to 1963; House Committee on Government Operations, for the years 1947 to 1963. No explanation was given as to why the committees in each instance needed the returns.

2. States which have Federal-State Co-operative Agreements, and the dates on which they were signed are: Wisconsin, 2/6/50; North Carolina, 2/6/50; Montana, 7/16/51; Kentucky, 7/16/51; Colorado, 3/28/52; Minnesota, 5/27/57; Kansas, 7/5/60; California, 1/5/61; Utah, 2/2/61; Ohio, 8/21/61; Indiana, 10/31/61; Oregon, 12/14/61; Missouri, 6/13/62; West Virginia, 10/15/62; Iowa, 12/13/63; Maryland, 1/10/63; District of Columbia, 2/14/63; Illinois, 3/13/63; Arkansas, 5/22/63; Virginia, 6/21/63; Nebraska, 8/26/63; Florida, 9/17/63; Tennessee, 10/28/63; Washington, 11/15/63; Oklahoma, 11/15/63; New York, 11/19/63; Massachusetts, 12/10/63; New Mexico, 12/13/63; Wyoming, 2/10/64; Idaho, 3/31/64; New Hampshire, 5/13/64; South Dakota, 7/7/64; Maine, 8/19/64; South Carolina, 8/24/64; North Dakota, 9/14/64; Michigan, 3/20/65; Vermont, 6/4/65; Pennsylvania, 4/19/65; Delaware, 6/29/65; Hawaii, 8/18/65; New Jersey pending. States having no broad-based personal income tax at the time of signing the agreement were: Ohio, Illinois, Florida, Tennessee, Washington, Wyoming, New Hampshire, South Dakota, Maine, Michigan and Pennsylvania.

3. *New York Times,* August 1, 1966, 27:1.
4. *New York Times,* January 9, 1967.
5. *Hearings,* The Computer and Invasion of Privacy, p. 17.
6. *Saturday Review,* July 23, 1966.
7. *Ibid.*
8. *U.S. News,* May 16, 1966, p. 59.
9. *Civil Liberties,* September, 1966.
10. *New York Times,* January 9, 1967, p. 143.
11. *Hearings,* The Computer and Invasion of Privacy, p. 31.
12. *Ibid,* p. 33.
13. *New York Times,* August 7, 1966, IV, 9:4.
14. Logan White.

CHAPTER 5—*How private is our mail?*

1. *Hearings,* Senate Subcommittee on Administrative Practice and Procedure (Invasions of Privacy), p. 216.
2. *Ibid.,* pp. 277, 241.
3. *Ibid.,* pp. 117-18.
4. *Ibid.,* p. 94. Government agencies that have requested mail covers in-

clude: Bureau of Immigration and Naturalization; Department of Justice; U.S. District Attorneys; Army Intelligence; Navy Intelligence; U.S. Air Force Intelligence; National Security Agency; NASA; FBI; Treasury Department; Department of Labor; Securities and Exchange Commission; U.S. Marshal; State Attorneys General; State Bureaus of Criminal Apprehension; State Divisions of Parole; County Chief Probation Officers; Assistant Commission of Finance Department; State Police; Local Police; Sheriffs.

5. *Hearings, op. cit.*, p. 500.
6. *Hearings, op. cit.*, p. 373.

CHAPTER 6—*Authority to bind and to loose*

1. *New York Times*, April 28, 1965, 28:3.
2. *New York Times*, April 14, 1965.
3. *Hearings*, Senate Subcommittee on Administrative Practice and Procedure (Invasions of Privacy), *op. cit.*, pp. 1057-58.
4. *United Pharmacal Corp. v. United States*.
5. *Science*, September 25, 1964, p. 1418.
6. *Ibid.*, p. 1419.
7. *Life*, August 26, 1966.
8. *New York Times*, March 19, 1966, 1:3.
9. *Time*, December 2, 1966.
10. *Coronet*, November, 1966.
11. CBS Radio Network, May 12, 1963, 9:15 A.M.
12. Sen. Edward V. Long, *The Intruders* (New York: Frederick A. Praeger, 1967).

CHAPTER 7—*Publicity as punishment*

1. *Hearings*, Senate Subcommittee on Administrative Practice and Procedure (Invasions of Privacy), pp. 942-43.
2. *Ibid.*, p. 808.
3. *Saturday Review*, November 24, 1962, p. 15.
4. *Hearings, op. cit.*, p. 252.
5. *Hearings, op. cit.*, p. 274.
6. Robert Payne, *Zero: The Story of Terrorism*, N.Y.: 1959.
7. *Hearings, op. cit.*, p. 823.
8. *Hearings, op. cit.*, p. 1099.

CHAPTER 8—*Programing our youth for bondage*

1. H. H. Remmers and D. H. Radler, *The American Teenager,* (Indianapolis: Bobbs-Merrill, 1957), pp. 16-17.
2. *Newsweek,* March 21, 1966, p. 62.
3. *Hearings,* The Computer and Invasion of Privacy, pp. 24-25.
4. *Civil Liberties,* September, 1966, p. 2.
5. *Ibid.*
6. *Ibid.*
7. *New York Times,* February 5, 1967.
8. R. H. Towner, *Philosophy of Civilization,* 2 Vols., N.Y., 1923.
9. *New York Times,* February 18, 1967, 1:1; 14:7.
10. *New York Times,* February 16, 1966.

CHAPTER 9—*The partners in anti-crime*

7. *Hearings,* Wiretapping, Eavesdropping and the Bill of Rights, Dec. 15 and 16, 1959.
2. *New York Times Magazine,* June 3, 1962, p. 21.
3. Transcript of Record, *U.S. v. Coplon* 191 F.2d 749 (D.C. Cir. 1950). FBI press release on wiretapping policy, January 15, 1950. Ruling of Attorney General Biddle, *New York Times,* May 29, 1942.
4. *New York Times Magazine,* June 3, 1962.
5. *New York Times,* June 21, 1961.
6. *Ramparts,* November, 1966.

CHAPTER 10—*Little bugs have big ears*

1. *Collier's,* February 10, 1955.
2. *Hearings,* Senate Subcommittee on Administrative Practice and Procedure (Invasions of Privacy), p. 1681.
3. *People v. Tarrantino,* 45 Cal. 2d. 590, 593 (1955).
4. *Hearings, op. cit.,* 1294-95.
5. *Hearings, op. cit.,* Exhibits.
6. *Ramparts,* November, 1966, p. 54.
7. Quoted in Fred J. Cooke, *The FBI Nobody Knows,* p. 24.
8. *Hearings, op. cit.,* p. 35.
9. *Hearings, op. cit.,* p. 904.
10. *Hearings, op. cit.*

11. *Goldman v. United States,* 316 U.S. 129 (1942).
12. *Diplomat,* June, 1966.

CHAPTER 11—*The command of our heritage*

1. Report of the New York Joint Legislative Committee to Study Illegal Interception of Communications (1956).
2. *New York Times,* November 23, 1966.

CHAPTER 12—*Paul Pry in Britain*

1. *New York Times,* November 22, 1966.
2. *Economist,* October 22, 1965.
3. *News of the World,* July 24, 1966.

Index

General Development Corporation, 147–48
General Services Administration, 11
Genetic manipulation, 73
George, Walter, 114–15
Georgetown University, 180–81
Gestapo, 178, 220
Gifts, bugging of, 212–13
Goddard, Dr. James Lee, 131–33, 135–36, 137–39
    campus spies of, 169–70
Goldman v. United States, 213, 215
Gottesman, Mr. (Cohn's co-defendant), 110
Gourley, Wallace S., 29
Great Britain, 234–50, 253
    admission of electronic evidence in, 236–37, 241–42, 244–48
    proposed teenage undercover squad in, 236
Gross, H. R., 190–91
Gross, Martin L., *The Brain Watchers,* 57
Grossman, Richard, 148
Gronouski, John A., 108–11
Gugas, Chris, 69

Hall, Durward G., 8
Hannah, Harvey H., 9
Hanselman, John J., 199
Hardy, Porter, Jr., 65
Harlem Hospital (N.Y.C.), 78–79
Harmon, Joseph, 37–38
Harriman, Averell, 212
Hathaway, Dr. Starke R., 53, 55, 59
Health, Education and Welfare, Department of, 84, 86, 123
    inquires about students, 164–65
    See also Food and Drug Administration
Heart Diseases and Strokes, Commission on, 80
Helms, Richard, 174
Henderson Novelty Company, 187

Hennings, Thomas C., 115
Heydrick, Reinhard, 162
Hitchcock (Kansas City police detective), 201
Hitler, Adolf, 252
Hochman, Bruce I., 29–30
Hoffa, James, 151–58
Holeman, Bonnie, 38–39
Holmes, Oliver Wendell, Jr., 9
Homme, H. Gordon, 202
Hoover, J. Edgar, 94, 130, 180
    R. Kennedy's debate with, 190–93
    Gov. Sawyer's demand to, 186–88
Horn (IRS agent), 31
Horton, Frank, 83
House of Representatives, U.S., 119, 132, 181
    investigations by
        data-collection, 85, 91–92, 100, 103
        FDA practices, 136
        hearings on censorship, 254
        hearings on polygraphing, 64–66, 70
        hearings on wiretapping, 197–98
    Operations Subcommittee of, 54
    scrutinizes tax returns, 86
Houston, Lawrence R., 173
Hussain, Ashiq, 245–48
Hypnosis
    as defense against polygraphs, 67–68
    as investigative tool, 76–77
    recommended ban on, 229

Illinois, wiretapping ban in, 12
Immigration Service, 44
Impersonation, 38, 127, 176
Inadmissable evidence, 189–90
    from bugging, 185, 189
    from involuntary confessions, 77
    from wiretaps, 181–83, 202, 205
Inbau, Fred E., 65